Oxford AQA History

A LEVEL AND AS
Component 2

The Crisis of Communism: the USSR and the Soviet Empire, 1953–2000

Rob Bircher

SERIES EDITOR
Sally Waller

OXFORD

OXFORD
UNIVERSITY PRESS

Great Clarendon Street, Oxford, OX2 6DP, United Kingdom

Oxford University Press is a department of the University of Oxford. It furthers the University's objective of excellence in research, scholarship, and education by publishing worldwide. Oxford is a registered trade mark of Oxford University Press in the UK and in certain other countries

First published in 2015

British Library Cataloguing in Publication Data
Data available

978-0-19-835465-9

10 9 8 7 6 5 4 3 2 1

Paper used in the production of this book is a natural, recyclable product made from wood grown in sustainable forests. The manufacturing process conforms to the environmental regulations of the country of origin.

Printed in Great Britain by Bell and Bain Ltd., Glasgow.

Approval message from AQA

This textbook has been approved by AQA for use with our qualification. This means that we have checked that it broadly covers the specification and we are satisfied with the overall quality. Full details of our approval process can be found on our website.

We approve textbooks because we know how important it is for teachers and students to have the right resources to support their teaching and learning. However, the publisher is ultimately responsible for the editorial control and quality of this book.

Please note that when teaching the AQA A Level History course, you must refer to AQA's specification as your definitive source of information. While this book has been written to match the specification, it does not provide complete coverage of every aspect of the course.

A wide range of other useful resources can be found on the relevant subject pages of our website: www.aqa.org.uk.

Please note that the Practice Questions in this book allow students a genuine attempt at practising exam skills, but they are not intended to replicate examination papers.

FSC www.fsc.org MIX Paper from responsible sources FSC® C007785

Contents

Contents (continued)

Introduction to features

The ***Oxford AQA History*** series has been developed by a team of expert history teachers and authors with examining experience. Written to match the new AQA specification, these new editions cover AS and A Level content together in each book.

How to use this book

The features in this book include:

TIMELINE

Key events are outlined at the beginning of the book to give you an overview of the chronology of this topic. Events are colour-coded so you can clearly see the categories of change.

LEARNING OBJECTIVES

At the beginning of each chapter, you will find a list of learning objectives linked to the requirements of the specification.

SOURCE EXTRACT

Sources introduce you to material that is primary or contemporary to the period, and **Extracts** provide you with historical interpretations and the debate among historians on particular issues and developments. The accompanying activity questions support you in evaluating sources and extracts, analysing and assessing their value, and making judgements.

A LEVEL AS LEVEL PRACTICE QUESTION

Focused questions to help you practise your history skills for both AS and A Level, including evaluating sources and extracts, and essay writing.

STUDY TIP

Hints to highlight key parts of **Practice Questions** or **Activities**.

ACTIVITY

Various activity types to provide you with opportunities to demonstrate both the content and skills you are learning. Some activities are designed to aid revision or to prompt further discussion; others are to stretch and challenge both your AS and A Level studies.

CROSS-REFERENCE

Links to related content within the book to offer you more detail on the subject in question.

A CLOSER LOOK

An in-depth look at a theme, event or development to deepen your understanding, or information to put further context around the subject under discussion.

KEY CHRONOLOGY

A short list of dates identifying key events to help you understand underlying developments.

KEY PROFILE

Details of a key person to extend your understanding and awareness of the individuals that have helped shape the period in question.

KEY TERM

A term that you will need to understand. The terms appear in bold, and they are also defined in the glossary.

AQA History specification overview

AS exam

Part One content

Crisis in the Soviet Union, 1953–2000

1. De-Stalinisation, 1953–1964
2. Years of stagnation, 1964–1985
3. The Gorbachev revolution, 1985–2000

Part Two content

Crisis in the Soviet Empire, 1953–2000

4. Soviet satellites, 1953–1968
5. 'Real existing socialism', 1968–1980
6. The collapse of the Soviet Empire, 1980–2000

A Level exam

AS examination papers will cover content from Part One only (you will only need to know the content in the blue box). A Level examination papers will cover content from both Part One and Part Two.

The examination papers

The grade you receive at the end of your AQA AS History course is based entirely on your performance in two examination papers, covering Breadth (Paper 1) and Depth (Paper 2). For your AQA A Level History course, you will also have to complete an Historical Investigation (Non-examined assessment).

Paper 2 Depth study

This book covers the content of a Depth study (Paper 2). You are assessed on the study in depth of a period of major historical change or development, and associated primary sources or sources contemporary to the period.

Exam paper	Questions and marks	Assessment Objective (AO)*	Timing	Marks
AS Paper 2: Depth Study	**Section A: Evaluating primary sources** One compulsory question linked to two primary sources or sources contemporary to the period (25 marks) • The compulsory question will ask you: *'with reference to these sources and your understanding of the historical context, which of these sources is more valuable in explaining why…'* **Section B: Essay writing** One from a choice of two essay questions (25 marks) • The essay questions will contain a quotation advancing a judgement and <u>could</u> be followed by: *'explain why you agree or disagree with this view'*.	AO2 AO1	Written exam: 1 hour 30 minutes	50 marks (50% of AS)
A Level Paper 2: Depth Study	**Section A: Evaluating primary sources** One compulsory question linked to three primary sources or sources contemporary to the period. The sources will be of different types and views (30 marks) • The compulsory question will ask you: *'with reference to these sources and your understanding of the historical context, assess the value of these three sources to an historian studying…'* **Section B: Essay writing** Two from a choice of three essay questions (2 x 25 marks) • The essay questions require analysis and judgement, and <u>could</u> include: *'How successful…'* or *'To what extent…'* or *'How far…'* or a quotation offering a judgement followed by *'Assess the validity of this view'*.	AO2 AO1	Written exam: 2 hours 30 minutes	80 marks (40% of A Level)

*AQA History examinations will test your ability to:

AO1: Demonstrate, organise and communicate **knowledge and understanding** to analyse and evaluate the key features related to the periods studied, **making substantiated judgements and exploring concepts**, as relevant, of cause, consequence, change, continuity, similarity, difference and significance.

AO2: **Analyse and evaluate** appropriate source material, primary and/or contemporary to the period, within the historical context.

AO3: **Analyse and evaluate**, in relation to the historical context, different ways in which aspects of the past have been interpreted.

Visit **www.aqa.org.uk** to help you prepare for your examinations. The website includes specimen examination papers and mark schemes.

Introduction to the *Oxford AQA History* series

Depth studies

The exploration of a short but significant historical period provides an opportunity to develop an 'in-depth' historical awareness. This book will help you to acquire a detailed knowledge of an exciting period of historical change, enabling you to become familiar with the personalities and ideas which shaped and dominated the time. In-depth study, as presented here, allows you to develop the enthusiasm that comes from knowing something really well.

However, 'depth' is not just about knowledge. Understanding history requires the piecing together of many different strands or themes, and depth studies demand an awareness of the interrelationship of a variety of perspectives, such as the political, economic, social and religious – as well as the influence of individuals and ideas within a relatively short period of time. Through an 'in-depth' study, a strong awareness of complex historical processes is developed, permitting deeper analysis, greater perception and well-informed judgement.

Whilst this book is therefore designed to impart a full and lively awareness of a significant period in history, far more is on offer from the pages that follow. With the help of the text and activities in this book, you will be encouraged to think historically, question developments in the past and undertake 'in-depth' analysis. You will develop your conceptual understanding and build up key historical skills that will increase your curiosity and prepare you, not only for A Level History examinations, but for any future studies.

Key Term, Key Chronology and **Key Profile** help you to consolidate historical knowledge about dates, events, people and places

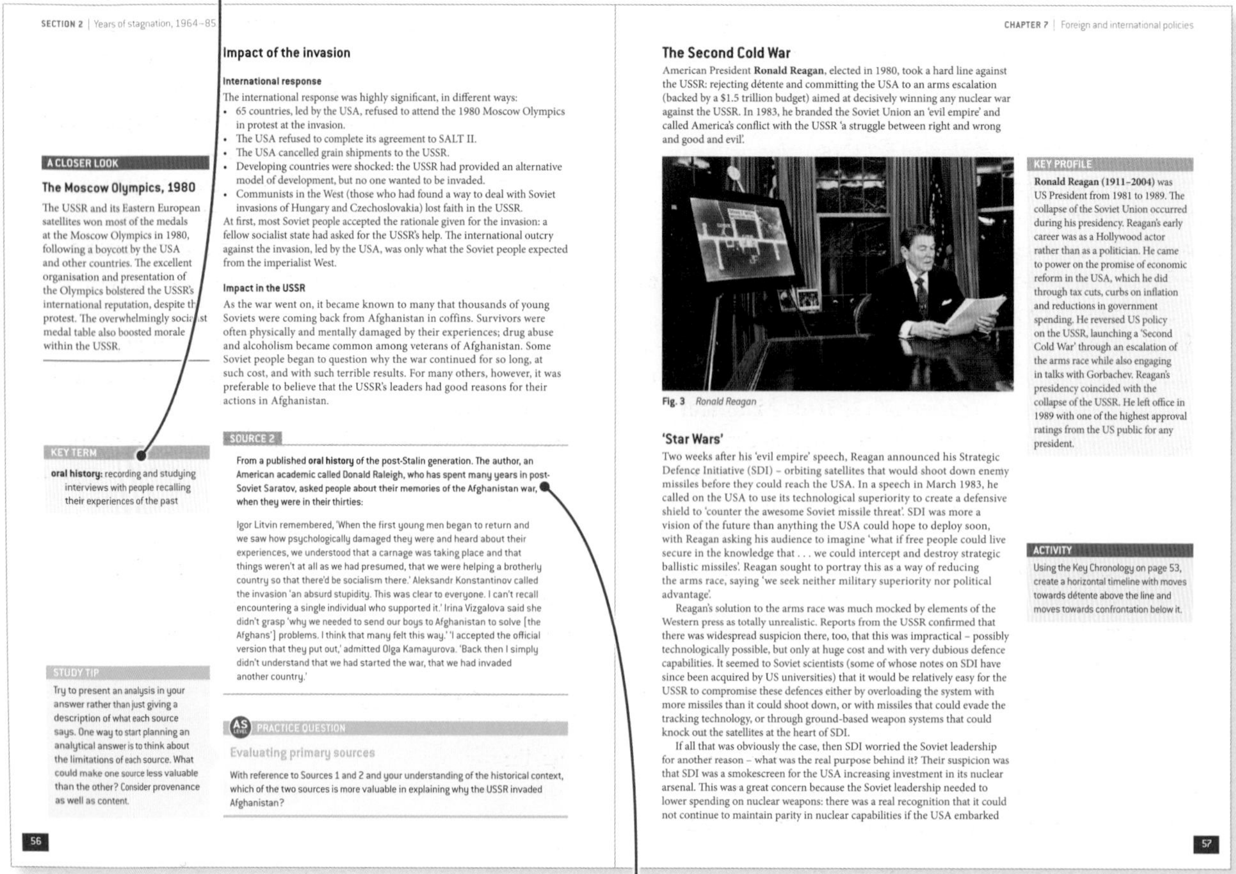

SECTION 2 | Years of stagnation, 1964–85

Impact of the invasion

International response

The international response was highly significant, in different ways:

- 65 countries, led by the USA, refused to attend the 1980 Moscow Olympics in protest at the invasion.
- The USA refused to complete its agreement to SALT II.
- The USA cancelled grain shipments to the USSR.
- Developing countries were shocked: the USSR had provided an alternative model of development, but no one wanted to be invaded.
- Communists in the West (those who had found a way to deal with Soviet invasions of Hungary and Czechoslovakia) lost faith in the USSR.

At first, most Soviet people accepted the rationale given for the invasion: a fellow socialist state had asked for the USSR's help. The international outcry against the invasion, led by the USA, was only what the Soviet people expected from the imperialist West.

Impact in the USSR

As the war went on, it became known to many that thousands of young Soviets were coming back from Afghanistan in coffins. Survivors were often physically and mentally damaged by their experiences; drug abuse and alcoholism became common among veterans of Afghanistan. Some Soviet people began to question why the war continued for so long, at such cost, and with such terrible results. For many others, however, it was preferable to believe that the USSR's leaders had good reasons for their actions in Afghanistan.

A CLOSER LOOK

The Moscow Olympics, 1980

The USSR and its Eastern European satellites won most of the medals at the Moscow Olympics in 1980, following a boycott by the USA and other countries. The excellent organisation and presentation of the Olympics bolstered the USSR's international reputation, despite the protest. The overwhelmingly socialist medal table also boosted morale within the USSR.

KEY TERM

oral history: recording and studying interviews with people recalling their experiences of the past

SOURCE 2

From a published oral history of the post-Stalin generation. The author, an American academic called Donald Raleigh, who has spent many years in post-Soviet Saratov, asked people about their memories of the Afghanistan war, when they were in their thirties:

Igor Litvin remembered, 'When the first young men began to return and we saw how psychologically damaged they were and heard about their experiences, we understood that a carnage was taking place and that things weren't at all as we had presumed, that we were helping a brotherly country so that there'd be socialism there.' Aleksandr Konstantinov called the invasion 'an absurd stupidity. This was clear to everyone. I can't recall encountering a single individual who supported it.' Irina Vizgalova said she didn't grasp 'why we needed to send our boys to Afghanistan to solve [the Afghans'] problems. I think that many felt this way.' 'I accepted the official version that they put out,' admitted Olga Kamayurova. 'Back then I simply didn't understand that we had started the war, that we had invaded another country.'

STUDY TIP

Try to present an analysis in your answer rather than just giving a description of what each source says. One way to start planning an analytical answer is to think about the limitations of each source. What could make one source less valuable than the other? Consider provenance as well as content.

AS LEVEL PRACTICE QUESTION

Evaluating primary sources

With reference to Sources 1 and 2 and your understanding of the historical context, which of the two sources is more valuable in explaining why the USSR invaded Afghanistan?

56

CHAPTER 7 | Foreign and international policies

The Second Cold War

American President **Ronald Reagan**, elected in 1980, took a hard line against the USSR: rejecting détente and committing the USA to an arms escalation (backed by a $1.5 trillion budget) aimed at decisively winning any nuclear war against the USSR. In 1983, he branded the Soviet Union an 'evil empire' and called America's conflict with the USSR 'a struggle between right and wrong and good and evil'.

Fig. 3 *Ronald Reagan*

KEY PROFILE

Ronald Reagan (1911–2004) was US President from 1981 to 1989. The collapse of the Soviet Union occurred during his presidency. Reagan's early career was as a Hollywood actor rather than as a politician. He came to power on the promise of economic reform in the USA, which he did through tax cuts, curbs on inflation and reductions in government spending. He reversed US policy on the USSR, launching a 'Second Cold War' through an escalation of the arms race while also engaging in talks with Gorbachev. Reagan's presidency coincided with the collapse of the USSR. He left office in 1989 with one of the highest approval ratings from the US public for any president.

'Star Wars'

Two weeks after his 'evil empire' speech, Reagan announced his Strategic Defence Initiative (SDI) – orbiting satellites that would shoot down enemy missiles before they could reach the USA. In a speech in March 1983, he called on the USA to use its technological superiority to create a defensive shield to 'counter the awesome Soviet missile threat'. SDI was more a vision of the future than anything the USA could hope to deploy soon, with Reagan asking his audience to imagine 'what if free people could live secure in the knowledge that . . . we could intercept and destroy strategic ballistic missiles'. Reagan sought to portray this as a way of reducing the arms race, saying 'we seek neither military superiority nor political advantage'.

Reagan's solution to the arms race was much mocked by elements of the Western press as totally unrealistic. Reports from the USSR confirmed that there was widespread suspicion there, too, that this was impractical – possibly technologically possible, but only at huge cost and with very dubious defence capabilities. It seemed to Soviet scientists (some of whose notes on SDI have since been acquired by US universities) that it would be relatively easy for the USSR to compromise these defences either by overloading the system with more missiles than it could shoot down, or with missiles that could evade the tracking technology, or through ground-based weapon systems that could knock out the satellites at the heart of SDI.

If all that was obviously the case, then SDI worried the Soviet leadership for another reason – what was the real purpose behind it? Their suspicion was that SDI was a smokescreen for the USA increasing investment in its nuclear arsenal. This was a great concern because the Soviet leadership needed to lower spending on nuclear weapons: there was a real recognition that it could not continue to maintain parity in nuclear capabilities if the USA embarked

ACTIVITY

Using the Key Chronology on page 53, create a horizontal timeline with moves towards détente above the line and moves towards confrontation below it.

57

▲ The Crisis of Communism: the USSR and the Soviet Empire, 1953–2000

Source features support you with assessing the value of primary materials

This book also incorporates primary source material in the **Source** features. Primary sources are the building blocks of history, and you will be encouraged to reflect on their value to historians in trying to recreate the past. The accompanying questions are designed to develop your own historical skills, whilst suggestions for **Activities** will help you to engage with the past in a lively and stimulating manner. Throughout the book, you are encouraged to think about the material you are studying and to research further, in order to appreciate the ways in which historians seek to understand and interpret past events.

The chapters which follow are laid out according to the content of the AQA specification in six sections. Obviously, a secure chronological awareness and understanding of each section of content will be the first step in appreciating the historical period covered in this book. However, you are also encouraged to make links and comparisons between aspects of the period studied, and the activities will help you to relate to the key focus of your study and the key concepts that apply to it. Through intelligent use of this book, a deep and rewarding appreciation of an important period of history and the many influences within it will emerge.

Developing your study skills

You will need to be equipped with a paper file or electronic means of storing notes. Organised notes help to produce organised essays and sensible filing provides for efficient use of time. This book uses **Cross-References** to indicate where material in one chapter has relevance to that in another. By employing the same technique, you should find it easier to make the final leap towards piecing together your material to produce a holistic historical picture. The individual, group and research activities in this book are intended to guide you towards making selective and relevant notes with a specific purpose. Copying out sections of the book is to be discouraged, but recording material with a particular theme or question in mind will considerably aid your understanding.

There are plenty of examples of examination-style 'depth' **Practice Questions** for both AS Level, in Part One, and A Level in Parts One and Two of this book. There are also **Study Tips** to encourage you to think about historical perspectives, individuals, groups, ideas and ideology. You should also create your own timelines, charts and diagrams, for example to illustrate causation and consequence, analyse the interrelationship of the differing perspectives, consider concepts and identify historical processes.

It is particularly important for you to have your own opinions and to be able to make informed judgements about the material you have studied. Some of the activities in this book encourage pair discussion or class debate, and you should make the most of such opportunities to voice and refine your own ideas. The beauty of history is that there is rarely a right or wrong answer, so this supplementary oral work should enable you to share your own opinions.

Writing and planning your essays

At both AS and A Level, you will be required to write essays and, although A Level questions are likely to be more complex, the basic qualities of good essay writing remain the same:

- **read the question carefully** to identify the key words and dates
- **plan out a logical and organised answer** with a clear judgement or view (several views if there are a number of issues to consider). Your essay should advance this judgement in the introduction, while also acknowledging alternative views and clarifying terms of reference, including the time span
- use the opening sentences of your paragraphs as stepping stones to take an argument forward, which allows you to **develop an evolving and balanced argument** throughout the essay and also makes for good style
- **support your comment or analysis** with precise detail; using dates, where appropriate, helps logical organisation
- **write a conclusion** which matches the view of the introduction and flows naturally from what has gone before.

Whilst these suggestions will help you develop a good style, essays should never be too rigid or mechanical.

This book will have fulfilled its purposes if it produces, as intended, students who think for themselves!

Sally Waller

Series Editor

Timeline

The colours represent different types of events as follows:

Blue: Economic events · Yellow: Social events · Red: Political events
Black: International events (including foreign policy) · Green: Leadership changes

1948

- Split between Yugoslavia and the USSR
- Cominform ends different paths to socialism

1953

- **March** Death of Stalin
- **June** Riots in East Germany, suppressed by Soviet Army and GDR police
- **July** Imre Nagy becomes Premier in Hungary
- **December** Beria executed

1954

- **March** Todor Zhivkov becomes General Secretary of the Bulgarian Communist Party

1955

- **May** Warsaw Pact signed

1964

- **October** Khrushchev removed; Leonid Brezhnev elected First Secretary; Kosygin elected Premier

1965

- **March:** Nicolae Ceauşescu becomes General Secretary of the Romanian Communist Party

1968

- **January** Dubček replaces Novotny as First Secretary of the Czechoslovak Communist Party
- **April** An 'Action Programme' of reforms introduced in Czechoslovakia
- **August:** 200,000 Warsaw Pact troops invade Czechoslovakia to suppress the 'Prague Spring'
- **November:** Brezhnev Doctrine announced

1969

- The USSR achieves nuclear parity (equal balance of nuclear forces) with USA, by Soviet calculations
- **April** Gustáv Husák becomes First Secretary of the Czechoslovak Communist Party

1975

- **August** Helsinki Final Act is signed

1976

- KOR formed in response to repression of Polish strikes and unrest

1977

- **October** Members of the Czechoslovak dissident group Charter 77 are imprisoned

1978

- **October** Karol Wojtyła, archibishop of Kraków, is elected Pope

1956

- **February** Khrushchev's Secret Speech denounces Stalin: de-Stalinisation begins
- **October** Gomułka returns to power in Poland. Collectivisation ends.
- **October** Revolution in Hungary; Imre Nagy tries to withdraw from Warsaw Pact

1956

- **October** Suez Crisis takes international attention away from Hungary
- **October** János Kádár forms new pro-Soviet government in Hungary
- **November** Soviet Army enters Hungary; heavy fighting in streets

1958

- **March** Nikita Khrushchev becomes Premier as well as First Secretary of CPSU, consolidating his leadership
- **November** Khrushchev issues an ultimatum for the Western Powers to quit Berlin

1961

- **August** The border between East and West Berlin is closed

1970

- The term *nomenklatura* is first used (by a Soviet dissident) to criticise the Party elite
- **December** Gomułka is replaced by Edward Gierek as First Secretary of PUWP Polish Communist Party), following worker riots

1971

- **May** Erich Honecker becomes General Secretary of GDR

1972

- **May** SALT I signed
- **December** East Germany and West Germany sign the 'Basic Treaty' as part of Ostpolitik

1973

- **October** OPEC embargo on oil production increases the global price of oil by four times

1979

- A second global 'oil shock', following the Iranian revolution of February 1979
- **June** Pope John Paul II visits Poland
- **December:** USSR invades Afghanistan; end of détente

1980

- **January** leading Soviet dissident Andrei Sakharov exiled to Gorky
- **August** Gdansk shipyard workers demand independent trade union; Lech Wałęsa elected leader of strike committee
- **September** Stanisław Kania becomes first secretary of PUWP after Gierek is forced to resign

1981

- **October** General Jaruzelski replaces Kania as First Secretary of PUWP
- **December** Martial law declared in Poland following a bugged Solidarity meeting that appeared to discuss a coup

1982

- **November** Death of Brezhnev; Yuri Andropov elected General Secretary of CPSU

1984

- **February** Andropov dies; Konstantin Chernenko elected General Secretary

1985

- **March** Chernenko dies; Mikhail Gorbachev elected General Secretary

1986

- **April** Chernobyl disaster
- *Perestroika* and *glasnost* begin

1987

- **December** Gustáv Husák replaced as General Secretary of CPCz by Miloš Jakeš

1990

- **March** Hungarian parliamentary elections end Communist Party rule
- **March** Gorbachev appointed President of the USSR
- **October** Unification of Germany

1991

- **February** Warsaw Pact dissolved
- **July** Boris Yeltsin elected president of RSFSR
- **August** Coup against Gorbachev
- **December** Collapse of the USSR
- **December** Gorbachev's resignation as leader of the USSR

1992

- **December** End of Czechoslovakia as a country

1993

- **October** Russian constitutional crisis: attack on White House

1988

- **January** Communist parade turns into demonstration for greater freedoms in GDR
- **May** Kádár replaced as General Secretary of the Hungarian Socialist Workers Party by Károly Grósz
- **August** 'Round table' negotiations between Solidarity and the Polish government begin

1989

- **February** Final withdrawal of Soviet troops from Afghanistan
- **March** Elections to the USSR's Congress of People's Deputies
- **July** Gorbachev declares the USSR will not interfere in internal affairs of the satellite states
- **August** Poland's communist government collapses
- **September** Hungary allows thousands of East Germans to cross its border into Austria

1989

- **October** 10,000 East Germans leave the GDR through West German embassies in Warsaw and Prague
- **November** GDR's Politburo resigns; all border crossings, including the Berlin Wall, are opened
- **November** Todor Zhivkov resigns as General Secretary of Bulgarian Communist Party

1989

- **November** Violent suppression of a demonstration in Prague leads to resignation of CPCz Politburo; Miloš Jakeš resigns as First Secretary of the CPCz
- **December** The Ceauşescus order troops to fire on demonstrators, flee, are recaptured and shot after an improvised military trial

1994

- **December** First Chechen War begins

1996

- **July** Yeltsin re-elected as president

1999

- **March** Czech Republic, Hungary and Poland join NATO
- **August** Second Chechen War begins

2000

- **March** Vladimir Putin elected as leader

Introduction to this book

KEY TERM

communism: a theory or system of social organisation in which there is a classless society; production is organised to provide for what people need, without any requirement for money; everything is owned by everyone; there is no private property

Soviet: Russian word for council; workers' councils played an important part in the Bolshevik Revolution of 1917, which overthrew the temporary Russian government of the time

Marxism: theories following the writings of Karl Marx (1818–83), who developed an economic and political argument for the inevitable triumph of communism over capitalism

Bolshevik: member of the Russian Social-Democratic Workers' Party, which, under the leadership of Lenin, became the dominant political power in Russia in 1917

satellites: a political term that refers to a country that is formally independent, but under heavy political and economic influence or control by another country

proletarian: member of the proletariat; a working-class person whose contribution to the State is their labour

In the 1950s and 1960s, **communism** did not appear to be in crisis. The single party-state of the **USSR** (the Union of **Soviet** Socialist Republics) emerged after the **Bolshevik Revolution of 1917**, and became an economic and military powerhouse, the world's second superpower. Its victory in the Great Patriotic War of 1941–45 (the Russian name for the Second World War) extended the Soviet political, economic, and social system to seven states in Eastern and Central Europe: these states became its '**satellites**', part of a Soviet 'Empire'. Developing countries looked to the USSR's model of economic development as a proven way of achieving rapid industrialisation and modernisation. However, this powerhouse stagnated in the 1970s and then fell apart through the 1980s. Its satellite states overthrew the Soviet model in 1989 and the USSR ceased to exist in 1991. Economic and political chaos resulted throughout the former Soviet Empire in the 1990s, as each country tried to find its way from the discredited socialist model towards something new.

A CLOSER LOOK

The founding of the USSR (1922)

The USSR came into being in December 1922 with the Treaty on the Creation of the USSR, signed by the different Soviet republics and setting up the federal structures that would rule the USSR.

This book will explore the workings and collapse of the Soviet system in depth. There are many different interlinked arguments and explanations for the collapse of Soviet communism through the period 1953–91. Some believe that the reason for its defeat was due to the West taking a leading role during the Cold War. Others see the Soviet system as inherently flawed, that it was not a sustainable system economically, socially, or politically. If that is the case, then the question is not so much why did the system collapse, but how did it manage to keep going for so long? After all, it lasted for 74 years.

A CLOSER LOOK

The USSR: socialist or communist?

There are many different theories and definitions of **socialism**, but basically it is when production is owned by the State, rather than owned by private individuals. Individuals are rewarded by the system according to the contribution they have made to it. Socialism promised a more equal society. **Marxists** believed this would be achieved when a **proletarian** (workers') revolution overthrew the **bourgeoisie** (the capitalist class who, under a 'free' system, exploit the workers to make profits for themselves). However, socialism itself was not the final goal: society would reach classless perfection under communism, in which the community would own all property and each person would contribute to the community according to his abilities, and receive from the community according to his needs. Technically, the Soviet system set up in 1917 was committed to implementing socialism with the aim of becoming communist.

The main focus for this book is the internal dynamics of the Soviet system and, in particular, attempts to reform the system from within after **Stalin**'s death in 1953. This includes key terms such as de-Stalinisation,

glasnost (openness), ***perestroika*** (restructuring), and ***demokratizatsiya*** (democratisation), which will be introduced in this book. The crisis of communism had its roots in the basic conflict between reforming the system and yet maintaining the **legitimacy** of the Communist Party. Under the Soviet system, the Party had complete control. Any failure resulting from reform was blamed on individuals because the Party could never be wrong. That made the role of leading the Party and leading reform a difficult balancing act.

KEY TERM

legitimacy: rightful control, which means the acceptance of authority by the people under that authority

Fig. 1 *Stalin lying in state in his coffin in Moscow, March 1953. Huge crowds gathered to pay their respects; 500 people were crushed to death as the crowds surged forward*

KEY PROFILE

Joseph Stalin (1878–1953) was the leader of the Soviet Union after Lenin. He was a totalitarian ruler (dictator), and his policies turned the Soviet Union into a powerful, modern nation. His form of government was later called Stalinism.

Vladimir Lenin (1870–1924) was a Russian communist and leader of the Bolshevik Party. He led a coup, known as the October Revolution, against the Russian provisional government in October 1917 that marked the start of communist Russia (the USSR itself came into being in 1922). After Lenin's death in 1924, there was a power struggle for leadership which Stalin won, and Lenin was raised to a status similar to that of a saint. A popular slogan of the USSR and its satellite states was 'Lenin is with us'.

Part One of this book is about the crisis of communism in the USSR, starting with the death of Stalin in 1953 and ending with the collapse of communism by 2000. In order to understand the history of the USSR and its satellite states, in these years you will need to understand the significance of Lenin and Stalin, and the political situation of the USSR before 1953.

Political context of the USSR before 1953

The Communist Party of the Soviet Union (CPSU) was a political party founded by **Vladimir Lenin** in 1912. After the 1917 Revolution, it became the ruling organisation of the USSR. No other political party was allowed.

- The Party's 'leading role', and complete power, was justified in two main ways. Firstly, the Party followed the ideology of Marxism–Leninism, believed to be scientifically infallible. Secondly, the Party represented the will of the proletariat, or the workers. Because socialism was only weakly developed in the early days of the USSR, Lenin saw the Party, led by intellectuals like himself, as acting on behalf of the workers until they had fully understood their leading role for themselves.
- The Soviet Union was another term for the USSR: a shorter way of referring to the union (joining together) of republics organised on the basis of soviets. Because soviets represented the workers' demands against their capitalist masters, they fitted in well with Lenin's communist ideology, and the idea of soviets was introduced into the way the USSR was governed. Soviets were integrated into all levels of the system.
- A founding myth of the USSR was that socialism was more important than nationalism, that the glorious goals of socialism brought workers of all nations together and united them. In practice, socialist internationalism gave way to nationalist fervour under Stalin, particularly during the Great Patriotic War.

Fig. 2 *Vladimir Lenin, first leader of communist Russia*

CROSS-REFERENCE

See Fig. 3 on page xviii for a diagram showing how the USSR was organised.

CROSS-REFERENCE

The structure of the satellite states is summarised in Chapter 13, page 105.

KEY TERM

Chairman of the Council of Ministers: a position equivalent to a premier (prime minister or first minister); the title of premier will be used for the holder of that office throughout this book

rubber-stamped: a phrase that describes the process where authorisation is given to something just as a matter of course, often because the decision to do that something has already been made somewhere else (where the real power is)

Politburo: short for Political Bureau, this was the executive committee carrying out the decisions of the CPSU (Communist Party of the Soviet Union)

legislative: law-making; the legislature is the body that makes laws

Presidium: the committee which functioned as the legislative authority between meetings of the Supreme Soviet

Marxism–Leninism: the social and economic principles of Marx as interpreted and put into effect by Vladimir Lenin in the Soviet Union; it was the guiding ideology, as suggested by Stalin, for the USSR and its satellite states

CROSS-REFERENCE

Stalinism is explained in Chapter 1.

The '**cult of personality**' is described in Chapter 1, page 1.

- Socialism was also 'collective'; individual rights did not matter in anything like the same way as in the West today. The State provided jobs, education, health, and housing for the people, and the people, in turn, worked hard for the common goal of building socialism, with the later aim of becoming a communist society.
- The socialist idea of everyone being equal (where even Stalin himself was a 'comrade', a title everyone used to show they were equal) proved to be an unrealistic ideal: the Party elite lived far better lives than ordinary citizens. The Communist Party had a huge hierarchy, where different levels had different amounts of authority, and with supreme authority at the top at the level of the USSR. The Central Committee of the Communist Party was the main decision-making body of both the Party and of the government of the USSR. The satellite states had a very similar structure.

Political structure of the USSR

In the USSR, government was technically separate from the Party and had its own hierarchy, but it was the Party that decided what the laws and policies carried out by government should be, and senior government officials were also senior Party members.

- The Council of Ministers was the highest body of the USSR's government hierarchy, and it was led by the chairman. Again, this same approach was found in the satellite states, too.
- The Presidium of the Supreme Soviet was the legislative body of the USSR, its parliament. In theory, it held all the power to make laws, but in practice, it merely **rubber-stamped** decisions made by the Party. The Supreme Soviet comprised elected deputies from all over the USSR. However, these were not free, multi-party elections: in most cases, there was only one candidate, approved by the local Party. The **Presidium** of the Supreme Soviet was a committee that operated in between meetings of the Supreme Soviet. The chairman of the Presidium was the equivalent of a head of state, and it was this role that evolved into the role of president in 1990. In the satellite states, the **legislative** bodies performed the same role, although other political parties were part of the legislature too (even if all still followed Party decisions).

Marxism–Leninism

Even after his death in 1924, Lenin continued to be the ultimate source of authority in the USSR and throughout the satellite states. While the German political philosopher Karl Marx (1818–83) had set out the theory for the transition from socialism to communism, he did not supply any practical details. Lenin helped to provide those, and his writings inspired and directed Party decision-making. Lenin's theories became known as Marxism–Leninism.

Stalinism

Stalinism is the term used to describe Stalin's view of socialism and what it meant for how the USSR should operate. Stalin added to the slogans with which communism was associated. These included:

- **'Socialism in one country'**: this was a defining feature of **Stalinism**, his theory that it was possible for the USSR to become a fully socialist country on its own. Stalin's aim was to build, at all costs, a strong, industrialised, socialist USSR that could protect itself against all the enemies of communism, both within and outside the USSR. Stalin's opponents in Stalin's struggle for power had argued that the USSR would only survive if it could encourage proletarian revolution in other countries around the world but Stalin's view became accepted from around 1928.

- **Victory over fascism:** This was Stalin's crowning achievement. His **cult of personality** was built on the myth that he almost single-handedly defended the USSR against the Nazis and led the Red Army to its crushing victory over Nazi Germany in 1945. This brought many of the satellite states of Eastern Europe, including the eastern part of defeated Germany, into the Soviet 'Empire'. The victory came at the cost of an estimated 27 million Soviet deaths.
- **Planned economy and the Five Year Plans:** these were another lasting legacy of Stalinism. Rather than letting **market forces** steer the economy, the State took control of the entire economy under Stalin, and directed every aspect of production through a state planning commission (*Gosplan*). Every production unit, factory, organisation, and department was told what they needed to produce to achieve their quota; collectively, these quotas delivered the plan targets. Stalinism prioritised heavy industry, so that the USSR industrialised rapidly. The planned economy was an essential aspect of the USSR and was also found wherever else the Soviet system was applied.

The Soviet Satellite States

The dominant Soviet Union ruled the satellites through 'puppet leaders' (communists who were born in the states they led but whose education and training took place in the USSR). During Stalin's time, leaders in the satellite states were described as 'little Stalins', who did whatever Stalin commanded. However, the relationship was not always so simple. Sometimes, satellite state leaders were reluctant to follow the USSR's lead, and some even tried to go their own way and deviate from the Soviet model in order to fit the specific needs of their country. There were situations when opposition to the Soviet model threatened to cause a break between a satellite state and the USSR, as occurred in Germany in 1953, Poland and Hungary in 1956, Czechoslovakia in 1968, and Poland in 1980. On these occasions the USSR decided to reimpose its control by force, with enormous repercussions for the future.

The Soviet system was very different from a Western, individualist, democratic system of government. In this book, you will discover more about the way the Soviet system worked, both in the USSR itself and in Eastern Europe.

A CLOSER LOOK

There were seven Soviet satellite states in Eastern and Central Europe:

- the Czechoslovak Socialist Republic (1948–89)
- the German Democratic Republic (1948–89)
- the Hungarian People's Republic (1949–89)
- the Polish People's Republic (1944–89)
- the People's Republic of Bulgaria (1946–90)
- the People's Republic of Romania (1947–89)
- the People's Socialist Republic of Albania (1944–60).

Part Two of this book focuses on the first four in this list; in addition, Bulgaria and Romania are discussed in the final chapters. Yugoslavia, which is not on this list, had a Communist Party leadership, but was not a Soviet satellite.

KEY TERM

fascism: an authoritarian and nationalistic right-wing system of government that opposes communism and tends to include a belief in the supremacy of one national or ethnic group, a contempt for democracy, and an insistence on obedience to a powerful leader

cult of personality: the creation through the media of an image of a leader as an idealised hero

market forces: economic factors that determine the price of, demand for, and availability of a product; for example, the price of something rises if demand for it rises

A CLOSER LOOK

The Stalinist economy was a planned economy. In a market economy, what gets produced depends on what customers want and how much they will pay. In a planned economy, the State decides what should be produced. In the USSR, planning happened centrally and targets for every kind of production were then circulated, down to individual factories and workers. This high degree of economic centralisation produced a very hierarchical system.

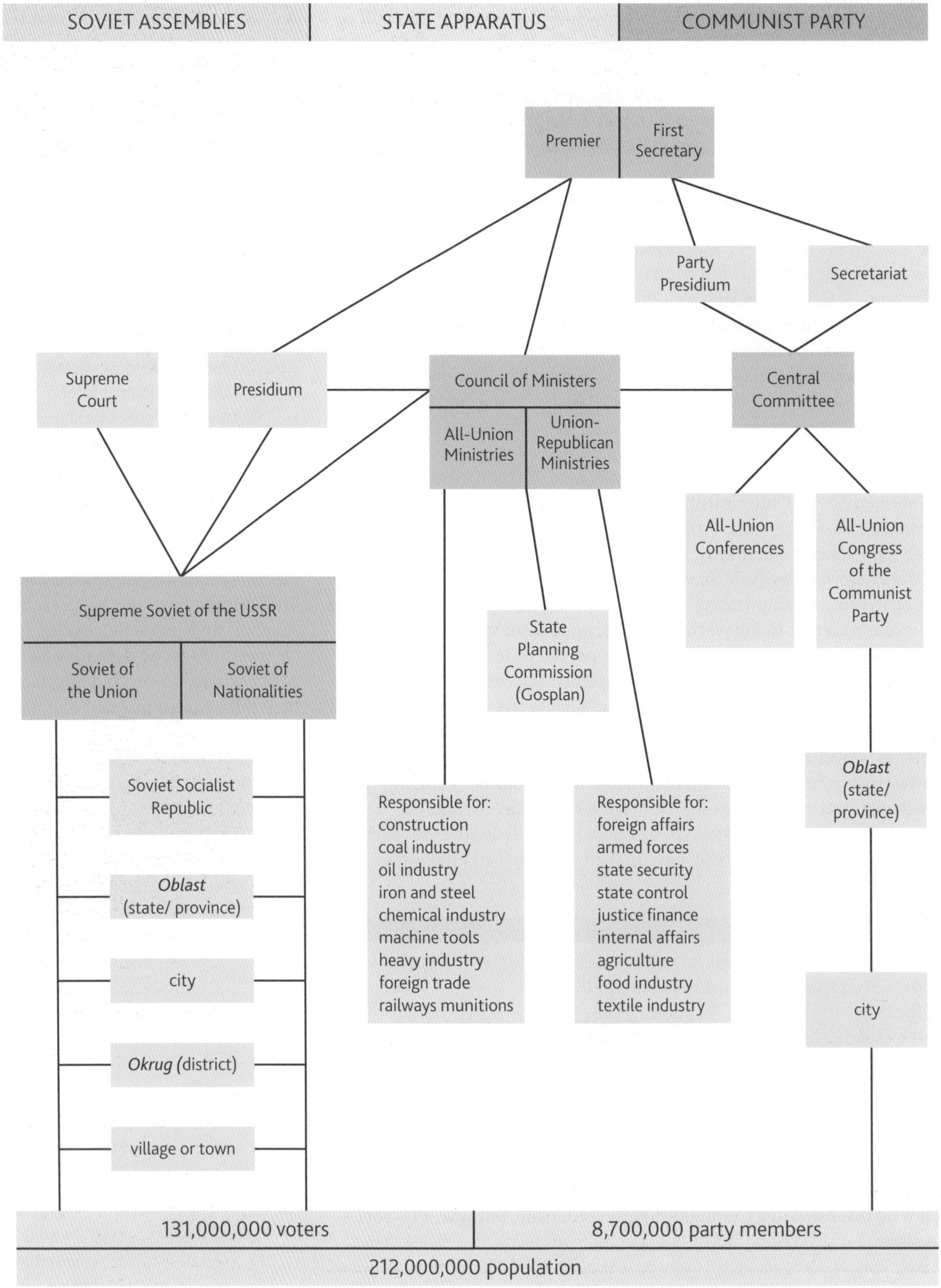

Fig. 3 *Organisation of the legislature, government, and Party in the USSR c1960*

1 De-Stalinisation, 1953–64

1 The USSR in 1953

The Stalinist legacy

Key features of the Stalinist State by 1953 included:

- collectivised agriculture: individual peasant farms had been merged into collective farms; peasant resistance to this process in the 1930s meant collectivisation was enforced
- an economy dominated by heavy industry: Stalin had brought rapid industrialisation through his planned economy
- centralised power and 'socialism in one country'
- totalitarian control: a state system in which everyone was compelled to follow a single ideology and any dissent or alternative political view was ruthlessly crushed by the police
- a 'cult of personality': the creation through propaganda of an attitude of extreme reverence towards a leader
- the dominance of 'socialist realism': a policy that required all art (e.g. literature, film, music) to educate the Soviet people about socialism and why it was good.
- a state protected by foreign invasion by a collection of buffer states in Eastern Europe, a strong military force and high defence spending

Stalin's immediate successors were all Stalinists – they had been Stalin's '**henchmen**' – and yet there was a rapid switch after Stalin's death, in 1953, to a policy known in the West as '**de-Stalinisation**'. This was because Stalin's legacy left deep economic, social, political, and cultural problems for the USSR.

LEARNING OBJECTIVES

In this chapter you will learn about:

- the legacy Stalin left when he died in 1953, including: his legacy of terror and paranoia; economic centralisation
- the power vacuum after Stalin and the contenders for leadership
- how Khrushchev succeeded in becoming leader of the USSR.

Fig. 1 *Alexander Solzhenitsyn on the day of his release in 1953 from eight years in the Gulag, as part of the 'de-Stalinisation' process*

ACTIVITY

Compile your own glossary of key terminology as you go through this course and try to use relevant terminology in your written work. Use the Key Terms and the glossary in this book to help you.

A CLOSER LOOK

'Socialism in one country'

One defining feature of Stalinism was Stalin's theory that the USSR could become a fully socialist country on its own. Previously, the agreed Marxist–Leninist view was that Russia's revolution would not survive on its own against the capitalist and imperialist powers that surrounded it unless there were **proletarian** revolutions in those countries too. The impact of 'socialism in one country' was Stalin's drive to build at all costs a strong, industrialised, socialist USSR that could protect itself against the enemies of communism, both outside and within the USSR.

KEY TERM

henchman: a faithful follower or political supporter, especially one prepared to engage in crime or violence by way of service

de-Stalinisation: a term that was used in the West at this time to describe attempts to remove the negative aspects of Stalinism from Soviet society, politics, and economy

proletarian: working people, the working class

Problems of the Stalinist legacy

The legacy of Stalinism meant that the USSR in 1953 was an uncomfortable place to live in for all but a tiny fraction of its population.

KEY TERM

kolkhoz: a collective farm operated by a number of peasant families on state-owned land, where the peasants lived rent-free but had to fulfil state-procurement quotas; any surplus was divided between the families according to the amount of work put in, and each family also had a small private plot

Gulag: the state organisation responsible for running the USSR's system of forced labour camps; an acronym for Main Camp Administration

CROSS-REFERENCE

Return to the introduction to this book for information on **Stalinist economy** and an explanation of who **Bolsheviks** were.

- Half the population lived in rural areas in 1953, with one third living on collective farms (***kolkhozes***). These people were not allowed to travel from their district. They lived in poverty and were extremely unproductive farmers. Agriculture was in crisis in 1953: production was lower than before the October Revolution of 1917 that had brought the **Bolsheviks** to power.
- There was nowhere near enough housing in the cities: often several families shared a single cramped apartment. Working conditions were also difficult. Stalin had made it a crime to be absent from work, and lack of safety equipment and workplace drunkenness meant accidents were common. Although women were equally as important in the workplace as men, they were expected to do all the domestic work too.
- The **economy** was based on heavy industry (like iron and steel manufacture), which depended on masses of workers, most of whom were working quite inefficiently. The military sector was very large, while production for consumer goods was limited. Although bread, potatoes, and vodka were almost always available, anything else was likely to be in short supply. The Party elite, however, lived in big apartments, travelled in chauffeur-driven limousines, and could purchase a wide range of products from special shops.
- Stalin's rapid programme of industrialisation took place at the expense of agriculture. By forcing peasant farmers into collective farms, Stalin ensured that the State could extract food products from the countryside very cheaply. Even during famine years, Stalin insisted that food be taken from the starving countryside, and delivered to the cities or exported for foreign currency.
- Some of the work in the Soviet system was done by prison labour. Under Stalin, millions of people had been sent to camps in the **Gulag** where conditions were often horrendous. Fear of being sent there kept people compliant with the system.
- Stalin's attitude to international politics meant that the USSR was cut off from the world economy and from international research developments. Anyone caught talking to a foreigner was likely to be arrested as a spy. As Western economies began to move from heavy industry to chemicals and plastics, consumer products (TVs, fridges, cars), and computing, the Soviet economy's dependence on heavy industry started to look outdated.
- Power in the USSR was highly centralised. In Stalin's last years, he restricted decision-making to a small inner circle – or, often, just to himself. It was impossible for just a few men to make all the decisions needed to run the country effectively.

Terror and paranoia

Stalin believed that the USSR was threatened from outside and from within by its enemies. Any problems in agriculture or industry were blamed on 'enemies of the people' who were sabotaging production to bring down the USSR. Because anyone could be arrested as an enemy of the people, no matter how high in the Communist Party or how low on the factory floor they were, Stalin's paranoia spread through the whole of society. People's fears were well-founded. Stalin's **purges** had turned the non-violent process of expelling potential political enemies from the Communist Party into an instrument of mass terror. The Great Purges of 1936–38, which affected every part of society and left thousands dead and hundreds of thousands exiled to the Gulag, continued to impact on everyone's lives. Not only was there general fear that the Great Purges could occur again, but a sequence of political purges and purges against ethnic minorities continued to the end of Stalin's life.

KEY TERM

purge: literally a 'cleaning out of impurities'; under Stalin it came to mean the removal (often through imprisonment or execution) of anyone deemed a political enemy

A CLOSER LOOK

The Doctors' Plot, 1952

In 1952, Stalin put it about that Jews, in the pay of the USA and Israel, were using their positions in the Soviet medical profession to harm the USSR. Hundreds of doctors were arrested and tortured, and thousands of Jews were rounded up and deported to new Gulag camps. The nine doctors first accused of the plot were sentenced to execution, but Stalin died before the sentence could be carried out. Those at the top of the Party hierarchy had suspected that they might be targeted for purging, too. Whether this paranoia was justified or not, these men had good reason to welcome Stalin's death.

Stalin's paranoia about enemies seeking to destroy the USSR extended to a powerful cultural control. Anything 'poisoned' by a suspected Western influence was condemned, and this was accompanied by anti-Semitism (Nazi atrocities were portrayed in literature and film, for example, without any mention of the Holocaust). If authors, intellectuals, composers, film-makers, and artists wanted their work to be seen, they needed to conform closely to Marxist–Leninist teachings, praise Russia's historic achievements, and denounce everything Western. Academic scholarship was greatly hindered as a result. For example, Stalin published his own views on economics, which no one dared challenge.

The Stalinist system depended on fear: people were coerced into compliance through fear of punishment. The fact that almost anyone could denounce another to the **NKVD** meant that people at all levels of society were very careful about what they said. People lived in a constant state of fear and shame, afraid to talk honestly even to their wives or husbands. After Stalin's death in 1953, the Party leadership decided to release Gulag prisoners in the so-called 'rehabilitations'. Yet Stalin's legacy persisted, because not only were there millions of survivors of the camps, but also millions who had survived by denouncing others to the NKVD.

KEY TERM

NKVD: Stalin's secret police, the People's Commissariat of Internal Affairs; replaced by the KGB – the Committee for State Security – in 1954

SOURCE 1

From a memoir written by Nadezda Mandelshtam in 1970. Mandelshtam was a writer and wife of the poet Osip Mandelshtam, who died in 1939 en route to a Siberian Gulag:

They thought that everyone sent to the camps had been eliminated once and for all. It never entered their heads that these ghosts might rise up and call their grave diggers to account. During the period of rehabilitations, therefore, they were utterly panic-stricken. They thought that time had gone into reverse and that those they had dubbed 'camp dust' had suddenly once more taken on flesh and reassumed their names. They were seized by terror.

ACTIVITY

Evaluating primary sources

1. According to Source 1, how did Stalin's legacy of fear and paranoia persist in the Soviet Union even after his death?
2. Source 1 is from a memoir, written some years after the event it describes. What are the strengths and limitations of this type of source for the historian?

The power vacuum and contenders

When Stalin died, Georgii Malenkov took up the role of Premier and also leadership of the Party. Everyone had expected this: Malenkov was Stalin's deputy and seen as Stalin's natural successor. Yet to the surprise of all, it was Nikita Khrushchev, not Malenkov, who went on to lead the USSR until 1964, following a struggle for power among Stalin's old inner circle.

Who were the contenders?

KEY PROFILE

Malenkov

Fig. 2

Georgii Malenkov (1902–88) earned Stalin's approval during the purges of the 1930s, and was a member of a small team, headed by Stalin, that controlled every aspect of life in the USSR during the Great Patriotic War. He worked on all Stalin's highest priority projects, including the development of a nuclear bomb, and had responsibility for removing rivals to Stalin's power.

Khrushchev

Fig. 3

Nikita Khrushchev (1894–1971) was the son of a peasant, from a village on the border with Ukraine. He worked in mining and metalwork, then joined the Party and worked his way up the hierarchy. Khrushchev was a commissar in the Great Patriotic War, ensuring the army acted as the Party wished, and took part in the Battle of Stalingrad. As Stalin's Party boss in Ukraine, he was away from Moscow at the height of the purges, but actively supported them. He became a member of Stalin's inner circle in the late 1940s. Soon after Stalin's death, he became Party First Secretary.

Beria

Fig. 4

Lavrenti Beria (1899–1953) was from Georgia, like Stalin, and had organised purges for Stalin in the Great Terror of the 1930s. Stalin had made him Head of the Ministry for State Security, which meant he was in charge of the secret police. He became Deputy Premier after Stalin's death, and was in charge of the MVD (the Ministry for Internal Affairs) and of the newly named **KGB**.

KEY TERM

KGB: the Committee for State Security; the successor to Stalin's feared NKVD

Molotov

Fig. 5

Vyacheslav Molotov (1890–1986) helped Stalin in his rise to power in the 1920s and was one of his longest-serving supporters. He was Stalin's Foreign Minister and ran collectivisation and the First Five Year Plan. He was the architect, with Stalin, of the purges. After Stalin's death, Malenkov made him Foreign Minister again.

Collective leadership

After just a week with Malenkov as Premier and Party Secretary, the Presidium – the ten men at the top of the Communist Party – decided that it was wrong for one man to have all this power. No one wanted a new Stalin, and the aim was to get back to Lenin's ideas about Party organisation, based on 'collective leadership', with decisions following discussion and debate. Asked to choose one role or the other, Malenkov decided to stay as Premier.

ACTIVITY

Explain the difference between the role of Premier and the role of Party Secretary. The introduction has information to help with this on page xviii.

A power vacuum

In practice, collective leadership simply created an arena for Stalin's inner circle, including the four main contenders, to battle for the top job. Initially, Khrushchev had much less influence in the Party than the others. Malenkov, Molotov, and Beria formed a ruling 'triumvirate', based on their huge influence in the government.

Beria's downfall

Beria launched a campaign for sole leadership. He did this with criticism of Stalin and a radically reformist agenda: a million people were released from prison camps on his orders. He also considered a unified, non-socialist Germany, in return for massive financial recompense from the USA for the USSR if the Soviet Union gave up East Germany.

CROSS-REFERENCE

The accusations made against **Beria** are listed in source 2 on page 7.

Beria's reformist motives upset Party conservatives, while his sudden lurch towards moderate policies alarmed his rival contenders. Riots in East Germany in June 1953 convinced Malenkov that Beria's ideas were dangerous and gave his rivals the opportunity they had been looking for. When Khrushchev acted to bring Beria down, Malenkov did not stop him.

Beria's downfall shows Khrushchev's political skills in action. Beria had the backing of the secret police forces, but Khrushchev had powerful friends in the army. On 26 June 1953, making sure he had the support of other leadership members, Khrushchev used the army to arrest Beria at a meeting of the Presidium. In December 1953, Beria was accused of treason and terrorism against the USSR in a secret trial at which Khrushchev and Molotov led the accusations. Beria was sentenced to death and shot.

Why was Beria executed?

In Khrushchev's rise to power, his rivals usually lost their jobs or, at worst, their Party membership. This was because Khrushchev wanted to end the fear associated with Stalin's leadership. However, Beria was a different case because he:

- was a 'Stalin-in-waiting': brutal, ruthless, and sadistic
- knew everyone's secrets: his spies had bugged senior Party members for years
- led the secret police, which had purged the Party before
- could be directly blamed for Stalin's crimes if he was dead.

Malenkov's demotion

Malenkov also set out a programme of reform. He acted to:

- reduce the power of the secret police
- improve agricultural productivity
- shift the focus from heavy industry to light industry: making consumer goods.

Khrushchev's tactics here were to ally himself with heavy industry and argue against Malenkov's approach to reform. In 1954, he started to put forward his scheme to develop underused and 'virgin' land, as an alternative to Malenkov's 'new course' in agriculture. When, by February 1955, Malenkov's policies had failed to prevent continued food production decline, Khrushchev had the Party support he needed to replace Malenkov, as Premier, with Bulganin: someone Khrushchev could easily manipulate.

ACTIVITY

1. Make a chart to show the strengths and weaknesses of the positions of Malenkov, Beria, and Khruschev in the period 1953–54. You could use a 'living graph' approach.
2. Research the main contenders and produce speeches setting out their programmes and views:
   a) immediately after Stalin's death
   b) at the time of Beria's arrest
   c) following Beria's execution.

Khrushchev's success

By 1956, Khrushchev was clearly the leader of the USSR. He had achieved this due to his:

- forceful character – more dominant than Malenkov
- political awareness – like Stalin, he was adept at building alliances to attack enemies
- Party role – as Party Secretary he had control of the Communist Party and important appointments
- power base – he put his loyal supporters in key positions, promoting them into the regional Party leadership (a significant portion of the Central Committee membership)
- war record – the army trusted him as one of their own
- time in Ukraine – as Party boss in Ukraine, he was not in Stalin's inner circle during the purges, so was less implicated in them than Malenkov, Molotov, Beria, and others.

Khrushchev used an approach learned from Stalin to weaken his rivals. First, he isolated an individual by linking them to past crimes or present failures. Second, he encouraged everyone else to criticise them – or be judged along with them. For example, he damaged Molotov by blaming his hard-line tactics for Yugoslavia's decision to split from USSR influence in 1948. Once he had isolated a rival in this way, Khrushchev could then often get a supporter of his own promoted to take over from that individual, as when Bulganin took over from Malenkov as Premier.

Khrushchev also changed the way the Party was organised, to consolidate his hold on power. He bolstered the strength of the Party against his rivals in government (see the diagram in the introduction on page xviii, which shows Party and government organisation).

- When Stalin died, Khrushchev was made a Party secretary (one of several). By the end of 1953, he had managed to be appointed First Party Secretary, a position that had not existed before.
- Khrushchev then used his position as leader of the Party to appoint his supporters to key Party roles in the regions of the USSR, creating a large power base in the Central Committee of the Party.

After Malenkov's demotion in 1955, Khrushchev and Bulganin acted as joint leaders until 1958, with Khrushchev surviving a concerted attempt to unseat him in 1957, when he and Bulganin were in Finland. Khrushchev's successful outmanoeuvring of the 'Anti-Party Group' demonstrates why he was the winning leadership contender.

ACTIVITY

Write a newspaper editorial for *Pravda*, the official Communist newspaper, celebrating the victory of Khrushchev in the leadership struggle after Stalin's death.

The Anti-Party Group, 1957

Malenkov and Molotov instigated the May 1957 political attack on Khrushchev. Together with Kaganovitch, another of Stalin's inner circle, they felt Khrushchev was wrong in attacking Stalin. A majority of Presidium members voted against Khrushchev, but Khrushchev used his allies in the Central Committee of the Party to outvote the Presidium. He also benefited from the support of Soviet army hero Marshal Zhukov, who had been brought back into power as Deputy Minister for Defence. Malenkov, Molotov, and Kaganovitch were denounced as the 'Anti-Party Group', accused of involvement in the purges of the 1930s, and voted out of the Presidium (29 June 1957). They were demoted to relatively low-grade jobs in places far from the centre of power: Malenkov as manager of a power station in

Kazakhstan, and Molotov to the Soviet embassy in Mongolia.

However, Khrushchev was not comfortable with being reliant on others. In October 1957, Marshal Zhukov was dismissed and a propaganda campaign launched against him. In March 1958, Bulganin was accused of encouraging the Anti-Party Group and forced to step down. At this point, when Khrushchev took on the role of Premier (heading the government) as well as that of Party Secretary, his success was complete.

SOURCE 2

From the indictment of the Central Committee on the 'criminal anti-Party and anti-state' activities of Beria, which was sent out as a confidential letter to all party organisations on 7 July 1953:

As is now evident, Beria wormed his way into the trust of Stalin. Beria's criminal anti-Party and anti-state activity, deeply concealed and masked during the life of Stalin, began to be revealed step by step after his death. Becoming insolent and unrestrained, Beria began in the recent period to reveal his genuine face as an enemy of the Party and the Soviet people. By treacherous intrigues Beria tried to cut off and split the Leninist-Stalinist leading core of our Party, to discredit individually the leading figures in the Party and government, in order to heighten his own 'authority' and realise his criminal anti-Soviet designs. As has been established by the facts, Beria impeded in every way the resolution of the most important pressing questions regarding the strengthening and development of agriculture. Now there is no doubt that this miserable enemy of the people made it his goal to disrupt the collective farms and create difficulties for the country's food supply.

SOURCE 3

From a statement to the Supreme Soviet by Malenkov on his resignation as Chairman of the Council of Ministers on 8 February 1955:

I ask you to bring to the notice of the Supreme Soviet of the USSR my request to be relieved from the post of chairman of the Council of Ministers of the USSR. I clearly see that the carrying out of the complicated and responsible duties of chairman of the Council of Ministers is being negatively affected by my insufficient experience. I also consider myself bound to say that now, when the Communist Party of the Soviet Union and the workers of our country are concentrating special efforts for the most rapid development of agriculture, I see particularly clearly my guilt and responsibility for the unsatisfactory state of affairs which has arisen in agriculture, because for several years past I have been entrusted with the duty of controlling and guiding the work of central agricultural organs and the work of local Party and administrative organisations in the sphere of agriculture.

CROSS-REFERENCE

The role of the Chairman of the Council of Ministers is defined in the Introduction, page xiv.

ACTIVITY

Summary

Make a list of the different aspects of Stalin's legacy. As you read through this book, note down examples of Stalin's legacy in action.

STUDY TIP

Make sure you read the details of attribution of the source. Information about provenance will contribute to your answer. Also consider content and tone, and apply your own contextual knowledge in your evaluation.

AS LEVEL PRACTICE QUESTION

Evaluating primary sources

With reference to Sources 2 and 3 and your understanding of the historical context which of these two sources is more valuable to an historian studying Khrushchev's rise to power in the years immediately after Stalin's death.

STUDY TIP

When you are asked to agree or disagree with a view, try to include your own point of view in your introduction. Remember that it is possible to either agree or disagree depending on your view of the evidence. You should balance points of agreement and disagreement in your answer, but in the conclusion emphasise why your view is the more convincing.

AS LEVEL PRACTICE QUESTION

'It was Khrushchev's position in the party that enabled him to come to power in the Soviet Union by 1956.' Explain why you agree or disagree with this view.

2 Khrushchev as leader

Khrushchev's character, ideology, and aims

Khrushchev's character and style of leadership

Nikita Khrushchev's style of leadership in the USSR was much influenced by his character. The way he went about making his reforms owed much to his personality. His rivals for power saw aspects of Khrushchev's character as weaknesses in a leader of the USSR:

- **impulsive and reckless**: sometimes announced policies without thinking them through – these became known as Khrushchev's 'hare-brained schemes'
- **uncultured**: had not had much of an education; was not sophisticated
- **bullying**: like all Stalin's henchmen, he could be a violent thug
- **manipulative**: critics said his intelligence was 'peasant cunning'
- **arrogant**: like Stalin, trusted his 'intuition' to solve problems
- **populist**: looked for, popular solutions that oversimplified complex challenges.

Against this charge sheet of character flaws, Khrushchev's character as leader was clearly an improvement on Stalin's:

- **anti-Terror**: apart from Beria, Khrushchev's rivals were not murdered or imprisoned; Khrushchev sincerely regretted his part in the Great Terror
- **open to new ideas**: Khrushchev travelled around the USSR discussing its problems with ordinary people, looking for practical solutions
- **internationally minded**: while Stalin had been isolationist, Khrushchev was keen to build bridges with both socialist countries and capitalist countries
- **power sharing**: while Stalin had been a dictator, Khrushchev shared power – as little as possible with his rivals, it is true, but he sought to give the regions more say and reduce centralisation
- **energetic**: while Stalin had become reclusive and the USSR had closed in on itself, Khrushchev launched a blizzard of reforms and promoted many of them personally and publicly
- **idealistic**: Khrushchev believed wholeheartedly in the USSR's historic mission to first build socialism and then achieve Marx and Lenin's workers' paradise of full communism; this gave his reforms ideological legitimacy.

Khrushchev's aims

Fundamentally, Khrushchev's aims were not radically different from those of Stalin. For example:

- Ideologically, Khrushchev was a firm believer that the USSR would become a Communist state through Stalin's '**socialism in one country**' route.
- Khrushchev thought the economy should still be centrally planned by the State, but more efficiently. Food production should still be from collective farms, but bigger ones, with better technology.
- The Party should still have the monopoly on power, but with less bureaucracy (complicated administrative procedures).
- People still needed to be motivated, but not through fear. Khrushchev wanted grand schemes to inspire people, and better standards of living so they (and the West) could see that socialism was delivering on its promises.

However, Khrushchev's critics saw his aims as being acutely dangerous for the USSR, because he was also ready to turn away from some aspects of 'Stalinism':

- By criticising Stalin, he was undermining the huge achievements of the USSR under Stalin: industrialisation and victory in the Great Patriotic War.

LEARNING OBJECTIVES

In this chapter you will learn about:

- Khrushchev's character, ideology, and aims, and his style of leadership
- the Secret Speech and de-Stalinisation within the USSR
- political and legal reforms
- changes to Party organisation.

Fig. 2 *Nikita Khrushchev was considered a man of enormous energy and drive; talkative and sociable, but also tough and shrewd.*

CROSS-REFERENCE

See page xvi for more on Stalin's '**socialism in one country**'

- By allowing more power to go to local areas, he was weakening central control, which could lead to unrest and dissent against Soviet rule, both in the USSR and in Eastern Europe.
- By seeking closer relations with the West, he was making the USSR appear weak to its enemies.
- By identifying problems within the USSR that were the result of the Soviet system, he was admitting that both Marx and Lenin had not foreseen everything correctly and that the Party had made mistakes.

ACTIVITY

Create a diagram to show Khrushchev's aims as leader of the USSR.

The Secret Speech and de-Stalinisation

In February 1956 Khrushchev gave a speech to the Twentieth Congress of the Communist Party of the Soviet Union (CPSU) entitled 'On the cult of personality and its consequences.' In it he set out the justification for political and legal reform by highlighting the ways in which, he alleged, Stalin had led the country astray. This speech was known as the 'Secret Speech' because it was delivered at an unpublicised, closed session of Communist Party members. It came as a bombshell to the Party members who had been educated never to criticise the great leader. Khrushchev said that Stalin had corrupted Lenin's intentions for the USSR, and explained how the Communist Party would put things right again. Although criticism of Stalin had begun with Beria, it was Khrushchev's Secret Speech that really started de-Stalinisation.

The Secret Speech included the following criticisms of Stalin:

1. Lenin had not trusted Stalin, because Stalin was rude and had too much power.
2. Stalin was personally responsible, with Beria, for the illegal arrests, imprisonments, and executions of thousands of loyal Party members who had been tortured into confessing to fictional crimes.
3. Stalin had not been the hero of the Great Patriotic War. Stalin's incompetence and arrogance nearly caused the USSR's defeat.
4. Stalin had created a cult of personality that, together with his intense paranoia, meant that all the proper organs of power in the USSR were ignored and overruled.
5. Stalin's arrogance also led to serious errors in foreign policy. For example, he believed he had only to 'wag his little finger' and Tito, the Yugoslav leader, would disappear. Instead, Tito's Yugoslavia split from the USSR.
6. Stalin's mania also led him to persecute ethnic minorities within the USSR itself because of groundless suspicions about their loyalty to the Soviet Union.

A CLOSER LOOK

How secret was the Secret Speech?

Despite Khrushchev's speech having been delivered to a closed session of the Twentieth Congress, details soon leaked out. A printed version was circulated to local Party organisations and read out at thousands of meetings in March 1956. It is thought unlikely that Khrushchev planned to keep it secret from the people of the USSR – a BBC reporter believes that Khrushchev himself may have authorised details of the speech being passed to him.

SOURCE 1

Adapted from the Secret Speech given by Khrushchev to the Twentieth Congress of the CPSU in February 1956:

Stalin acted not through persuasion, explanation, and patient cooperation with people, but by imposing his concepts and demanding absolute submission to his opinion.

Mass arrests and deportations of thousands of people, execution without trial created conditions of insecurity, fear and even desperation.

The power accumulated in the hands of one person, Stalin, led to faulty methods of directing the nation and the Party.

Stalin energetically popularised himself as a great leader; he tried to convince the people that all victories gained by the Soviet nation during the Great Patriotic War were due to his genius and nothing else.

ACTIVITY

Evaluating primary sources

What evidence can you find in Source 1 to support the six criticisms listed on page 10?

Fig. 2 *Khrushchev delivering his Secret Speech to 1400 Party members in a closed session of the Twentieth Congress; on the wall behind him looms a giant statue of Lenin*

The limitations of the Secret Speech

The speech caused utter shock among delegates. Some became unwell as they listened: 30 are reported to have fainted; some even had heart attacks. But in fact, the speech deliberately held a lot back. There was no discussion of:

- repressions and executions carried out by the Party before Stalin's rule was fully established
- the millions of '**kulaks**' and '**wreckers**' who were purged – Khrushchev could not afford to undermine confidence in collectivisation or industrialisation
- the purges of the '**old Bolsheviks**' – Khrushchev and his colleagues were only in senior positions because Stalin had wiped this original leadership out
- the involvement of the current leadership in Stalin's excesses.

KEY TERM

kulaks: 'rich' peasants, blamed under Stalinism for resistance to collectivisation

wreckers: a term used for 'enemies of the people' accused of sabotaging industrial production

old Bolsheviks: people who had joined the Party in its early days and had taken part, with Lenin, in the October Revolution of 1917

Why did Khrushchev make the speech?

Khrushchev's plans to speak out against Stalin were opposed by others in the leadership who feared that their own participation in the purges would be revealed. But Khrushchev thought the opportunity to blame Stalin for the USSR's problems outweighed the risk. The speech aimed to:

- distance Khrushchev and the Party from Stalin
- clear the way for economic reform
- allow for better foreign relationships.

For Khrushchev personally, it marked him out as a leader who would say what others feared to.

A CLOSER LOOK

De-Stalinisation in practice

De-Stalinisation took many different forms; in fact, the definition of what was 'Stalinist' was often vague. For example, there was a search for a new architectural style that was freer than that preferred by Stalin. Other targets were much clearer. Statues of Stalin were removed from public squares, his portraits and busts were taken out of Party offices, and streets and towns named after him were renamed (Stalingrad became Volgograd). In 1961, the Presidium removed Stalin's mummified body from its place beside Lenin in Red Square, and buried it instead inside the Kremlin. Although Stalin's reburial was carried out in secret, the other symbolic acts of de-Stalinisation were very public and generated a real atmosphere of hope and change within Soviet society.

ACTIVITY

Create a poster on the theme of 'de-Stalinisation'. You could use pictures, cartoons and words to create a vivid visual impact.

ACTIVITY

Copy and complete the table below to summarise the key aspects of de-Stalinisation, to collect evidence of reforms, and to evaluate how far the reforms went.

Aspects of de-Stalinisation	Legal or political reform	How far did reform go?
Decentralisation of decision-making		
End of the cult of personality associated with Stalin		

CROSS-REFERENCE

Khrushchev's reforms to industry, agriculture, and social conditions and living standards are discussed in Chapter 3.

Legal and political reforms

Khrushchev's reforms were in five main areas: law, politics, industry, agriculture, and social conditions and living standards. Each area of reform brought changes from Stalinism, although there were also elements of continuity.

Legal reform

The Secret Speech provided justification for reform of the legal system, which had already started to happen since Stalin's death. Under Stalin, the Secret Police had acquired arbitrary powers to arrest and sentence anyone, so that no one had the right to a fair trial. The reforms ensured:

- the release of millions of victims of Stalinism from the Gulag and a process of rehabilitating the reputations of those unjustly accused
- the KGB no longer had the right to judge and sentence suspects: the courts took this back
- people could not be accused of intending to commit a crime, or accused of catch-all offences like 'being an enemy of the people', or tortured into confessing to crimes
- 'comradely courts' – community tribunals – were brought back: where the community shamed offenders and could hand out community service punishments.

Legal reform was a key aspect of de-Stalinisation but, in practice, change was limited. The Party still controlled every aspect of people's lives. People were not free to go where they wanted or do what they wanted. The KGB found new ways to control and intimidate – for example, by committing political troublemakers to psychiatric hospitals.

Political reform

While Stalin had blamed individual 'enemies of the people' for political and administrative corruption, Khrushchev's reforms recognised that the system was itself to blame for giving government bureaucrats too much power and privilege. Khrushchev's Secret Speech criticised Stalinism for its excessive centralisation. His reforms sought to decentralise some powers.

- Under Stalin, bureaucrats in one ministry held on to resources rather than let another department have them. In 1957, Khrushchev partially decentralised the system so that 105 ***sovnarkhozy***, controlled industrial resources, not central ministries.
- Khrushchev put an end to many perks of office that senior bureaucrats enjoyed (including cash bonuses in unmarked envelopes), and placed a limit on how long they could stay in office.
- Technical experts were brought into senior ministerial posts so that key decisions were made by people with relevant experience and understanding of the problems facing the USSR.

The government bureaucrats were extremely angry at the changes. Many had to move out to the provinces and lost numerous privileges.

Changes to Party organisation

Stalin's death brought changes in the balance of power within the Soviet Union. As a result of the leadership struggle, the institutions of the Party and the government assumed a renewed importance as centres for debate and decision-making – the collective leadership that the contenders for power vowed to restore was a direct response to so much power being concentrated in the hands of just one person. Initially, a third institution – the police – competed with them for influence. However, with Beria's arrest and execution in 1953, the police were again placed under the authority of the Party and government, and their powers of arbitrary arrest and sentencing were ended, as described above. By 1957, Khrushchev had the backing he needed to decentralise the ministries and transfer power to the regional *sovnarkhozy*. The regional Party leaders, appointed by Khrushchev, approved the initiative and gained control over industry in their regions.

In 1962 Khrushchev introduced a radical change to Party organisation that split the Party into urban and rural sections at all levels. One half of the Party was made responsible for agriculture, with the other half responsible for industry. This division went from the lowest branches of the Party all the way to the Central Committee. This change was supposed to emphasise the Party's role in driving economic production, but was probably more to do with Khrushchev's attempts to remain in control when some of his policies were being criticised.

Summary

Khrushchev took a huge risk in speaking out about Stalin's crimes against the Party and linking his own leadership so directly to de-Stalinisation. Politically, although Khrushchev could promote his supporters to key positions, the majority of Party members were not helped by de-Stalinisation: they owed their jobs to Stalinism and so resisted change.

ACTIVITY

Make a chart. On one side list Khrushchev's legal and political reforms; on the other the results of these reforms.

KEY TERM

sovnarkhozy: ('Council of National Economy') system of regional economic councils across the USSR; there were 105 such regional councils under Khrushchev

CROSS-REFERENCE

The problems resulting from the *sovnarkhozy* reforms are described in Chapter 3, page 18.

CROSS-REFERENCE

The political structure of the USSR is detailed in the Introduction to this book, page xvi.

CROSS-REFERENCE

The failures in Khrushchev's policies to reform industry and agriculture are discussed in Chapter 3.

A CLOSER LOOK

Unrest in Eastern Europe

The Secret Speech had significant consequences. in Eastern Europe. It was taken as a sign of a 'thaw' in the repressive Soviet system. As de-Stalinisation spread to the USSR's satellite states in Eastern Europe, unrest flared up, most notably in Hungary in 1956.

Socially and culturally, Khrushchev's de-Stalinisation only went so far in exposing Stalin's crimes against the Soviet peoples. He stopped short of examining how the Party had allowed Stalin's purges, or contributed to Stalin's cult of personality, because so many in the Party were deeply implicated in them.

Economically, Khrushchev cleared the way for a new approach, but Stalinism had created a staggeringly rapid transition to an industrialised superpower. Khrushchev's economic reforms would be judged in comparison to Stalin's achievements.

SOURCE 2

Taken from a summary of questions posed by local Party members following the distribution of the Secret Speech; the summary was sent to the Party's Central Committee from the Department of Party Organs in 1956:

'Why was Khrushchev's report so limited in its contents?'
'Why was there no open discussion of the report?'
'What guarantees are there that there will not be another cult of personality?'
'Are other Presidium members also guilty? They must have known what was happening under Stalin but will not admit it.'
'Is there not also a cult around Lenin?'
'How could the newspapers lie for so long and now change track so easily?'

SOURCE 3

From a political leaflet created by a forestry worker, Boris Generozov, in 1956, after the Secret Speech became public. He was arrested in the same year after reading his leaflet to co-workers:

The Stalinist Communist Party has nothing to do with Lenin's Party. It is now criminal and against the people. The Party hides Stalin's crimes from the country and is now run by cowards and **degenerates**.

All of the country is striving for communism, we do not need exploiters. Is it possible to believe in this government? No! Never!

For three years the Party has hidden Stalin's crimes and now exposes them only because they are under pressure from public opinion.

KEY TERM

degenerates: immoral, corrupt people

SOURCE 4

From an interview in 2006 with the former Soviet First Secretary, Mikhail Gorbachev, who was present when the Secret Speech was read out in 1956 at a meeting of the Party District Committee where he lived. Gorbachev was an official in the Party's youth wing, Komsomol, at the time. After the Committee's copy of the speech was taken away, he did not see it again until it was finally published in the USSR in 1988:

I remember how my grandfather was arrested. When the Revolution happened, his family got land [and] he became a communist. He was the chairman of a kolkhoz for many years. Then, suddenly, in 1938, he is an enemy of the people! This is why, in this sense, I was prepared for the speech and interpreted it differently than others. But even I was haunted by the question: Was it really like that? Can it be?!

I think this is exactly what Khrushchev must be credited with. They say he trembled while he read the speech, but he read it nonetheless. I think this is where we begin our difficult, dramatic separation from Stalinism and everything it bore.

A LEVEL PRACTICE QUESTION

Evaluating primary sources

With reference to Sources 2, 3 and 4, and your knowledge of the historical context, assess the value of these sources to an historian studying the reaction to Khrushchev's Secret Speech in the USSR.

STUDY TIP

Provenance means where a source comes from, from when it dates, in what context it was created, to whom it was addressed, and for what purpose it was made. Starting with provenance is a possible way to begin your answer. Source 3 is from 1956, but comes from a police arrest: how might that affect how we view this source? Source 2 comes from an internal Party document: how might this affect what it reported and what it did not? After looking at provenance, consider the content and tone of each source and try to provide a supported judgement on the value of each one.

AS LEVEL PRACTICE QUESTION

'The release of political prisoners was the most important aspect of de-Stalinisation.' Explain why you agree or disagree with this view.

STUDY TIP

If you agree with this view, then try to show both why the release of political prisoners was important and why other aspects of de-Stalinisation (political and legal reforms, for example) were less important. To disagree with the view, you do not need to suggest that the release of prisoners from the Gulag was not important, but you might want to suggest that other aspects of de-Stalinisation had a greater impact.

3 Economic and social developments

Fig. 1 *Khrushchev in 1962, carrying a bumper crop of maize. Khrushchev had been impressed by the yields of maize crops that he saw on a visit to the USA, and was convinced new crops and new techniques could solve the problems of Soviet agriculture*

LEARNING OBJECTIVES

In this chapter you will learn about:

- the reasons for and results of Khrushchev's reforms of industry and agriculture, including partial decentralisation and the Virgin Lands Scheme
- social conditions and living standards
- the extent of 'the Thaw' culturally.

Khrushchev's industrial reforms

Stalinism starved agriculture of investment and focused industrial production on the heavy industries, like steel-making. Khrushchev attempted to shift industrial production more towards that of consumer products, in an attempt to improve everyday life for the Soviet population.

As a planned economy, in theory it was simple to make the USSR's industries produce more consumer products: set higher production targets for them. This was set out in Khrushchev's Seven Year Plan covering the period 1959–65: light industry and production of consumer goods were supposed to grow faster than heavy industry. But heavy industry carried on outpacing production of consumer goods, meaning that the needs of the Soviet people continued to be very badly served. The quality of consumer products was also very poor.

The reason for this weak performance was the planned economy itself.

- Central planning worked well for heavy industrial production which was concentrated in a relatively small number of enormous factories with clear supply chains. However, resourcing the individual consumer needs of 210 million Soviet people through central planning was far too complex a task.
- Central planning worked by setting targets for output, not quality. Factory managers manipulated the system to meet their targets. If their targets were set according to weight, for example, they would make each product as heavy as possible.
- Central planning was inherently conservative. Planners used data on past production to set targets, and factories were disinclined to do anything differently in case things went wrong and they missed their targets. Innovation was not part of the system.
- The state and party officials linked to heavy industry were also too powerful to allow investment to be moved from them to consumer products. Heavy industry and the military blocked Khrushchev's reforms. The booming space industry also used up scarce resources and skilled workers.

CROSS-REFERENCE

The space programme under Khrushchev is discussed in Chapter 4, page 32–33.

CROSS-REFERENCE

The ***sovnarkhozy*** are introduced in Chapter 2, page 13.

Partial decentralisation

The ***sovnarkhozy*** reforms were designed to improve the efficiency of Soviet industry by decentralising economic control down to the regional level, which would, in theory, mean that resources reached where they were needed rather than being hoarded by individual ministries. As well as adding substantially to government opposition to Khrushchev, however, this partial decentralisation also failed to improve the efficiency of the system. In fact, it made it worse.

- The central ministries had organised the supply chains between industries, which often crossed regions. Without the ministries, these chains often broke down.
- A new problem of 'localism' emerged, in which the regions organised their production with no consideration for the needs of other regions or of the USSR as a whole.
- All the problems of central planning still remained: while production resourcing was decentralised, planning was not.

As problems mounted up, Khrushchev sought to patch up the system by merging the *sovnarkhozy* so their number reduced from 105 to 47 in 1963, by splitting up central planning into different functions, and by introducing new committees that replicated some of the role of the old ministries. The Party itself was split into industrial and agricultural halves in 1962. However, the result of all this tinkering was that no one really knew who was responsible for what.

ACTIVITY

1. Imagine that production of coffee in the UK was centrally planned, with one or two enormous suppliers producing all the coffee for the whole country. What might this mean for:
   a) the quality and variety of coffee?
   b) the price of coffee?
   c) the reliability of delivery of the coffee for your school or college?
2. If the production of coffee was centrally planned, what do you think you would do to ensure you always had an adequate supply?

ACTIVITY

Copy and complete the table below

Advantages of Stalin's focus on heavy industry	Disadvantages of Stalin's focus on heavy industry	How did Khrushchev's reforms aim to change the system?	How successful were Khrushchev's reforms?

Khrushchev's agricultural reforms

The legacy of the Stalinist agricultural system was that food production in 1953 was lower per head of population than in 1913. The necessity for reform was therefore very pressing: new ways had to be found to ensure the Soviet population had food. Khrushchev's reforms were in three main areas:

- Increase the prices paid to collective farms (*kolkhozes*) for their agricultural products (grain production rose by around 25 per cent between 1953 and 1956).
- Open up new crop-growing regions – the Virgin Lands Scheme (see page 20).
- Introduce crop changes – maize to feed to livestock; increase butter and milk production.

Khrushchev's reforms did increase agricultural production – but historians argue about how sustainable the changes were, and how far he actually reformed the system.

Partial decentralisation

As with industry, Khrushchev placed the implementation of his agricultural reforms into the hands of local Party organisations. The Ministry of Agriculture's powers were thus reduced so that it became little more than a consultative and advisory body.

Price rises and other incentives

Raising the prices that the State paid for agricultural products produced a rapid increase in production. Soviet figures show that there was an increase in *kolkhoz* average incomes of 68 per cent from 1952 to 1958. The US government made their own estimate of 27 per cent from 1953 to 1958. However, although procurement prices increased, Khrushchev did not increase the prices that Soviet citizens paid for food. This caused tension within the Soviet economy.

Several other changes were introduced to encourage peasants to produce more:

- State procurement quotas were reduced, so that *kolkhozniks* had the incentive to produce more for sale (of which they would receive a share).
- Taxes were reduced and made payable on plot size rather than on what the *kolkhozniks* owned (for example, livestock), which meant more money to invest in improving production and an incentive for meat and dairy farming.
- Quotas on *kolkhozniks'* private plots were cut: produce from these plots could be sold at markets, bringing in money direct to the household rather than the *kolkhoz*. These plots were often more productive than the collective farm.
- Collectives were allowed to set their own production targets and choose how to use their land, on the basis that this involvement in decision-making would be an incentive for increased production.

State farms

Alongside the *kolkhozes* (the collective farms) were the state farms, the *sovkhozes*. While the *kolkhozniks* owned the land of their farm collectively, the State owned the land of the *sovkhoz*, and its workers earned a wage instead of the redistribution of farm earnings (as in the case of the collective farm). State farms were generally much bigger, more mechanised, more efficient, and employed more skilled workers than the collective farms. Under Khrushchev, collective farms were encouraged to join together to form state farms. The result was that the number of collective farms was halved between 1950 and 1960. *Sovkhozes* were used, in particular, to develop previously uncultivated 'virgin lands'.

SOURCE 1

From a report written in 1960 for the Central Intelligence Agency (CIA) of the USA about problems in verifying the economic statistics published (from 1956) by the USSR:

Through most of the years of the Soviet regime, the final authority for estimating crop production lay with the Office of the Chief Inspector for Estimating Crop Yields, attached to the Council of Ministers. This office relied on a staff of local agents to inspect reports and used historical correlations of weather conditions with crop yields to check the validity of local reports and determine output. It is interesting that US intelligence officers now use this same technique to judge the reasonableness of official Soviet claims for agricultural crop production. The agricultural delegations which have gone to the USSR under the exchange program have provided few, if any, checks on the published figures.

A CLOSER LOOK

Soviet economic statistics

The economic statistics published by the USSR acted as propaganda: the State used them to show how the Soviet system was better than the capitalist system in meeting its citizens' needs. The USA was equally obsessive in calculating its own (lower) estimates of Soviet economic production, which means historians often have a lower and a higher figure to compare. Historians working with economic statistics must therefore think carefully about why the figures were produced and how that could affect reliability.

ACTIVITY

Evaluating primary sources

1. Source 1 indicates some ways in which the CIA made checks on the agricultural production statistics issued by the USSR. Explain what they were and decide how valid you think those verification processes would be.
2. Which sources are more reliable: Soviet economic statistics or the CIA's estimates of Soviet economic production? Identify the strengths and weaknesses of both.

Soviet definitions and usage are often not explicitly defined, and their meaning must be determined by laborious cross-checking. For these reasons, the statistics released by the Soviet Union must be screened very carefully and not assumed to be comparable to US figures unless so proved by rigorous analysis.

A CLOSER LOOK

Khrushchev's special interest in agriculture

Khrushchev prided himself on his agricultural expertise. Coming from a peasant background himself, he enjoyed spending time in the countryside, talking with the peasants in an 'earthy' language which at least suggested (and probably meant) he was interested in farming matters. He contrasted his agricultural knowledge and experience with Stalin's lack of interest in agriculture which came, Khrushchev felt, from Stalin being misinformed about the amazing potential of socialist agriculture.

The Virgin Lands Scheme

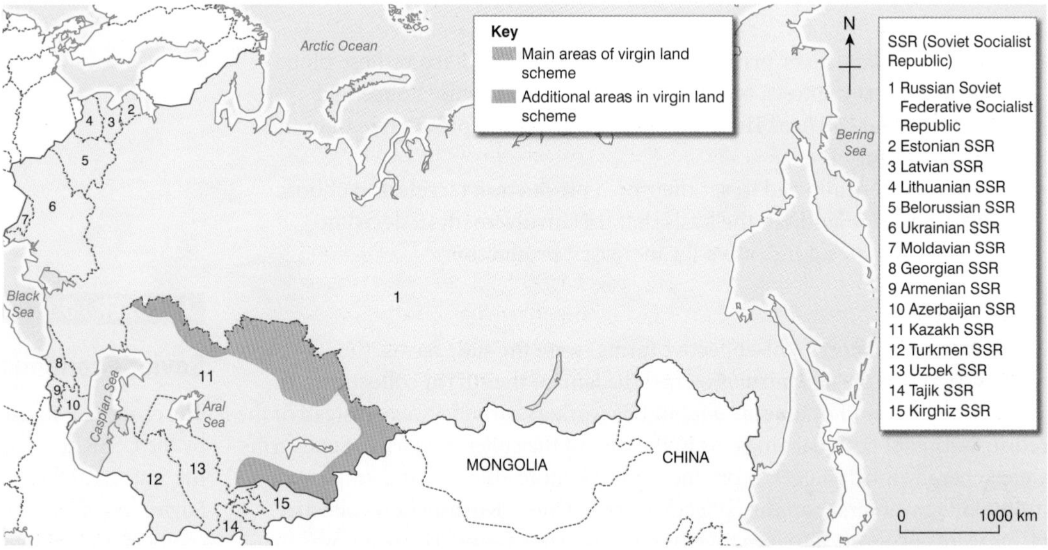

Fig. 2 *The areas targeted for the Virgin Lands Scheme were mainly in the north of present-day Kazakhstan. In total, the area ploughed up was the size of England: 42 million hectares*

By ploughing up the semi-arid grasslands of the Kazakh SSR (Soviet Socialist Republic), Khrushchev aimed to increase grain production dramatically. There were objections within the Party:

- Malenkov thought the area chosen was too drought-prone for grain. Khrushchev countered with arguments about improved fertilisers.
- Millions of people had to move to these sparsely populated areas, plus all the machinery needed, plus the distribution system to store and move the crops. Khrushchev's answer was financial incentives and propaganda to inspire young Soviets to go and farm the virgin lands.

Results

The Virgin Lands Scheme did increase production, but in a way that ended up damaging Khrushchev's authority as leader.

- The USSR's grain harvest increased substantially: up 40 per cent between 1953 and 1958, with 1958's harvest the biggest ever and 75 per cent higher than before the Virgin Lands Scheme came on stream. However, virgin land production declined year on year because the overworked soil tended to blow away.

- Higher wages and housing loans were attractive, but few stayed: conditions were hard, housing sub-standard, and the locals not always welcoming. Those inspired by propaganda were young, idealistic – but unskilled.
- Khrushchev's habit of promising constant increases each year was unrealistic given the huge impact of weather conditions on Soviet harvests. The harvest of 1963 was very poor across the USSR (due to drought) and this damaged Khrushchev. A famous *anektdot* (Soviet joke) of the time was 'What is Khrushchev's hairstyle called? The harvest of sixty-three.' (Khrushchev was completely bald by this time.)

SOURCE 2

From a CIA report of August 1954 on agriculture in the USSR, entitled 'Soviet Agricultural Results: Future Plans and Prospects', which looked forward to the likely consequences of the Virgin Lands Scheme:

The most spectacular and widely publicized facet in the change in acreage patterns has been the program for expanding food-grain acreage in the areas of 'inadequate rainfall'. This expansion, by itself, will increase overall grain acreage by 12 per cent. One-third of this expansion will take place on state farms. In these dry steppelands, the USSR can expect almost complete crop failures every 5 years. At best, the USSR can expect to sustain this part of the grain expansion program for only a few years. [Other problems include] the problem of utilization and maintenance of tractors in the new areas. Throughout the agricultural economy there is a shortage of maintenance facilities, primarily of repair shops equipped with machine tools. The other important input is the labour force. Although it is estimated that the total labor force required for the entire project will not exceed 400,000, there will be a serious drain on the skilled or semi-skilled labor force that will manage the farms and operate and repair the machinery. The rest of the agricultural economy is hardly in a position to supply experienced machine operators, agronomists or engineers without weakening their own operation.

AS LEVEL PRACTICE QUESTION

Evaluating primary sources

With reference to Sources 1 and 2 and your understanding of the historical context, which of the two sources is more valuable to an historian studying agricultural production in the USSR under Khruschev?

STUDY TIP

Remember that it is not only sources from the former Soviet Union that may be affected by ideological bias.

How successful were Khrushchev's agricultural reforms?

In 1961, Khrushchev boasted that the USSR would overtake the USA in meat production per head of population. Instead, in 1963, the USSR had to import grain to feed its people – a humiliation. In retrospect, the collective farm system was too inefficient to do what Khrushchev wanted. Wages were so low (even after the increases) that farm managers spent all their time trying to persuade *kolkhozniks* to do their work on the farm rather than farm their own little plots (where they grew the food they lived on themselves).

ACTIVITY

Thinking point

1. Was the Virgin Lands Campaign an extension of the Stalinist system or a reform of the system into something new?
2. To what extent did the way Khrushchev handled agricultural reform affect his authority as leader?

The reforms did increase production significantly, but they did so by extending the existing system. The Virgin Land farms were mostly *sovkhozy* (state farms): super-sized kolkhozes. They were still subject to the same limitations as collective farming under Stalin, except now without the fear of the Gulag to coerce workers into productivity.

ACTIVITY

Copy and complete the table below

Advantages of Stalinist agricultural system	Disadvantages of Stalinist agricultural system	How did Khrushchev's reforms aim to change the system?	How successful were Khrushchev's reforms?

ACTIVITY

Khrushchev's era is seen as a golden age for Soviet jokes. For example:
'A woman goes into a shop and looks at the empty shelves. "Oh, I see you have no sausage," she says.
"No, we are the shop with no cheese," says the shopkeeper. "The shop with no sausage is round the corner."
Are jokes a reliable source of information about how Soviet society viewed Khrushchev's reforms? What are their strengths and weaknesses as source material?

A CLOSER LOOK

Khrushchev's education reforms

Khrushchev was concerned that education had become too academic, and that this might explain why students were not showing much enthusiasm for working in industry and agriculture. He launched a campaign in 1958 to increase the amount of vocational training. As well as the academic curriculum they had been focusing on, secondary schools needed to provide all students with opportunities for regular work experience in local industry or on local farms. Universities had to change their admission policies, too, so that 60 per cent of places were allocated to applicants with two years' work experience.

Social conditions and living standards

Stalin's rapid industrialisation programme had no concern for the social needs of the Soviet people in the short term. Millions had moved from the country to the cities for work, but there was a huge shortage of housing and most people lived in squalor. Living conditions in the country side were difficult, too: there was poverty due to low wages and very few facilities.

Khrushchev's reforms aimed to effect a rapid improvement in social conditions and living standards.

- He led a huge effort to tackle the housing shortage crisis through the building of millions of new prefabricated apartment blocks (known as *khrushchyovka* ever since): 108 million people moved into new housing between 1956 and 1965.
- There were big increases in pensions and social security benefits, a reform of wages that led to pay rises for most, the introduction of a minimum wage, shorter hours of work, longer holidays and maternity leave, and the repeal of Stalin's war-time rule that made repeated absence from work a criminal offence.
- Pay rises for farm workers and an improvement in their living conditions came as part of the agricultural reforms.
- There was reform of the **education system**, so more higher education opportunities went to workers.

As with Khrushchev's other reforms, success was only partially achieved.

- The new apartments were a big improvement on before, but they were still low-quality, hastily built, and sometimes unsafe.
- Pay rises for farm workers came at a cost: the state farms often reduced the amount of land that workers had for their own crops (which they used to live on and to sell for money).
- Incomes did rise for Soviet citizens generally (30 per cent between 1960 and 1964 according to US government calculations), but shortages meant there was often nothing to spend it on.
- Education reforms caused resentment among Party bureaucrats whose children then had to compete with workers for university places.

Fig. 3 *A postcard from the 1950s by artist V. Govorkov. The construction worker is showing a modern new apartment. The caption says: 'Built to last and ready ahead of time' (a slogan that rhymes in Russian)*

The extent of the 'Thaw' culturally

Khrushchev's programme of de-Stalinisation was intended to recover the spirit of the October Revolution when people felt inspired to work for a communist future, rather than being forced to work through fear. Khrushchev hoped that some relaxation of the levels of control, at the same time as improving social conditions, would enable ordinary people to reconnect with the Party and its mission to achieve communism.

This relaxation of control is often referred to as the 'Thaw', especially in relation to a time of more freedom in Soviet culture.

- Writers were allowed to publish books that were critical of Stalinism.
- There was more freedom of expression in art, comedy, and music.
- Soviet people had more access to foreign books, radio, and films.
- Some foreigners were allowed to visit the Soviet Union.

The period of the Thaw was a very exciting one for young people, but there was often conflict between this younger, post-war generation and the older people who controlled the cultural organisations, who were much more conservative. Soviet culture during the Thaw was contested, with heated arguments in congresses and literary journals.

ACTIVITY

Khrushchev claimed that the USSR needed to show the world that the people in the Soviet Union were now free, they were not forced into work, and they chose to support Socialism. Using your own understanding of the Soviet system, to what extent would you say people in the soviet Union were free, worked willingly, and were 'building socialism' because they believed in it?

The Sixth World Festival of Youth

In 1957, Moscow hosted the World Festival of Youth. The intention was that young people from capitalist countries would be impressed by what the USSR was trying to achieve for its youth, compared with the inequalities and individualism of their own countries. Instead, however, the young people of the USSR were exposed, as never before, to the fashion, music, and youth culture of the West.

Fig. 4 *American participants of the World Festival of Youth, held in Moscow in 1957, travel through Moscow to the opening ceremony in the Lenin Stadium*

Even under Stalin, a few young people (known as *stilyagi*, from 'style') had tried to dress in a Western style. But after the 1957 Festival, demand for Western clothes and records increased massively. The demand was met by the black market.

For conservatives, it looked as though Khrushchev's Thaw was spinning out of control; most significantly in Eastern Europe (where it released uprisings against the USSR) but also within the culture of the USSR. It looked to them that young people were not reconnecting with the Party and its mission, but were instead being drawn towards Western culture and ideals.

The extent of the Thaw

Khrushchev's relaxation of control allowed Soviet artists more freedom in their descriptions of Soviet life. However, the limit was quickly reached.

- When Boris Pasternak tried to publish *Dr Zhivago* in the USSR in 1956, the censors refused on the grounds that its depiction of the Revolution and Civil War was anti-Soviet. It was published abroad, after which Pasternak was furiously denounced by the Soviet establishment.
- Writers **Alexander Solzhenitsyn** and Yevgeny Yevtushenko, who had seen critical work published during the Thaw, pushed further with later works and saw them banned.
- Khrushchev's own tastes were also influential. Visiting an art exhibition in 1962, he took offence at modern art, describing works as degenerate and asking one sculptor, 'Why do you disfigure the faces of Soviet people?' and saying to him, 'Only the grave straightens the hunchback' (a Stalin-style threat).

SOURCE 4

From a poem by Yevgeny Yevtushenko called 'Stalin's Heirs'. This poem first appeared in *Pravda,* the official newspaper of the Communist Party, in 1962, following Khrushchev's insistence that it be published:

We sowed our crops honestly.
Honestly we smelted metal,
Honestly we marched, joining the ranks
But Stalin feared us.
We carried him from the mausoleum
But how to remove Stalin's heirs.
Some of his heirs tend roses in retirement
Thinking in secret
Their enforced leisure will not last
Others from platforms, even heap abuse on Stalin
But, at night, yearn for the good old days
They, the former henchmen,
Hate this era of emptied prison camps
And auditoriums full of people listening to poets

KEY PROFILE

Alexander Solzhenitsyn (1918–2008) was arrested in 1945 for making derogatory remarks about Stalin (a common political crime) and went to prison for eight years (see the picture of him in Chapter 1, page 1). He was released in 1953, following Stalin's death, and his story of life in the Gulag, *One Day in the Life of Ivan Denisovitch,* was published in 1962. Khrushchev himself made the decision to allow its publication. From 1968, he came under attack from conservatives and in 1974 he was deported from the USSR.

ACTIVITY

Analysing primary sources

1. What message does Yevtushenko give about 'Stalin's heirs' in Source 4?
2. Why do you think Khrushchev was keen for this poem to be published, and published in *Pravda*?
3. Using what you know about the Thaw, to what extent was it a real liberalisation of cultural expression rather than a way for Khrushchev to attack his Stalinist rivals?

Summary

The key problem of the Soviet economy that Khrushchev wanted to reform was the poor supply of consumer products in industry and the low productivity of Soviet agriculture. However, while central planning for huge heavy industry factories worked comparatively well, meeting complex and dynamic consumer demands was very difficult to achieve through one central plan. And while increasing the amount of land used for farming led to short-term increases in agricultural production, the land used was marginal – it would only do well when climate conditions were extremely favourable. That meant that Khrushchev's reforms did not tackle the underlying productivity problems of the Soviet collective farming system. In his social and cultural reforms, Khrushchev made enemies amongst conservatives whose interests were put directly under threat by the changes. But for young Soviets of the time, the post-war generation, Khrushchev's reforms were exciting and filled with promise for what the USSR would become.

ACTIVITY

Summary

Compare the tables you completed for Khrushchev's industrial and agricultural reforms. Which reforms would you consider to be most successful?

AS LEVEL PRACTICE QUESTION

'Khrushchev's economic reforms were a failure.' Explain why you agree or disagree with this view.

STUDY TIP

Consider presenting some material to support the idea as a failure and some to challenge it. Weigh up arguments for and against, and provide a well-supported judgement.

4 Soviet foreign and international policies

Khrushchev and foreign relations

Foreign policy under Stalin was dominated by the fear of invasion from Germany and the need to make the USSR strong against attack. Stalin's paranoia meant all foreigners were viewed with fear and distrust. When Stalin died, Khrushchev appeared to reverse these policies, travelling the world, portraying himself as a leader for world peace. This was ironic considering how close he would bring the **Cold War** to becoming 'hot' in 1962.

Khrushchev's goals in foreign affairs can be summarised as:

- repairing splits in the 'family' of socialist states so that communism could provide a strong, united front
- establishing a policy of '**peaceful coexistence**' with the USA and the West.

These both involved strong elements of de-Stalinisation. For example, Khrushchev blamed Stalin directly for **Yugoslavia's split** from the USSR in 1948. Khrushchev's failures in relation to his goals, especially in regard to the split with Communist China and growing tensions with the West over Berlin and Cuba, were among the reasons why conservatives within the USSR organised his removal from power in 1964.

A CLOSER LOOK

Yugoslavia had a communist government but, unlike many of the Soviet satellite states, communism was 'home-grown' in Yugoslavia rather than imposed or encouraged by the Soviet Union. Yugoslavia was keen to follow its own route to socialism and communism rather than follow the Stalinist route prescribed from Moscow. Stalin was unable to tolerate this, and ties between the USSR and Yugoslavia were severed in 1948. In 1955, Khrushchev tried to repair the split, inviting Yugoslavia back into the 'family' of socialist states but, at the same time, accepting that it was possible to interpret Marxism in a different way from the Soviet model, which weakened the idea of an ideological united front.

The split with China

China's Communist Party had come to power in 1949 and had expressed some solidarity with the USSR – telling its people, for example, that 'the Soviet Union today is our tomorrow'. However, there was always tension in **Sino-Soviet** relations, too. The USSR had aided **Mao Zedong's** fight against the Japanese in China's north, but Stalin had not done much to help Mao in his battle against Jiang Jieshi Nationalists. Ideologically, the USSR's Marxist–Leninist path was focused on the proletariat, while in China, the vast majority of the population (over 90 per cent) were peasants, and Maoist theory therefore showed how socialism could follow directly from peasant revolution.

Reasons for the split with China (1960):

- Khrushchev's Secret Speech, criticising Stalin, came as Mao was using Stalin's example to consolidate his own cult of personality and to carry through collectivisation and rapid industrialisation – the Great Leap Forward. (The resulting famine killed an estimated 30 million people.) Khrushchev had also given Mao no warning of the speech, which infuriated him.
- Mao saw Khrushchev as a '**revisionist**', abandoning proper socialist ideology and becoming far too friendly with the USA. Khrushchev saw Mao as a '**dogmatist**', sticking to mistaken hard-line, Stalinist policies. For

LEARNING OBJECTIVES

In this chapter you will learn about:

- the split with China
- Khrushchev's policy for peaceful coexistence with the West
- negotiations with the West over Berlin
- the Cuban Missile Crisis
- the space programme.

KEY TERM

the Cold War: the state of political hostility that existed between the Soviet Empire and the Western powers from 1945 to 1990; the terrifying consequences of nuclear war stopped the two sides ever turning the 'cold' war into a 'hot' war of open conflict

peaceful coexistence: a policy of mutual toleration between states or groups that hold different beliefs, ideologies or outlooks; the foreign policy of the Soviet Union stated that socialist countries should be able to maintain peaceful trade relations and diplomatic relations with capitalist countries

KEY PROFILE

Mao Zedong (1893–1976), the son of a peasant, joined the National People's Party, but when Jiang Jieshi took over as leader, he purged the Party of communists, including Mao. Deciding that they must go north to safety, the communists embarked on a long march of 6000 miles, experiencing terrible hardships. When the Japanese invaded China in the Second World War, Mao's communists joined with the Nationalists to fight them, then turned on the Nationalists once the Japanese were beaten. By 1949, the communists had taken control of all China, which became the People's Republic of China, with Mao as Party Chairman.

example, Khrushchev was appalled when Mao said a nuclear war would be good for socialism if capitalism were defeated as even if half the world's population were killed, numbers would soon recover.

- For the Chinese Communist Party, unrest in Eastern Europe in 1956 was deeply worrying: they wanted no encouragement of dissent in places like Tibet.
- The Chinese also reacted badly to Soviet attempts to station troops in China, fearing that the USSR was hoping to make China into another of its 'colonies'.

The split widened to the point, in 1963–64, when the USSR and China openly criticised each other. Even after Khrushchev was removed from power, the split continued, as Mao then became worried that Soviet policy was to encourage the Chinese to remove their leader, too.

KEY TERM

Sino–Soviet: Chinese–USSR

revisionist: a criticism made of those who moved away from the official (orthodox) interpretation of Marxism

dogmatist: person who fervently expresses ill-founded opinions

ACTIVITY

1. The Soviet Union had seen itself as the leader of world communism, of countries united in ideology against capitalism. How do you think the split with China affected the USSR's image of itself internationally?
2. How might Khrushchev's enemies in the USSR have viewed the split with China?

Fig. 1 *Mao Zedong with Khrushchev*

Peaceful coexistence with the West

Khrushchev hoped to reduce the USSR's enormous military expenditure to allow more investment in improving living conditions for its people. To achieve this, he needed to confront the 'steel-eaters' – the complex of military industries and their heavy industry suppliers within the USSR, who were used to receiving the bulk of investment. His policy of peaceful coexistence with the West was designed to lower the threat of war.

Peaceful coexistence suggested that the ideologies of the USSR and the USA would continue to conflict, but that the governments of the two countries did not need to be hostile to one another.

This ideological battle to influence countries to choose one system over the other was a key feature of the Cold War, but instead of happening alongside peaceful relations between the governments, it instead led to flashpoints of tension and an atmosphere of increasing threat. This was exacerbated by the other side to Khrushchev's argument: that conventional armed forces could be reduced in the USSR because nuclear weapons would now be the Soviet Union's main defence against the capitalist countries.

A CLOSER LOOK

The Warsaw Pact, 1955

After its experiences in the 1941–45 Great Patriotic War, the USSR had every reason to fear a re-militarised, reunited Germany, and therefore it viewed with trepidation the 1955 inclusion of the **Federal Republic of Germany (FRG)** (West Germany) into **NATO**. Its response was the Warsaw Pact, which bound the USSR and seven satellite states together in a collective defence treaty saying that given the military threat of NATO, 'the peaceable European states must take the necessary measures to safeguard their security'.

Negotiations with the West over Berlin, 1958–61

One of the flashpoints contradicting any 'peaceful coexistence' between the USSR and USA was Berlin. Berlin was deep in the **German Democratic Republic (GDR)** but, like Germany as a whole, the city was divided into East and West by its occupying powers: the USSR for the East; and the USA, Britain, and France for the West. The existence of West Berlin caused huge problems for the Soviet Union and its **client state**, the GDR. It was part of the occupation agreement that citizens of Berlin could travel freely between the sectors. Citizens of East Berlin only had to look across a street to be able to compare socialism and capitalism, and what they saw convinced hundreds of thousands of them to cross over into the West and start their lives again in the **FRG**. Numbers reached a high point of 330,000 in 1953, following Stalin's death and the suppression of unrest in East Germany.

- In November 1958, Khrushchev issued an ultimatum to the Western powers: they were to withdraw from Berlin within six months, after which the USSR would also withdraw its occupation from Berlin. The city would become part of the GDR.
- The Western powers refused: although the existence of a militarised city split between occupying powers was clearly problematic, West Berlin was very important for Western propaganda and was where Western spies obtained most of their information about the Soviet bloc.
- Although the ultimatum was withdrawn, this was in return for more talks: a meeting of foreign ministers in 1959. The talks went on for three months, and although they did not solve the Berlin situation, they did lead to Khrushchev's visit to the USA in September 1959, which concluded with a joint statement by Khrushchev and President Eisenhower that committed the USA and USSR to solving 'all outstanding international questions . . . not by the application of force but by peaceful means through negotiations.'
- A Paris summit was arranged in May 1960, but was derailed when a US U-2 spy plane was shot down over the USSR on 1 May. A serious international crisis developed which saw the USA maintaining its right to gather information on the USSR in this way, in defence of US citizens and the 'free world', because of the USSR's 'excessive secrecy'. Khrushchev responded by threatening strikes on bases used by the USA in neighbouring countries (the U-2 had taken off from Pakistan).
- There were further attempts at a diplomatic solution to the Berlin crisis, but after the new US **President John Kennedy** also refused to surrender West Berlin, Khrushchev seemed to give up, telling the Twenty-Second Party Congress that the new ultimatum deadline of 31 December 1961 was 'not so important as all that'. By June 1961, Khrushchev was apparently convinced by the GDR First Secretary, Walter Ulbricht, that a wall was needed to divide East from West.

KEY PROFILE

John Fitzgerald Kennedy (1917-1963), commonly referred to as 'JFK', was US president from 1961 until his assassination in November 1963. Key events in the Cold War took place during his presidency, including the Berlin crisis and the building of the Berlin Wall, the space race and the Cuban Missile Crisis (which followed a US-backed invasion attempt of Cuba). During the Cuban Missile Crisis, Kennedy went against the advice of the majority of his advisors, who recommended an air assault on the missile bases, which could well have precipitated a nuclear war.

ACTIVITY

Create a timeline of Khrushchev's foreign policy. Use colour coding to show events in Europe, Asia and America.

KEY TERM

Federal Republic of Germany (FRG) – West Germany: a state made up of the parts of Germany occupied by the USA, Britain, and France in 1945

NATO – the North Atlantic Treaty Organization: an organisation based on a treaty of 1949 in which its members agreed to help defend each other from an armed attack by a state outside NATO

German Democratic Republic (GDR) – East Germany: a state in Eastern Europe that governed the part of Germany occupied by the USSR in 1945

client state: a state that is dependent on another state

ACTIVITY

Group work

Working in groups, create a poster for the East German government in 1961 explaining how the Wall benefited East Berliners. Match this with one for the West Berliners protesting about the Wall (the official FRG name for the Wall was the 'Anti-Fascist Protection Rampart', and Berlin city government referred to it as the 'Wall of Shame').

A CLOSER LOOK

Khrushchev's visit to the USA, September 1959

This was the first visit of a Soviet leader to the USA and represented Khrushchev's 'peaceful coexistence' policy, while also allowing Khrushchev to promote Soviet achievements to the American people.

A CLOSER LOOK

The Berlin Wall

Before the Berlin Wall (which divided East Berlin from West Berlin) was built, some 3.5 million people in the GDR had left for the FRG, most of them through Berlin. Although the decision to build the Berlin Wall came from the GDR's leadership, not the Soviet leadership, it solved an embarrassing problem for the USSR: if socialism was working so well, why did millions of East Germans want to leave? However, for the same reasons, it was difficult to justify the Wall. In his memoirs, Khrushchev (after describing the problem the GDR had of thousands of FRG citizens coming to East Berlin to buy its cheap food products) admitted that the problem was that 'West Germany has more material goods than the GDR. If we had at our disposal more ability to supply our material needs, there's no question but that our people would be content with what they would have and they would no longer try to cross over to the West in such numbers that the drain has become a major threat to a state like the GDR.'

The Berlin crisis had been of Khrushchev's making. He had issued the ultimatum to the Western powers in the hope that diplomacy would bring him real gains:

- the end of the costly Soviet occupation of East Berlin
- an end to the constant stream of refugees from East to West that undermined the legitimacy of the GDR regime
- agreements with the USA on a reduction in the size of armed forces that would have enabled him to reduce spending on the military.

Unfortunately, the U-2 crisis gave the Soviet military a major boost: proof that the enemy was constantly on the lookout for any weakness. Khrushchev's policy of peaceful coexistence with the West was left in tatters and foreign relations took on a harder edge.

The Cuban Missile Crisis, 1962

Cuba, a Caribbean island just 90 miles from the USA, had become a socialist state after Fidel Castro overthrew the corrupt Fulgencio Batista in 1959. Batista had been propped up by wealthy American businessmen (many as corrupt as he was), and Castro's revolution was very unpopular in the USA. Batista fled Cuba with all the island's gold reserves and the USA was so hostile to Castro that it backed a disastrous attempted invasion of Cuba in 1961 which was defeated at the Bay of Pigs. Castro turned to communism in order to access the support of the Soviet Union. Some historians think that in 1962 Khrushchev suggested to Castro that Cuba could be used as a base for Soviet nuclear weapons, despite having given the USA specific assurances that this would not happen. Having its missiles this close to its Cold War enemy would be strategically good for the USSR:

- NATO had installed missile bases in Turkey, near the USSR, in 1961. Putting Soviet missiles on Cuba was possibly intended as a bargaining tool: the USSR would remove them if NATO removed its missiles from Turkey.
- The USSR only had 20 **ICBMs** that could reach the USA, and their accuracy was not very good.
- Khrushchev may have hoped that he could use the missiles in Cuba to barter for getting the West out of Berlin.
- Khrushchev may have convinced an initially reluctant Castro that the missiles would also stop the USA attacking Cuba again.

KEY TERM

ICBMs: intercontinental ballistic missiles; nuclear missiles capable of flying from one continent to another (for example, from launch sites in the USSR to targets in the USA)

Fig. 2 *US reconnaissance photo of a Soviet missile site on Cuba, 1962. Evidence that the USSR was installing missiles on Cuba began the Cuban Missile Crisis, which brought the world close to nuclear war*

Khrushchev faced opposition within the USSR to his plans because of America's likely reaction if it found out about the missiles. When, on 14 October 1962, US spy planes identified the missile site under construction, tense negotiations followed, during which the world waited for the onset of nuclear war. President Kennedy's decision not to bomb the sites or sink the Soviet ships bringing the missiles to Cuba went against the advice of his military chiefs.

KEY CHRONOLOGY

The 'Thirteen Days' of 1962

16 Oct Kennedy learns of the Soviet plans for missiles on Cuba
20 Oct Kennedy sets up a naval blockade to prevent missiles reaching Cuba
22 Oct Kennedy announces the blockade in a live television speech
23 Oct Khrushchev orders the Soviet ships to stop around 750 miles from Cuba
24 Oct Khrushchev refuses to remove the missiles and accuses the USA of wanting to start a war
25 Oct Both sides reach highest alert levels; Kennedy asks Khrushchev to withdraw the missiles
26 Oct Khrushchev agrees, if Kennedy will guarantee not to invade Cuba and to withdraw US missiles from Turkey
27 Oct Kennedy's brother Robert accepts the deal, but only if the withdrawal from Turkey is kept secret
28 Oct Khrushchev accepts the secret deal

ACTIVITY

Extension

Watch the film 'Thirteen Days' or look at extracts from it on Youtube. This film recreates something of the tense atmosphere of the Cuban Missile Crisis.

ACTIVITY

Class debate

'Khrushchev made a serious error in placing nuclear weapons in Cuba.' Prepare speeches for and against and hold a class debate.

To resolve the crisis quickly, Kennedy agreed not to attack Cuba again and to withdraw from bases in Turkey, in return for the USSR dismantling its bases in Cuba and removing its missiles and any other military hardware that could threaten the USA. However, Kennedy's unilateral deal on Turkey remained secret because it would have caused serious problems with NATO. So, in the USSR it appeared as though Khrushchev's rash manoeuvre had brought the Soviet Union to the brink of war at which point, as in Berlin, their leader had capitulated and been forced to accept humiliating terms by the enemy.

The Cuban Missile Crisis made both the USSR and USA realise how close they had come to disaster, and how easily mistakes on either side could have led to nuclear war. Negotiations began to limit nuclear testing and a hotline was installed between the two governments so that communication in times of crisis could be assured.

SOURCE 1

***Pravda*'s headlines during the crucial week in the Cuban Missile Crisis in October 1962:**

Wednesday, 24 October: 'The unleashed American aggressors must be stopped! "Hands off Cuba!"'

Thursday, 25 October: 'The aggressive designs of the United States imperialists must be foiled! Peace on earth must be defended and strengthened!'

Friday, 26 October: 'Everything to prevent war'; 'Reason must prevail'

Saturday, 27 October: 'Peoples of all countries, be vigilant; unmask the imperialist warmongers! Struggle more actively for the preservation of a durable and indestructible peace!'

Sunday, 28 October: 'We must defend and consolidate peace on earth.'

Monday, 29 October: 'We must ensure the peace and security of all peoples.'

ACTIVITY

Read Source 2. Compose a reply from Castro to Khrushchev. (Note that Castro was angry because he had not been consulted about the USA/USSR deals.)

SOURCE 2

From a letter sent by Khrushchev to Fidel Castro on 30 October 1962:

As we learned from our ambassador, some Cubans have the opinion that the Cuban people want a declaration of another nature rather than the declaration of the withdrawal of the missiles. But we political and government figures are leaders of a people who doesn't know everything and can't readily comprehend all that we leaders must deal with. Therefore, we should march at the head of the people and then the people will follow us and respect us.

Had we, yielding to the sentiments prevailing among the people, allowed ourselves to be carried away by certain passionate sectors of the population and refused to come to a reasonable agreement with the US government, then a war could have broken out, in the course of which millions of people would have died and the survivors would have pinned the blame on the leaders for not having taken all the necessary measures to prevent that war of annihilation.

The space programme

In 1957, the USSR launched the world's first artificial satellite, named 'Sputnik' (Russian for 'travelling companion'). In 1959, the USSR landed the Soviet Red Flag on the moon; and in April 1961, Yuri Gagarin became the first man in space, with Valentina Tereshkova becoming the first woman in space in June 1963. These startling achievements threw the West into panic. The USA's first attempt to launch its own satellite, 'Vanguard I', in December 1957, was a spectacular failure.

Fig. 3 *Yuri Gagarin, the first man in space, is honoured at a celebration in Red Square on 1 May 1961. He is flanked by Khrushchev and Leonid Brezhnev (at this time Chairman of the Supreme Soviet Presidium).*

The Soviet space programme and the development of Soviet nuclear weapons were the crowning technological achievements of the post-war USSR.

- Khrushchev was able to glory in these technological achievements as proof to the West that socialism was superior to capitalism.
- The achievements of the USSR's space programme were also ones that all socialist countries could be proud of – a unifying force.
- The space programme's successes were powerful propaganda for attracting developing countries to follow a socialist path.
- The space programme gave Khrushchev the confidence to assert that the USSR would soon catch up with the West in all areas: in agricultural production, in industrial production, and in living standards.
- Rocket technology was also critical to the USSR's nuclear capability: the rocket design that was used to carry Sputnik into orbit in October 1957 was used first in August 1957 in a test flight of an intercontinental ballistic missile – the world's first.

However, the space programme was also problematic for the USSR's international relations:

- Sputnik's success overturned many Americans' belief in the USA's technical superiority. Soviet rocket technology meant they were not safe from nuclear attack. Relations between the USA and the USSR were underlined by increased paranoia, undermining Khrushchev's hopes for peaceful coexistence.
- Space exploration became a technological race between the USSR and the USA (and a huge drain on the USSR's economy) that quickly saw Soviet achievements eclipsed by the USA putting the first man on the moon in 1969.

AS LEVEL **PRACTICE QUESTION**

Evaluating primary sources

With reference to Sources 1 and 2 and your understanding of the historical context, which of these sources is more valuable to an historian studying the impact of the Cuban Missile Crisis of 1962?

ACTIVITY

Research

Search 'Sputnik' on YouTube and find the clip from a CBS TV special on 6 October 1957. As you watch the clip, make a note of the concerns expressed in the USA about the USSR's space programme.

STUDY TIP

Consider the historical context of these sources. You may find it useful to consider the discrepancy between what Khrushchev had hoped to achieve in Cuba and what he was eventually left with to justify his actions to the Party and the Soviet people. Try to establish the historical context before attempting to answer this question.

ACTIVITY

Summary

Working as a group, prepare a revision presentation on one of the following aspects of Soviet foreign and international policies.

- the split with China
- peaceful coexistence with the West; the Cuban Missile Crisis
- negotiations with the West over Berlin
- the space programme.

As a class, cover all the aspects in this chapter.

STUDY TIP

A Level questions of this type are looking for you to consider different sides to the question and make a judgement. You will need to analyse what is meant by 'strengthen' and should examine different areas of foreign policy critically in relation to their outcome for the USSR.

A LEVEL PRACTICE QUESTION

To what extent did Khrushchev's foreign policy strengthen the USSR?

2 Years of stagnation, 1964–85

5 Brezhnev as leader

Fig. 1 *This photo from June 1963 shows Khrushchev and his protégé, Leonid Brezhnev. A little over a year after this photo was taken, Khrushchev would be ousted from power, with Brezhnev leading the attack on his former mentor.*

LEARNING OBJECTIVES

In this chapter you will learn about:

- the reasons for Khrushchev's removal from power and Brezhnev's ascendancy
- the character, views, and aims of Brezhnev and his associates in government
- the *nomenklatura* system and corruption.

KEY CHRONOLOGY

1964	Khrushchev removed Leonid Brezhnev elected First Secretary Kosygin elected Premier
1966	Politburo reintroduced Stalin partly rehabilitated Brezhnev becomes General Secretary
1970	Term *nomenklatura* first used to criticise Soviet elite

Reasons for Khrushchev's removal from power and Brezhnev's ascendancy

In 1964, at the age of 70, Khrushchev promoted both **Leonid Brezhnev** and **Nikolai Podgornyi** to deputy positions in the Central Committee Secretariat, marking them out as two potential successors. Khrushchev knew not to give one person too much power; they might then be tempted to make a grab for the leadership themselves.

KEY PROFILE

Leonid Brezhnev (1906–82) was the son of a metal worker and worked in steelworks in Ukraine himself before serving in the Great Patriotic War as a commissar (a Party representative in the armed forces). After the war, Stalin promoted him in the Party; he became a full member of the Presidium after he backed Khrushchev against the Anti-Party Group in 1957. After Khrushchev's removal, for which Brezhnev did the 'dirty work'; Brezhnev led the USSR for 18 years, although it took him many years to completely consolidate his hold on power. His leadership was characterised by economic and political stagnation, escalating military spending and repression of dissidents within the USSR.

Nikolai Podgornyi (1903–83) worked in the Ukrainian sugar industry before the Great Patriotic War. As head of the Ukrainian Party, he used his experience in reforming Ukrainian agriculture. Impressed, Khrushchev promoted him to a senior position in the Secretariat of the CPSU (Communist Party of the Soviet Union).

Both Podgornyi and Brezhnev were Khrushchev's **protégés** – they owed their senior Party positions to him. However, they combined forces to get

KEY TERM

protégé: someone whom an older/ more experienced person supports and advances in their career

Khrushchev ousted from power. The two took advantage of Khrushchev's absence from Moscow in October 1964 (for a holiday at a Black Sea resort in Georgia). Having first secured a majority of Central Committee members for removing Khrushchev from power, and with support from the KGB and the armed forces, Brezhnev phoned Khrushchev and urgently requested that he attend a meeting of the Presidium the next day. Khrushchev flew back to Moscow, with some reluctance, on 13 October and was immediately taken to the meeting. There he faced a barrage of criticism from Presidium members, including from his former supporters, and a unanimous vote for his removal. Seeing he lacked any support, even from old allies, he meekly accepted the Presidium's decision that he should retire. The Soviet people were told he had stepped down because of ill health. Only weeks later, however, *Pravda* denounced Khrushchev's 'hare-brained schemes, half-baked conclusions, hasty decisions, unrealistic actions, bragging, phrase-mongering and bossiness'.

ACTIVITY

Can you find examples of Khrushchev's policies and/or actions to match *Pravda's* criticisms of him?

Reasons for Khrushchev's removal from power

Khrushchev had lost the support of his colleagues because of his leadership style, policy decisions, and the disappointing results of his reforms and foreign relation initiatives. He had managed to alienate his old supporters.

- His *sovnarkhozy* reforms and anti-corruption drives had personally hurt many Party bureaucrats.
- He had undermined support in the armed forces with cuts to army numbers, humiliated the USSR over Berlin and Cuba, and failed to preserve a united front among socialist countries, especially regarding the split with China.
- Having positioned himself, against opponents, as the agricultural expert, his many agricultural reforms had not achieved the high targets he himself had set for them: there were limited improvements in grain production, but the virgin lands were too marginal to sustain high outputs; collective farmers still put all their real efforts into their own garden plots; maize as a crop was planted in too many unsuitable areas and failed; and, put together with unfavourable weather, in 1963, the USSR had to import grain, some of it from the USA.
- As his agricultural reforms and reorganisation campaigns had run into difficulties, he had stopped consulting with Presidium colleagues and increasingly made 'subjective' decisions by himself and with a small circle of advisers.
- His leadership style was problematic: his impulsive decisions led to 'hare-brained schemes', he was temperamental, lurching from one reorganisation to another (the decision to split the Party into two halves – agricultural and industrial – for example).

ACTIVITY

Revision

Complete a table, listing in one column the successes of Khrushchev's leadership of the USSR and, in the other, his failings. Then consider to what extent you feel that the Presidium was justified in removing Khrushchev from the leadership in 1964.

Brezhnev's ascendancy

The USSR needed stability, predictability, and an end to 'hare-brained schemes', and the Party saw collective leadership as the best way to achieve this. Brezhnev, as Party leader, shared power with **Alexei Kosygin**, as Premier. Both were men whom the Party elite thought they could control.

KEY PROFILE

Alexei Kosygin (1904–80) was from a working-class family in St Petersburg, worked in light industry for much of his early career, and became a minister for light industry under Stalin. Khrushchev promoted him to First Deputy Chairman of the Council of Ministers.

The character, views, and aims of Brezhnev and his associates in government

Brezhnev's character

On his foreign tours, Brezhnev was affable and charming where Khrushchev had been embarrassing. His speeches repeated the need for realism and objective calculations; he stressed the need to base planning targets on previous achievements rather than wishful thinking. To his Soviet audience, he personified the Soviet bureaucracy itself: serious-minded, conservative, impersonal; rather than outspoken, bragging, or coarse. Towards the end of his leadership, however, ill health had an effect on his public persona. His speech became slow and he sometimes seemed confused. There were many Soviet *anekdoty* about this, which suggests some of his legitimacy as leader was undermined in his later years.

Brezhnev was initially appointed First Secretary by the Presidium as a temporary Party leader; someone who was relatively weak in terms of support within the Party leadership. This would, the Party elite believed, prevent him from following Khrushchev's lead in overruling leadership colleagues and would allow the Party to return to collective leadership. As Brezhnev went on to stay at the top for 18 years (from October 1964 to November 1982), does this mean that his colleagues misjudged his character?

Brezhnev was ruthless enough to betray Khrushchev, to whom he owed his Party career, and seized the opportunity presented to him by his Central Committee colleagues (those who wanted Khrushchev removed but wanted someone else to do it because of the consequences for their careers if Khrushchev managed to hang on). Under Khrushchev, Brezhnev had been a loyal supporter, but once in power himself, Brezhnev modelled himself on being the opposite of everything Khrushchev stood for. As well as frequently criticising Khrushchev's 'hasty reorganisations' and '**subjectivism**', Brezhnev strongly promoted a new culture of steady improvement, 'cautiously, without fuss or haste'. First and foremost was the concept of his 'complete trust in **cadres**' (1965), which was a hugely reassuring message to the USSR's bureaucrats, who had been put under great pressure by Khrushchev's reforms and yearned for stability and security.

Despite this astute political positioning, it took Brezhnev a long time to consolidate his position. It was not until 1971 that the gradual process of promoting supporters and repositioning opponents into less influential roles made him really secure. This suggests that Brezhnev's role in Khrushchev's resignation was an opportunity he seized when it arose, rather than the result of a long campaign to build up the support required for a **coup**.

KEY TERM

subjectivism: Soviet criticism for letting personal feelings get in the way of objective decision-making

cadres: groups of reliable, politically dependable activitists in responsible, influential positions within the Party and government

coup: the overthrow of a government by force, often using a sudden, violent attack

A LEVEL PRACTICE QUESTION

'Khrushchev's removal from power in 1964 was above all the result of Brezhnev's ambition.' Assess the validity of this view.

STUDY TIP

A valid argument is a solid argument, so to assess the statement you should consider where there are weak points. There are various ways to do this. Does the argument about Brezhnev's ambition hold up on its own? What other reasons were there for Khrushchev's removal from power? To assess the validity try to come to a balanced conclusion.

Views and aims of Brezhnev and his associates in government

The Politburo under Brezhnev had an inner circle of five:

- Brezhnev – General Secretary of the CPSU
- Kosygin – Premier
- Podgornyi – Chairman of the Presidium of the Supreme Soviet (from 1965)
- Andrei Kirilenko – Brezhnev's organisational secretary in the Politburo
- Mikhail Suslov – Second Secretary of the CPSU.

Kosygin and Kirilenko were more liberal, and Suslov the most conservative, but there was broad agreement among the five that:

- while technical problems remained that modernisation and time would fix, socialism was now developed in the USSR
- relations with the West must be on the basis of the USSR matching or exceeding the USA's nuclear and conventional military capabilities
- socialist states should present a united front.

In contrast to Khrushchev's exhortations about overtaking the West and achieving the great goal of communism within the lifetime of the current generation of Soviet citizens, Brezhnev stated that socialism was already achieved – a 'developed socialist society has been built' – and in an address to the Twenty-fourth Congress of the CPSU in 1971, he spoke of a 'world socialist system' that he described as 'a well-knit family of nations, building and defending the new society together'.

As soon as Brezhnev and his associates were in control, they set about reversing Khrushchev's reforms:

- The ministries were resurrected and the *sovnarkhozy* reforms abandoned (in 1965).
- De-Stalinisation and the Thaw were reversed: liberal authors could be arrested for the new crime of 'anti-Soviet slander'; Stalin's achievements were praised in Party speeches.
- As part of this, the KGB cracked down on signs of nationalism among the republics of the USSR, which had found some expression during the Thaw.
- The Presidium became the Politburo again, as it had been under Stalin, and Brezhnev became the General Secretary, like Stalin, instead of First Secretary. This was a symbolic rejection of Khrushchev's political reforms.

Although the KGB was strengthened and grew significantly in power, there was no return to mass terror as a way of controlling the Soviet people: this legacy of Khrushchev *did* remain.

ACTIVITY

Pair discussion

1. With a partner, discuss what Brezhnev meant by 'a developed socialist society'. How did this position differ from Khrushchev's?
2. Brezhnev set out a positive picture of a 'family of nations'. Which role in the 'family' do you think Brezhnev saw the USSR occupying, and why?

A CLOSER LOOK

Nationalism

Nationalism is when people attach a great significance to the nation that they belong to. Nationalism was a challenge to the USSR because it wanted the population of its republics to consider themselves citizens of the USSR, committed to a socialist identity rather than any nationalist one.

The *nomenklatura* system and corruption

The term *nomenklatura* (from Latin for 'a list of names') was first used in 1970, by a **dissident** called Mikhail Voslenski, to describe an elite 'class' within the Soviet Union. Party bureaucrats controlled lists of Party and government positions into which they had power to appoint people, and also lists of people who were eligible for each position.

A CLOSER LOOK

The Party bureaucracy

Although the Soviet Union styled itself as a workers' state, the social group who actually benefited most from the system were the bureaucrats. Soviet ideology taught that the Communist Party must lead the transition to socialism until such a time as the proletariat was sufficiently developed to take over, at which point the State would 'wither away'. However, under Stalin, the bureaucracy grew into its own social class that became criticised (outside the USSR) as a new exploiter of the workers: the bureaucracy controlled the economy and the State, not the workers, and it was the bureaucracy that profited from the efforts of workers, not the workers themselves.

KEY TERM

dissident: someone who opposes the official policy of an authoritarian state

patronage: the power to appoint people to good jobs, privileged positions

faction: a group within the Party that shared a particular point of view

apparatchiks: ('agents of the apparatus') operators of the bureaucratic system; often these functionaries were moved from job to job rather than being specialists

The *nomenklatura* system was a recipe for corruption. People were put on the lists because they were relations of the bureaucrat in charge, or had promised political support for the bureaucrat, and/or had provided bribes. These relations spread to create a management system based on **patronage** and **faction**. Everyone owed their position to someone else. Brezhnev had his own faction of supporters, Kosygin had his, and rival factions competed to get their supporters appointed to key jobs. Below the *nomenklatura* was another bureaucratic 'class' – the **apparatchiks**.

Corruption resulting from the *nomenklatura* system had significant consequences:

- Frustration and resentment that bureaucrats usually expected 'favours' in return for doing their job.

- Widespread apathy: there was no opportunity for promotion if you lacked the right connections, removing incentives to work harder or innovate.
- Ordinary people knew that the *nomenklatura* had access to better housing, transport, food, clothing, and other consumer products than they did.

The Soviet bureaucracy was often officially criticised in the USSR: the Soviet humour magazine *Krokodil* frequently featured cartoons depicting the problems that the ordinary Soviet citizen had to face when dealing with the system. However, the *nomenklatura* system was too deeply embedded in the Party, and the Politburo, for Brezhnev to do anything to tackle the roots of the problems: he had seen what happened to Khrushchev's attempts to reform the system, after all.

ACTIVITY

Search for examples of *Krokodil* cartoons on the Internet. Create your own cartoon in the style of *Krokodil* depicting one or more of the problems faced by Soviet citizens when coping with officials.

ACTIVITY

Pair discussion

Why was the Soviet bureaucracy an obstacle to reform in the Soviet Union? Discuss with a partner.

Other forms of corruption

Despite frequent shortages, everything could be obtained, for a price, on the **black market**. The knowledge that the *nomenklatura* had special access to these same products undermined any legitimacy the Party had in condemning the black market. Bribery, *blat*, was also ubiquitous: the direct result of every aspect of people's lives being controlled by an inefficient state. For example, mortuary workers generally required bribes in return for finding a space for a grieving family's deceased person. Bribes also worked like favours: networks of acquaintances traded things they had for things they did not.

KEY TERM

black market: when products or services that are hard to obtain are traded illegally, usually for high prices

Fig. 2 *Not everyone was able to afford luxury products*

ACTIVITY

1. Imagine you lived in a society where most people would require a little *blat* to do their jobs. With a partner, role-play different situations from everyday life: getting some medicine to make your pet better, getting the smashed screen of your phone repaired, talking with your teacher about how you might improve your grades.
2. How differently would you feel about people in authority over you if they treated some people better because they were relatives or because they had done them favours?

SOURCE 1

From a Universal Newsreel report on 15 October 1964. Universal Newsreel was an American news service that produced films on current events for US movie theatre audiences in the period 1929–67 (i.e. before most people had televisions):

The Reds say ill health prompted Khrushchev to step down. Observers say his abortive feud with Red China that broke apart the front of monolithic [all-powerful] Communism was the real reason. The crowds that once cheered Khrushchev wildly were left in the dark as to just what went on when the Central Committee met to act on his 'retirement' and to name Leonid Brezhnev as the new leader of the Party, while Alexei Kosygin took the job as Premier. Brezhnev has lately been considered Khrushchev's heir apparent, but the question remains as to whether he had anything to do with hurrying his boss's departure. Brezhnev is known among Western diplomats as 'The Red in the Grey Flannel Suit', a man who is expected to continue peaceful coexistence with the West while trying to heal the breach with China.

SOURCE 2

From *Leonid Brezhnev: Pages from his Life* (1978), compiled by an author team from the USSR's Academy of Sciences.

The October 1964 plenary meeting of the Central Committee of the Communist Party of the Soviet Union relieved N.S. Khrushchev of his duties and elected L.I. Brezhnev as First Secretary of the Central Committee. Leonid Brezhnev's election to the post of First Secretary of the Central Committee of the Communist Party of the Soviet Union followed naturally from socialist democracy and the Soviet Union's political and social development, which creates conditions for promoting from the midst of the people outstanding organisers with extensive and diverse experience in political, economic, and state administration to leading party posts.

STUDY TIP

When judging the value of a source, consider the authority of the author: was he or she in a position to know vital information about the topic in question? Try to look at both provenance and context in your answer.

AS LEVEL PRACTICE QUESTION

Evaluating primary sources

With reference to Sources 1 and 2 and your understanding of the historical context, which of these sources is more valuable to an historian studying Brezhnev's rise to power.

Summary

Writing about Brezhnev in his memoirs (1995), Mikhail Gorbachev judged that Brezhnev had been selected as an easily controllable replacement for Khrushchev by the Soviet bureaucracy, and that 'Brezhnevism' was a conservative reaction against Khrushchev's attempts to reform the USSR. The 'years of stagnation' under Brezhnev were, to the Party cadres, far preferable to the uncertainty and instability of Khrushchev's leadership. But Brezhnev's character also helps explain the years of stagnation. He seems characteristic of the society he presided over: conservative, cautious, corrupt, complacent. While Khrushchev wanted to meet the people's needs by punching through the bureaucracy that prevented change, Brezhnev sided with the bureaucracy and put his 'trust in the cadres'.

6 Economic and social policies and problems under Brezhnev

Fig. 1 *General Secretary Leonid Brezhnev and Premier Alexei Kosygin in 1967, on a visit to Hungary. Kosygin was keen to introduce decentralising economic reforms, while Brezhnev wanted stability and an end to radical policy experiments*

LEARNING OBJECTIVES

In this chapter you will learn about:

- Kosygin's attempted reforms
- the Tenth Five Year Plan, industry, agriculture, and defence spending
- consumer goods, living standards, and lifestyles for the elite and the workers

KEY CHRONOLOGY

1965	Kosygin's economic reforms agreed
1968	Invasion of Czechoslovakia; Kosygin's reforms shelved
1970	One million cars on USSR's roads
1971	Ninth Five Year Plan
1976	Tenth Five Year Plan

CROSS-REFERENCE

See page 36 in Chapter 5 for information about Kosygin's rise to Premier.

Kosygin's attempted reforms

The context of Kosygin's reforms

Alexei Kosygin argued that giving more independence to factories and other enterprises would free the economy from problems caused by central planning. Against him was a **faction** representing the interests of the bureaucracy and Party ideology. They did not want the Party to lose control over enterprises and their workers. Very unusually, the argument between the factions appeared in Communist newspapers in May 1965: *Izvestia* for the Kosygin faction and *Pravda* for the **bureaucracy** (complicated administrative procedures).

- *Izvestia* argued that the Soviet economy should be allowed to operate according to 'economic laws' like **profit incentives**: allowing factories to aim to make a profit from their products instead of just meeting plan targets.

KEY TERM

faction: a small, organised, dissenting group within a larger organisation

profit incentives: allowing a small amount of capitalism; if businesses were allowed to keep some profits from their production, the 'profit incentive' would encourage them to produce what customers wanted, in order to maximise sales; they would also do so more efficiently, in order to minimise costs

- *Pravda* argued that profit incentives would promote individualism and selfishness, which were not socialist principles. Introducing elements of capitalism would be a **deviation** towards private interests instead of collective (community) interests.

ACTIVITY

Explain in your own words why *Pravda* objected to the argument for profit incentives in Soviet factories.

KEY TERM

deviation: Soviet criticism for those who strayed from the proper ideological route

Kosygin's reforms

Brezhnev was not on Kosygin's side – he called for the Party's authority to be strengthened. However, in 1965 neither Brezhnev nor Kosygin was in a strong enough position to push the other faction out. The result was that economic reforms *were* passed in September 1965, but they were ineffective.

Kosygin's reforms gave industry more economic independence, in the expectation that it would become more productive:

- The number of targets that enterprises had to meet were reduced, some targets were set for the numbers of products sold rather than the numbers produced, and for efficiency of production.
- Individual managers could make some decisions about what they produced (one fifth of investment could be spent this way), and they could keep some of the profit made to invest back into their enterprise.
- Their workers, too, would be paid not just according to their contribution, but would also share in the success of their company. Managers could even sack unproductive workers.

However, at the same time, Khrushchev's ***sovnarkhozy*** were cancelled and the central ministries re-established and given all their old powers back. This was a major concession to the bureaucracy faction. Kosygin's reforms were about economic decentralisation – moving control out from the centre to the industries themselves. The return of the ministries gave ultimate control of the economy back to the centre.

ACTIVITY

1. Create two columns headed 'The Brezhnev Faction' and 'The Kosygin Faction'. In them list the main points of difference between the two groups.
2. Write an article for either *Izvestia* or *Pravda* showing support for one of the factions.

CROSS-REFERENCE

The ***sovnarkhozy*** are introduced and explained in Chapter 2, page 14.

Results of the reforms

- By the end of 1967, 15 per cent of enterprises in 17 branches of industry worked under the new conditions, representing a third of all industrial output. While labour productivity did increase, it did not hit the reforms' targets.
- There was evidence of managers starting to use their new freedoms between 1965 and 1971, but this alarmed the bureaucrats, who feared economic control slipping away.
- There was also concern about workers being laid off under the reforms. Under the Soviet system, enterprises took on a large number of workers as this often helped to meet targets and maximise investment. Unemployment was almost unknown.
- The ministries reasserted their control on enterprises. Freedoms for managers were hedged with restrictions on the ways in which investment could be used. The number of targets was again increased.
- Similar reforms in Czechoslovakia triggered unrest against Soviet control in 1968. There was a backlash against the reforms in the USSR which damaged Kosygin. He was not weakened enough for Brezhnev to replace him as Premier, but his reforms were shelved.

CROSS-REFERENCE

There is more about the reforms in Czechoslovakia and the events of the Prague Spring in Chapter 16, pages 135–137.

The Tenth Five Year Plan

The Tenth Five Year Plan covered the period 1976 to 1980. Analysts in the West seized on the plan's lowered targets as evidence of economic problems, calling it 'the most modest plan in Soviet history' due to 'a long-term slowdown in the growth of the Soviet economy'.

Table 1 *Growth in output: targets and outcomes of the Ninth and Tenth Five Year Plans*

	Outcome of the Ninth Five Year Plan by 1975	Target for the Tenth Five Year Plan 1976–80
Soviet Union	43%	36%
Heavy industry	45.7%	38%
Consumer industry	36.7%	32%
Agriculture	13%	17%

Brezhnev referred the Tenth Five Year Plan as 'the plan of effectiveness and quality.' Explaining that lower rates of growth were due to a slowdown in technological progress, Brezhnev said that the plan aimed to modernise Soviet productivity: improving technology within plants to make workers more effective and the products they produced of higher quality.

ACTIVITY

Statistical analysis

What conclusions can be drawn from Table 1 about the Tenth Five Year Plan?

A CLOSER LOOK

Economic growth and socialism

In Soviet ideology, socialism was supposed to deliver economic growth year on year. Khrushchev had confidently predicted that the USSR would overtake the West economically by the 1970s, and would reach full communism by the 1980s. Brezhnev's ideological position was less ambitious, but any downturn in growth was troubling. The USSR's economic problems were not a state secret: they were widely discussed. But the discussion was about identifying the obstacles to the growth that socialism must produce, not about questioning whether the Marxist–Leninist theory was itself flawed.

Reasons for the economic slowdown

Economic growth slowed to 2 per cent a year in the 1970s. Several factors were involved in this:

- agriculture remained in crisis
- military spending siphoned money from the economy
- **bottlenecks in production** slowed down the economy
- living standards increased with higher wages, but there was little for people to spend their money on
- natural resources (e.g. oil, coal) were running out in European Russia, and production from Siberia was slow to develop
- a decline in 'plan discipline' – workers and managers lost motivation to meet targets
- demographic factors: the population was growing more slowly.

A CLOSER LOOK

Bottlenecks in production

These happen in complex production systems when one stage of production holds up everything else. For example, if one factory produced ball bearings that were used by a large number of other engineering plants, any delay in the delivery of ball bearings would hold up production everywhere else.

ACTIVITY

Make a diagram to show the reasons for the economic slowdown in the 1970s and use the information in this chapter together with further research to provide two bullet points of detail to accompany each reason.

A CLOSER LOOK

Soviet exchange rates

The USSR set an exchange rate of one US dollar being equivalent to 0.8 roubles: so 19 billion roubles was officially worth 23.8 billion dollars. But this official exchange rate had no basis in reality since the rouble was not traded on the international monetary markets and it was illegal to take roubles out of the USSR.

Agriculture

The Tenth Five Year Plan announced an increase in investment for agriculture. Khrushchev had increased agriculture's share of investment from almost nothing under Stalin to 16 per cent. Brezhnev increased it to 27 per cent. Prices for agricultural products were again increased, which meant higher incomes for the farm workers. But the result was that existing inefficient farming practices continued to be subsidised by the State. The need to keep the price of food low in the cities (the Party worried that there would be unrest otherwise) meant that the State could not pass on its higher costs for food to the consumers, making agriculture a burden on the economy. In 1977, the subsidy to agriculture cost the USSR 19 billion rubles.

The tension between the need to reward agricultural production with high procurement prices and the necessity of fixing the price of staple foods at a low rate for consumers had serious impacts on agriculture itself as it removed incentives to improve production. Worker productivity was extremely low in collective agriculture, with individuals shirking work if they could. Instead they put their efforts into their private plots, the produce from which could feed the family and also potentially provide surplus income when sold at markets. Although increased procurement prices from the State meant more income to share between kolkhoz members, and although those who worked more received more, it made more economic sense to take the minimum payment for collective work and maximise output on the private plots.

KEY TERM

GDP: (gross domestic product) the income of a country in one year; Soviet statisticians actually used a different measure, which had to be adjusted for comparisons with GDP

Defence spending

Fig. 2 *Soviet Army parade in the 1970s. The Red Army was formed in 1918 and continued to be called that in the West until the end of the Soviet Union in 1991, though it actually changed its name to the Soviet Army in 1946.*

ACTIVITY

Pair discussion

Discuss with a partner the rationale behind the USSR's drive to achieve parity in nuclear capability with the USA. Try to think of three reasons why, for Brezhnev, the cost of this military spending was justified.

The USSR made achieving parity (equal status) with the USA in its nuclear forces its top priority. The military budget increased five-fold between 1965 and 1969 (thought to be the equivalent of $42 billion in 1969), and Brezhnev increased military spending eight-fold over the course of his rule so that by 1982, 15 per cent of the USSR's **GDP** was spent on the military. This put a strain on the rest of the economy, which the leadership admitted: Brezhnev stated in 1971 that while socialism was strong enough to allow both defence spending and economic development, the Soviet economy would have developed more quickly if defence spending had not been required.

A CLOSER LOOK

Research priorities

Research and development in the USSR was primarily devoted to the military. Closed cities were cities and towns which were off limits to foreign tourists because of their military connections (e.g. military research centres or industrial centres). Residents required permits to live there. Because the research had military implications, the towns were secret and the results of their research were not shared with non-military industries. A technological gap widened between the USSR and the West.

Consumer goods, living standards, and lifestyles

Brezhnev put a high priority on improving living standards for the Soviet people: a better supply of higher-quality goods in the shops, better housing, higher wages, lower prices. Production in the light industries that made consumer goods was boosted in the Five Year Plans of the Brezhnev era, including the Tenth. In an address to the Party Plenum in 1965, Brezhnev stressed the need for the Soviet people to know how much the Party and government cared about increasing both their material well-being and also their cultural well-being.

Fig. 3 *A mother and her daughter shopping in Murmansk, in the north west of the USSR, in 1970 or 1971*

Brezhnev delivered on this commitment. The Soviet people enjoyed virtually full employment and job security; high-quality education and healthcare were free; radios, refrigerators, and telephones were common; and televisions and cars were much more available than previously (by 1970, there were a million private cars on the USSR's roads). Today's Russians regularly vote Brezhnev as the best leader of the twentieth century and remember his era as a 'golden age' of material satisfaction and international prestige.

By prioritising rising living standards, Brezhnev forged a 'social contract' with the Soviet people: replacing Stalin's coercion and Khrushchev's campaigns and ideological enthusiasm with a sort of **consumerism**. In return for relative comfort and security, the Soviet people did not challenge the Party politically, allowing the system to roll on as before – stagnation.

KEY TERM

consumerism: a culture or system that puts high value on being able to purchase and show off the new things you have bought to enhance your lifestyle

ACTIVITY

Extension

If you have not already done so, try to read George Orwell's satire on Stalinism, *Animal Farm* (1945). In this book the original slogan of the animals changes from 'All animals are equal' to 'All animals are equal, but some are more equal than others'. Discuss in your class what this means, and what it suggests about inequality in Soviet society before Brezhnev.

A CLOSER LOOK

Consumerism

Officially, there was no conflict between Soviet citizens enjoying the purchase of consumer goods and socialism, because socialism was supposed to deliver material abundance. However, consumerism undermined socialist ideology because it was individualistic rather than collective, and created inequalities in the system between those who could access better products and services, and those who could not. Socialist consumerism was an attempt to provide consumer products that everyone had the opportunity to purchase.

Fig. 4 *Cars being manufactured at the Leninist Communist Youth League Automobile Factory in Moscow, 1973. In 1972, for the first time in the USSR, more cars were manufactured than trucks*

KEY TERM

dacha: a country cottage (usually wooden) used for summer weekends and vacations

Lifestyles for the elite

At the top of the Soviet social hierarchy was the Party elite, who enjoyed exclusive lifestyles in the most important cities: chauffeured cars, big flats, country **dachas**, and access to special shops that sold luxury products. Their children went to schools and universities that had a strong connection with successful careers. They took holidays in the Black Sea in the warm south of the USSR. Understandably, these arrangements fed into the general view of a system that was not fair. Although the lavish lifestyles enjoyed by Brezhnev and the Party leadership were kept secret, there were clear indications that they were the social elite – for example, Moscow main roads had a special lane for the luxurious Zil cars of the Party *nomenklatura*.

The Party promoted a 'high culture' aesthetic for all of Soviet society, which meant that what would be considered elite cultural events (such as ballet, classical concerts, and theatre) had a mass audience. Soviet culture was also very literary, supported by virtually universal literacy from an education system that put a high value on everyone reading the classics of Russian literature. But there were strict controls on what was permitted in this high culture, which were frustrating for some of the highly educated elite who wanted to explore other ways of thinking and expressing themselves. This frustration, together with all the other restrictions on the elite (the ideological conformity, the clear contradictions seen every day between Party propaganda and reality, the lack of freedom to travel) resulted in growing resentment against the regime among a small percentage of the elite. An even smaller percentage – the dissidents – expressed their resentment openly, in defiance of the KGB.

Access to the elite was open to all in Soviet society, including Soviet ethnic minorities. In fact, a form of positive discrimination meant that the Party elite included representatives for all the ethnicities of the USSR. Soviet elite culture was conformist and Russian-orientated, but there were also limited opportunities for ethnic minority culture to develop and be promoted and valued within Soviet society. Within the republics of the USSR, Brezhnev's policy of 'trust in cadres' meant that republic-level Party elites were formed that were not all dominated by Russians. Although ethic minority Party elites in republics like the Kazakh SSR (Soviet Socialist Republic) outwardly conformed completely to Soviet expectations, they created centres for the future development of nationalism.

Lifestyles for the workers

Soviet society was not equal. At the bottom were the *kolkhozniks*, the collective farm workers who endured low wages and few amenities. Often, the village streets remained unpaved, village schools provided only a very basic education, and healthcare services were low-level. Any young person who could escape the *kolkhoz* and move to a city did so, meaning that the population left in the villages was increasingly elderly and unskilled. There was then a hierarchy of types of city, with Moscow at the top, where the biggest range of products, the best entertainment, and the best jobs could be found.

If life for the *kolkhozniks* had not improved greatly under Brezhnev, they were the exception, since for urban workers, many of whom were the children or grandchildren of peasants, life under Brezhnev had many positives. There were frustrations and difficulties to contend with in everyday life, which practically minded Soviet citizens found ways around. For example:

- Since a planned economy meant unexpected shortages of products frequently occurred (production was not geared to meeting market demand), Soviet citizens would stock up on items when they did come into shops.
- Families grew their own vegetables, gathered berries for jam, and collected mushrooms to supplement the food available in shops; markets selling food products from *kolkhoz* private plots performed the same role.
- The second economy (black market) supplied the products that the state-run shops did not, although for much higher prices.

Frustrating though shortages were on a day-to-day basis, there were also bigger frustrations about life opportunities. One of the most significant concerned the opportunities available to those in cities where residency was controlled: the 'closed cities'. Many of these were cities and towns with military industries and services, but they included also Moscow and Leningrad (the top of the city hierarchy and having the widest range of opportunities and

ACTIVITY

Use online photo libraries to find photos that illustrate some of the positives of life under Brezhnev, and also photos suggesting some of the frustrations and difficulties of this period in Soviet history.

the best supply of consumer products and food). Resident permits to live in Moscow, for example, were very hard to obtain for those outside the elite: only the most successful students, the most committed Party activists, the best-connected, or those willing to pay huge bribes could hope to gain permanent residency rights. There were thousands of workers living in Moscow on temporary work permits, or then living illegally once their permits had run out, trying to avoid detection.

SOURCE 1

From a 1981 US research survey of 3000 emigrants from the USSR. The research was funded by the US government and included questions about emigrants' perceptions of standards of living in the USSR:

When asked to score satisfaction with standard of living, a majority were either 'very' or 'somewhat satisfied' (59.2 percent). Only a minority were 'very dissatisfied' (14.4 percent). We were surprised that so many respondents expressed themselves as relatively satisfied with their standard of living. It was not expected from people who had chosen to leave their country. In general, our respondents were more satisfied with their housing than with their standard of living. Only one-third expressed any dissatisfaction. The strongest negative impact on respondents' satisfaction [was] Soviet goods shortages and their dissatisfaction with daily queues, inferior quality, and sporadic supply. Jobs were reported as the most satisfying aspect of life in the Soviet Union. The women in our sample were especially enthusiastic about their [Soviet] jobs. When our respondents were asked to name what the United States could learn from the Soviet Union, they often pointed to its healthcare system.

SOURCE 2

From a report by a Russian-speaking member of the Communist Party of Australia who attended the Twenty-fourth Congress of the CPSU in March 1971. The journal was the *Australian Left Review*, published by the Communist Party of Australia:

There is anxiety in the Party that the rise in living standards should continue, since this is an important factor in a general acceptance of policy. The events in Poland last December [see page 139] clearly made an impression and while nothing on that scale has taken place in the USSR, there are reports of relatively minor upsets in some provincial towns on economic questions. There was a considerable emphasis on consumer goods at the Congress. One factor for conformism and conservatism comes from progress itself. A growing proportion of young intellectuals come from families of industrial workers and peasants and the [lift this gives their families socially] partially at least [means they are more likely to accept] the **status quo**. In addition, the Soviet education system, good as it is, [does not really encourage] independent thought and debate. Cynicism is also widespread. After all, no-one earns a good living by disagreeing with the chiefs.

KEY TERM

status quo: the existing state of affairs, especially regarding social or political issues

STUDY TIP

When assessing the value of a source there are several different factors to consider. The content (what the source is actually saying), the provenance (who the author was and when the source was written), and the tone of the writing all impact on the value of a source. Try to link your existing knowledge of the period to the source when answering this type of question.

AS LEVEL PRACTICE QUESTION

Evaluating primary sources

With reference to Sources 1 and 2 and your understanding of the historical context, which of these sources is more valuable to an historian studying higher living standards in the time of Brezhnev?

A LEVEL PRACTICE QUESTION

'There was considerable improvement in living standards and lifestyles in the USSR during the time of Brezhnev.' Assess the validity of this view.

STUDY TIP

What evidence can you find that there was social improvement? Try to assess the extent to which Soviet people's lives improved and balance that against the ways in which they stayed the same or even declined. Don't forget that there were a number of different groups within 'society'.

ACTIVITY

Summary

Create a chart summarising the economic and social problems of the Brezhnev era. Divide your chart into five columns headed: agriculture, defence spending, consumer goods, living standards, and lifestyles, and three rows: 1) the main problems associated with each area, 2) any policies aimed at combatting these, and 3) the extent of success and any further comment.

7 Foreign and international policies

Détente with the West

Détente was the diplomatic term used in the West to describe the relaxing of international tensions. Brezhnev pushed hard for détente through his **1969 Peace Programme**, which coincided with the point at which the USSR calculated it had achieved nuclear 'parity' with the USA.

A CLOSER LOOK

The 1969 Peace Programme was Brezhnev's détente policy, presented to the 24th Congress of the CPSU as something that the USA had been keen to negotiate a result of its recognition of Soviet military supremacy. Brezhnev's programme stressed continuity rather than change: détente did not mean any change to the continued priority of military investment, it did not mean any Khrushchev-style 'Thaw' in Soviet domestic policy and it did not mean any reduction in the leadership's commitment to promoting the spread of communism amongst developing countries.

The benefits of détente for Brezhnev:

- Peaceful coexistence was a continuation of Marxist–Leninist ideology: it could be justified as the right path for the USSR to follow.
- American compromises were likely because the USSR had become its nuclear equal.
- Mutually reducing nuclear weapon numbers would reduce the strain on the USSR's economy.
- Soviet economic problems could be significantly reduced if the West would invest in Soviet oil and gas, and share technology with the USSR, and if the USSR could offset its agricultural deficiencies by purchasing grain from the West.

Within the context of Soviet foreign policy, détente, as the USSR understood it, still allowed the USSR to promote its ideology to what were then known as 'third world' countries (allied neither with the United States nor with the former Soviet Union). The USSR's self-appointed role at the head of the world's socialist countries made this strategically vital.

SOURCE 1

From a statement by Brezhnev to the Polish Party Congress in November 1968. The statement became known as the **Brezhnev Doctrine** and it accompanied a Soviet invasion of Czechoslovakia in the same year:

When internal and external forces, hostile to socialism, seek to reverse the development of any socialist country whatsoever in the direction of the restoration of the capitalist order, when a threat to the cause of socialism arises in that country, a threat to the security of the socialist commonwealth as a whole – this already becomes not only a problem of the people of the country concerned, but also a common problem and the concern of all socialist countries.

There were good reasons for the USA and its allies to work with détente:

- US President **Richard Nixon** was keen to pull the USA out of the hugely costly Vietnam War. He needed the USSR to help negotiate a treaty with North Vietnam.
- The USA had 300,000 troops stationed in Europe that cost a lot to maintain.
- The West needed new oil suppliers outside of the Middle East. West Germany in particular was keen to establish gas supplies from the USSR.
- The USSR was potentially a huge market for Western agricultural and industrial products.

LEARNING OBJECTIVES

In this chapter you will learn about:

- détente with the West
- the invasion of Afghanistan and the impact on the USSR
- the Second Cold War.

KEY CHRONOLOGY

1968	USSR invades Czechoslovakia
1969	USSR calculates it has nuclear parity with the USA
1972	SALT I signed
1975	Helsinki Final Act
1979	USSR invades Afghanistan; end of détente
1980	65 countries, headed by the USA, boycott Moscow Olympics
1983	Reagan's 'evil empire' speech; SDI proposed

CROSS-REFERENCE

You can read about the Soviet-led invasion of Czechoslovakia in Chapter 16, pages 135–37.

ACTIVITY

1. How many of the different elements of Brezhnev's hopes for détente can you identify in Source 1?
2. Compare Brezhnev's foreign policy aims with Khrushchev's (see Chapter 4). Make a diagram to illustrate the similarities and differences.

KEY PROFILE

Richard Nixon (1913–94) was US President from 1969 to 1974. He visited the USSR in 1972. Nixon established his political reputation as a fervent anti-communist, and had been Eisenhower's vice-president. As president, however, he showed a strong commitment to détente, visiting both China and the USSR (in 1972), agreeing an anti-ballistic missile treaty with the USSR and pulling US troops out of Vietnam. He was the only US president (to date) to resign as president, following a political scandal.

ACTIVITY

Extension

Find out more about the agreements between the two superpowers in the early 1970s. Try the US Department of State website (**www.state.gov/s/l/treaty**) for treaties and agreements about nuclear weapons.

CROSS-REFERENCE

You can read more about human rights in the Helsinki Final Act in Chapter 8 (page 62) and Chapter 9, page 156.

A CLOSER LOOK

The agreements on human rights in the Helsinki Final Act became problematic for the USSR because dissidents in the USSR and the satellite states realised that they could be used to challenge the regime. The Soviet leadership had signed up to respecting human rights, but dissident reports monitoring human rights abuses showed that the USSR was failing to honour this international agreement.

There was a flurry of agreements between the USSR and the USA in the early 1970s (20 between 1972 and 1973), of which the two most significant were SALT I and the Helsinki Final Act.

Strategic Arms Limitation Treaty (SALT)

Discussions with **President Nixon** about a SALT culminated in May 1972 with an agreement, known as SALT I, that both the USSR and the USA would freeze their number of missile systems and limit the number of anti-ballistic missile defence sites to two: one to protect their national capital, another to guard existing missile systems.

Fig. 1 *Nixon and Brezhnev sign the SALT I Treaty*

Helsinki Final Act

The USSR wanted recognition from the West of the boundaries created in Eastern Europe by the Red Army's advances in 1945. This was granted in the summer of 1975 at the Conference on Security and Cooperation in Europe, held in the Finnish capital Helsinki. The Helsinki Final Act also facilitated economic, scientific, and technological exchanges between East and West. However, the agreement was reached in return for some important compromises.

- Although the West agreed that these borders would never be challenged militarily, the USSR accepted that they could be changed by peaceful agreement.
- The USSR agreed to greater freedom in communication between Western and Eastern Europe.
- The agreements included the requirement that the USSR and its satellite states 'respect human rights and fundamental freedoms, including the freedom of thought, conscience, religion or belief, for all without distinction as to race, sex, language or religion', plus the commitment to publish the text of this agreement in their own countries for everyone to read.

From 1976, the West started to express concern that these agreements favoured the USSR. Critics in the US media claimed that while détente had promised a relationship of compromise, maturity, and give and take, it looked much more like the West was doing all the giving, and the USSR was doing all the taking. At the same time, aggressive Soviet actions in developing countries like Angola prompted an American rethink on where détente was leading.

On one side, it is possible to argue that the USA failed to understand that détente was not about the Soviet Union becoming more like the USA, but was a part of 'peaceful coexistence' for the USSR; that is to say, the continuation of the ideological struggle for the victory of socialism but without military conflict, leaving the USSR free to pump money and arms into revolutionary movements worldwide.

On the other side, there was confusion among the Soviet leadership about the West's concern for human rights in the USSR. Although they understood that the West would bring up the treatment of dissidents as a way of embarrassing the Soviet regime, this did not seem to be a serious issue to Soviet negotiators engaged in detailed discussions about arms reduction treaties. Raising human rights issues looked, instead, like a lack of real commitment to nuclear arms reduction, which made the USSR leadership suspect that the USA actually wanted to escalate the arms race.

ACTIVITY

Thinking point

What were the differences in understanding of détente between the USSR and the USA?

The invasion of Afghanistan and the impact on the USSR

Just as America had fought the North Vietnamese and Viet Cong troops backed by the USSR, in Afghanistan the Soviets fought **mujahideen** troops backed by US money and weaponry.

In December 1979, Soviet forces entered Afghanistan to protect a recently established Communist regime that had provoked a popular rebellion against its radical socialist programme. Brezhnev and his inner circle signed an order for 40,000 troops to enter the country, stating that the Afghan government had requested their help. In the nine years that followed, 14,500 Soviet troops, 90,000 mujahideen, and a million Afghan civilians were killed.

KEY TERM

mujahideen: Muslims engaged in jihad, Islam's struggle against oppression

Reasons for the invasion

There are several different explanations for the Soviet invasion, including:

1. The USSR had previously had military success in suppressing anti-socialist uprisings in Hungary (1956) and Czechoslovakia (1968).
2. Afghanistan was close to the USSR's 'soft underbelly' of the Central Asian republics. These were Muslim countries and the USSR had concerns about the spread of anti-Soviet Islamic politics.
3. The USA had also, in 1979, lost control of Iran as an ally and perhaps hoped to make Afghanistan its new ally on the USSR's border.
4. The **Brezhnev Doctrine** had stated that countries developing in a socialist direction must not be turned back to capitalism.
5. Brezhnev could barely sign his name to the decision to send in troops, being so heavily medicated for chronic illness. This has led to the assumption that the military pushed the decision through.

Fig. 2 *Afghan mujahideen stand on a downed Soviet Mi-8 transport helicopter in January 1981*

ACTIVITY

Extension

The 1988 film *Rambo III*, starring Sylvester Stallone, puts his Vietnam-veteran character John Rambo in Afghanistan, taking on the Soviet occupiers with the (eventual) help of the mujahideen. Watch a clip of the film and discuss what it suggests about the propaganda value of the Soviet invasion of Afghanistan for the West.

Impact of the invasion

International response

The international response was highly significant, in different ways:

- 65 countries, led by the USA, refused to attend the 1980 Moscow Olympics in protest at the invasion.
- The USA refused to complete its agreement to SALT II.
- The USA cancelled grain shipments to the USSR.
- Developing countries were shocked: the USSR had provided an alternative model of development, but no one wanted to be invaded.
- Communists in the West (those who had found a way to deal with Soviet invasions of Hungary and Czechoslovakia) lost faith in the USSR.

At first, most Soviet people accepted the rationale given for the invasion: a fellow socialist state had asked for the USSR's help. The international outcry against the invasion, led by the USA, was only what the Soviet people expected from the imperialist West.

Impact in the USSR

As the war went on, it became known to many that thousands of young Soviets were coming back from Afghanistan in coffins. Survivors were often physically and mentally damaged by their experiences; drug abuse and alcoholism became common among veterans of Afghanistan. Some Soviet people began to question why the war continued for so long, at such cost, and with such terrible results. For many others, however, it was preferable to believe that the USSR's leaders had good reasons for their actions in Afghanistan.

A CLOSER LOOK

The Moscow Olympics, 1980

The USSR and its Eastern European satellites won most of the medals at the Moscow Olympics in 1980, following a boycott by the USA and other countries. The excellent organisation and presentation of the Olympics bolstered the USSR's international reputation, despite the protest. The overwhelmingly socialist medal table also boosted morale within the USSR.

SOURCE 2

From a published oral history of the post-Stalin generation. The author, an American academic called Donald Raleigh, who has spent many years in post-Soviet Saratov, asked people about their memories of the Afghanistan war, when they were in their thirties:

Igor Litvin remembered, 'When the first young men began to return and we saw how psychologically damaged they were and heard about their experiences, we understood that a carnage was taking place and that things weren't at all as we had presumed, that we were helping a brotherly country so that there'd be socialism there.' Aleksandr Konstantinov called the invasion 'an absurd stupidity. This was clear to everyone. I can't recall encountering a single individual who supported it.' Irina Vizgalova said she didn't grasp 'why we needed to send our boys to Afghanistan to solve [the Afghans'] problems. I think that many felt this way.' 'I accepted the official version that they put out,' admitted Olga Kamayurova. 'Back then I simply didn't understand that we had started the war, that we had invaded another country.'

KEY TERM

oral history: recording and studying interviews with people recalling their experiences of the past

AS LEVEL PRACTICE QUESTION

Evaluating primary sources

With reference to Sources 1 and 2 and your understanding of the historical context, which of the two sources is more valuable in explaining why the USSR invaded Afghanistan?

STUDY TIP

Try to present an analysis in your answer rather than just giving a description of what each source says. One way to start planning an analytical answer is to think about the limitations of each source. What could make one source less valuable than the other? Consider provenance as well as content.

The Second Cold War

American President **Ronald Reagan**, elected in 1980, took a hard line against the USSR: rejecting détente and committing the USA to an arms escalation (backed by a $1.5 trillion budget) aimed at decisively winning any nuclear war against the USSR. In 1983, he branded the Soviet Union an 'evil empire' and called America's conflict with the USSR 'a struggle between right and wrong and good and evil'.

Fig. 3 *Ronald Reagan*

KEY PROFILE

Ronald Reagan (1911–2004) was US President from 1981 to 1989. The collapse of the Soviet Union occurred during his presidency. Reagan's early career was as a Hollywood actor rather than as a politician. He came to power on the promise of economic reform in the USA, which he did through tax cuts, curbs on inflation and reductions in government spending. He reversed US policy on the USSR, launching a 'Second Cold War' through an escalation of the arms race while also engaging in talks with Gorbachev. Reagan's presidency coincided with the collapse of the USSR. He left office in 1989 with one of the highest approval ratings from the US public for any president.

'Star Wars'

Two weeks after his 'evil empire' speech, Reagan announced his Strategic Defence Initiative (SDI) – orbiting satellites that would shoot down enemy missiles before they could reach the USA. In a speech in March 1983, he called on the USA to use its technological superiority to create a defensive shield to 'counter the awesome Soviet missile threat'. SDI was more a vision of the future than anything the USA could hope to deploy soon, with Reagan asking his audience to imagine 'what if free people could live secure in the knowledge that . . . we could intercept and destroy strategic ballistic missiles'. Reagan sought to portray this as a way of reducing the arms race, saying 'we seek neither military superiority nor political advantage'.

Reagan's solution to the arms race was much mocked by elements of the Western press as totally unrealistic. Reports from the USSR confirmed that there was widespread suspicion there, too, that this was impractical – possibly technologically possible, but only at huge cost and with very dubious defence capabilities. It seemed to Soviet scientists (some of whose notes on SDI have since been acquired by US universities) that it would be relatively easy for the USSR to compromise these defences either by overloading the system with more missiles than it could shoot down, or with missiles that could evade the tracking technology, or through ground-based weapon systems that could knock out the satellites at the heart of SDI.

If all that was obviously the case, then SDI worried the Soviet leadership for another reason – what was the real purpose behind it? Their suspicion was that SDI was a smokescreen for the USA increasing investment in its nuclear arsenal. This was a great concern because the Soviet leadership needed to lower spending on nuclear weapons: there was a real recognition that it could not continue to maintain parity in nuclear capabilities if the USA embarked

ACTIVITY

Using the Key Chronology on page 53, create a horizontal timeline with moves towards détente above the line and moves towards confrontation below it.

on another round of the arms race. It is likely that it was for this reason, then, rather than because it believed in SDI, that in 1986, in a summit in Reykjavik, the Soviet leadership offered substantial reductions in their nuclear arsenal if the USA dropped SDI. This was therefore an attempt to remove the smokescreen of SDI in full view of the international community and return to the negotiations that the USSR needed.

Since the collapse of the Soviet Union, there have been arguments over the importance of Reagan's apparent re-escalation of the arms race: the Second Cold War. Interpretations include:

- SDI brought about a recognition in the USSR that its economic system and technological know-how was simply not capable of competing with the West without fundamental reform.
- The Soviet leadership planned to use SDI as propaganda, portraying the USA as a warmonger in order to use world opinion to force the USA to return to détente.
- The Soviets were simply bemused by SDI – it clearly would not work in the way Reagan wanted it to, so why was the USA even talking about it? What were they trying to hide?

STUDY TIP

Validity is when something is logically and factually sound. Try to assess the validity of a view by examining the facts and arguments that support or contradict it.

A LEVEL PRACTICE QUESTION

Brezhnev's foreign policy, in the years 1964 to 1985, was a complete failure. Assess the validity of this view.

ACTIVITY

Summary

Draw a spider diagram centred on 'Pressures on détente', identifying the factors that made the policy of détente difficult to sustain.

8 Pressures for change and the reaction of the regime

Political dissidents and protest

Fig. 1 *Training in the photo-forensic room of the KGB training school in Moscow. Brezhnev used the state security services to suppress the dissident movement in the USSR*

LEARNING OBJECTIVES

In this chapter you will learn about:

- political dissidents and protest, including Alexander Solzhenitsyn and Andrei Sakharov
- the effect of the Helsinki Accords
- nationalist unrest
- new leaders and political developments: Andropov, Chernenko, and Gorbachev.

KEY CHRONOLOGY

1974	Solzhenitsyn exiled from USSR
1975	Helsinki Accords
1976	Helsinki monitoring groups set up in USSR
1980	Sakharov exiled to Gorky
1982	Brezhnev dies
1982	Andropov elected General Secretary
1984	Chernenko elected General Secretary
1985	Gorbachev elected General Secretary

Political dissidents

Before the end of the Soviet Union, it was very difficult for Western researchers to study what Soviets really thought about the USSR because people were very careful not to say anything that could get them into trouble with the KGB. The political dissidents who used international opinion to try to force political change in the USSR were one exception to this. In response, the regime portrayed them as traitors who wanted to damage socialism. The KGB harassed and persecuted dissidents either through the courts or in ways outside the law, including confining them to psychiatric hospitals. They monitored those suspected of 'anti-Soviet activities' very carefully, regularly updating assessments on the measures needed to keep their activities under control. A KGB crackdown on dissidents that began in 1977 reached a peak in 1983. By this point, the dissident movement had been almost completely suppressed. Two leading dissidents were Alexander Solzhenitsyn and Andrei Sakharov.

Alexander Solzhenitsyn

Solzhenitsyn's novel *One Day in the Life of Ivan Denisovitch* was published in 1962, during the Thaw, and became a bestseller around the world.

In 1970, Solzhenitsyn was nominated for a Nobel Prize for Literature. His novels *The Gulag Archipelago* and *Cancer Ward* had not been published in the USSR; the KGB had attempted to seize the manuscripts, but Solzhenitsyn had finished them in secret and had smuggled them out of the USSR to be published in the West. The works were highly critical of the Soviet system and implicated Lenin in the formation of the Gulag system. The Party launched a campaign against Solzhenitsyn in the press. His treatment in the USSR received a lot of publicity in the West. He was stripped of his Soviet citizenship and exiled from the USSR in 1974.

CROSS-REFERENCE

The KGB is explained in Chapter 1, page 4.
There is a Key Profile of **Alexander Solzhenitsyn** in Chapter 3, page 25.

ACTIVITY

Research

As part of what was known as 'The Thaw', Khrushchev relaxed cultural controls. Solzhenitsyn's novel was published due to Khrushchev's personal influence, as it exposed the harsh treatment of victims of Stalin's purges (which are covered in Chapter 1, page 2).

There are significant differences between *One Day in the Life of Ivan Denisovich* and *The Gulag Archipelago*, although both are condemnations of the Gulag system and its effects on its inmates. Using online reviews of both books, identify three differences that you think made one book publishable in the USSR, albeit during the Thaw, and one unpublishable.

Andrei Sakharov

Sakharov (1921–89) was a high-level Soviet physicist who had worked on developing thermonuclear weapons, but then, in the 1960s, became involved in movements for nuclear disarmament. In 1968, he wrote an article on disarmament and freedom of speech that circulated as ***samizdat***, was smuggled abroad, and published. As a result, Sakharov was not allowed to continue any research with military connections. He campaigned for human rights within the USSR and against the war in Afghanistan – campaigns that led to him being forced to live in 'internal exile' in the **closed city** of Gorky from 1980.

Fig. 2 *Andrei Sakharov with his wife Yelena*

A CLOSER LOOK

Samizdat means 'self published' and it referred to censored articles, books, speeches, and so on being copied out and secretly passed around groups. The punishment for anyone caught with banned material was severe.

ACTIVITY

Extension

Visit the Sakharov Archive website (www. sakharov-archive.ru/English/) and read through the selection of Sakharov's writings listed under 'Sakharov's works'. Produce a spider diagram summarising the main themes of his concerns.

CROSS-REFERENCE

Closed cities were described in Chapter 6, pages 46 and 49.

Protest

In the late 1970s and early 1980s, the Soviet system was under severe strain, owing to:

- international condemnation over human rights
- renewed pressure from the Second Cold War
- the economic and social strain of the war in Afghanistan
- unrest in the Eastern European satellite states
- Brezhnev's poor health
- a corrupt bureaucracy
- no real individual freedoms or political participation
- dependence on foreign imports of grain to feed its people
- a stagnating economy dominated by the dead weight of the military.

There was plenty to fuel the dissident movement but it had been largely shut down by 1982–83. The dissidents faced sustained and harsh repression from the KGB and fear of punishment must explain, in part, why the Soviet system survived under Brezhnev, despite its many problems.

A CLOSER LOOK

In 1984 and 1985, Sakharov twice went on hunger strike, during which he was hospitalised and force-fed, in an attempt to pressurise the government into letting his wife travel to the USA for heart surgery. She finally went to the USA for treatment in 1985, returning to the USSR the following year.

The number of dissidents actively involved in protest in the USSR was very small indeed: the Moscow Helsinki Watch Group (see next page) had only around 20 members. It was also heavily Westernised and geared towards an international audience rather than to the Soviet people.

Popular unrest involving 'ordinary' Soviet people had little connection with the dissident movement, therefore. When popular unrest happened, it was primarily connected with economic issues – wages, prices, shortages – and with nationalist issues.

In 1983, the US government's Central Intelligence Agency (CIA) produced a secret report on unrest in the USSR (what we might term 'open protest'). Any incident of unrest was usually kept out of the Soviet media, so the incidents in the report were from a variety of HUMINT (human intelligence) sources: diplomatic reporting, travellers, **émigrés, defectors**, and sensitive human sources (informers and spies). Table 1 was included in the report based on these sources – the report authors estimated that the actual number of incidents of unrest was probably double this.

Table 1 *CIA record of incidents of reported civil unrest in the USSR, 1970–82*

	Number of incidents	Percent of total
Total	281	100
Demonstrations	113	40
Strikes	105	37
Political violence	39	14
Riots	24	9

- Demonstrations had many different causes: about 60 per cent related to issues connected to nationalism in the non-Russian republics, or to protests over people not being allowed visas to emigrate; of the rest, quite a high proportion were connected to food shortages
- Strikes were almost all related to worker grievances, e.g. promised pay bonuses that had never happened.
- Political violence included extreme actions, like people setting fire to themselves in a nationalist protest, or the assassination of Soviet soldiers in response to the invasion of Afghanistan.
- Riots had lots of different causes, including the cancellation by the authorities of a rock concert in Leningrad and a riot against corrupt local officials in southern Russia.

Economic unrest was often not about challenging the regime itself, but was often conservative – a demand for prices to be kept as they were before, for example. When unrest had a nationalist element, however, it often challenged the Soviet system directly.

ACTIVITY

Pair discussion

1. The authors of the CIA report noted that while the activities of political dissidents had decreased drastically in the early 1980s, the number of incidents of 'popular' unrest appeared to have increased rapidly in the same time period. What explanations could you give for this?
2. Strikes, demonstrations, riots, and other forms of open resistance were surely rare occurrences in the USSR, even if there were more of them than Western observers first believed. Most people showed their lack of commitment to the regime through taking time off work, working slowly, stealing from work, and telling political jokes. Were these actions forms of protest, too?

A CLOSER LOOK

While countries like Britain used faraway colonies as dumping grounds for political troublemakers and habitual criminals, Russia had a long history of exiling people to remote locations within the country (internal exile). The USSR continued this tradition.

A CLOSER LOOK

In the 1970s and 1980s a dissident movement in Poland had gathered enormous support throughout the country, despite state repression. It made connections to Polish people's everyday concerns in a way that the Soviet dissident movement, dominated by intellectuals, never did.

KEY TERM

émigrés: people who have left one country to live in another

defectors: people who independently give up allegiance to a state; a term used to describe those who escaped the Soviet Union

The effect of the Helsinki Accords

The dissident movement in the USSR had its roots in popular reaction to Khrushchev's Secret Speech – and disappointment in the subsequent repression of freer speech and the clampdown on any discussion of an alternative to the Party line. Discontent about the political direction of the USSR rose significantly with Soviet suppression of a 'thaw' in Czechoslovakia – the Prague Spring – which showed to all that the USSR's brand of socialism was not sustainable without the threat of brutal suppression.

The Helsinki Final Act of 1975 gave the dissident movement a significant boost. It required the USSR to respect human rights, and activists and dissidents attempted to make the USSR live up to this requirement, both inside the USSR and its satellite states, and outside it, in the West. Activists set up 'Helsinki Watch Groups' to report infringements of human rights to the world's press. These groups were supported by similar groups in the West, but this could not prevent the Soviet groups being subject to intense KGB scrutiny and pressure, with members arrested, put in prison, confined to psychiatric hospitals, and beaten.

CROSS-REFERENCE

The Helsinki Final Act, as part of Soviet foreign policy, is discussed in Chapter 7 on page 54.

Internal exile is explained in A Closer Look, on page 61.

The Moscow Helsinki Watch Group was set up in 1976 by 11 people. Their initial spokesman was a scientist friend of Sakharov's called Yuri Orlov. The group invited Soviet citizens to report incidents of human rights abuses to them, which they sought to verify, travelling across the USSR to gather evidence and then collating this into reports. The types of human rights infringements in their reports related to:

- the freedom to leave the USSR (this applied particularly to Jewish citizens who wished to leave the USSR to live in Israel but were being blocked by the Soviet authorities)
- the freedom to leave the USSR and return
- the freedom to choose one's place of residence (especially for those in **internal exile**)
- the right to a fair trial
- the rights of political prisoners
- the rights of ethnic minorities within the USSR.

These collated reports were then signed by all the group members who had taken part in preparing them and copies were sent to the Politburo of the CPSU, the Moscow embassies of countries that were signed up to the Helsinki Final Act, and to foreign journalists.

The security services responded with a campaign of repression against the group, starting with hostile newspaper coverage and followed by threats and intimidation, with most of its members being arrested for periods of time. Some, like Sakharov, were forced into internal exile; others were made to emigrate, as with Solzhenitsyn; and some were committed to psychiatric hospitals. By 1982, the remaining members of the group were no longer able to continue.

ACTIVITY

Research

The National Security Archive (at Washington University, USA) includes a collection of English-language documents on its website (**http://nsarchive.gwu.edu**) relating to the Moscow Helsinki Watch Group and KGB responses to dissidents. Research the documents for evidence of the perceptions of the dissidents and their aims, assessment of their effectiveness, and the measures of repression used against them.

Nationalist unrest

Unrest amongst the nationalities was connected to a range of issues:

- cultural rights, e.g. Muslim burial rites not being permitted
- competition between the national language and Russian
- Russians coming to live in national territory
- competition for jobs, housing, and positions with Russians
- damage to the environment in national territory from Russian industries
- discrimination faced when living outside their territory, e.g. in Russia.

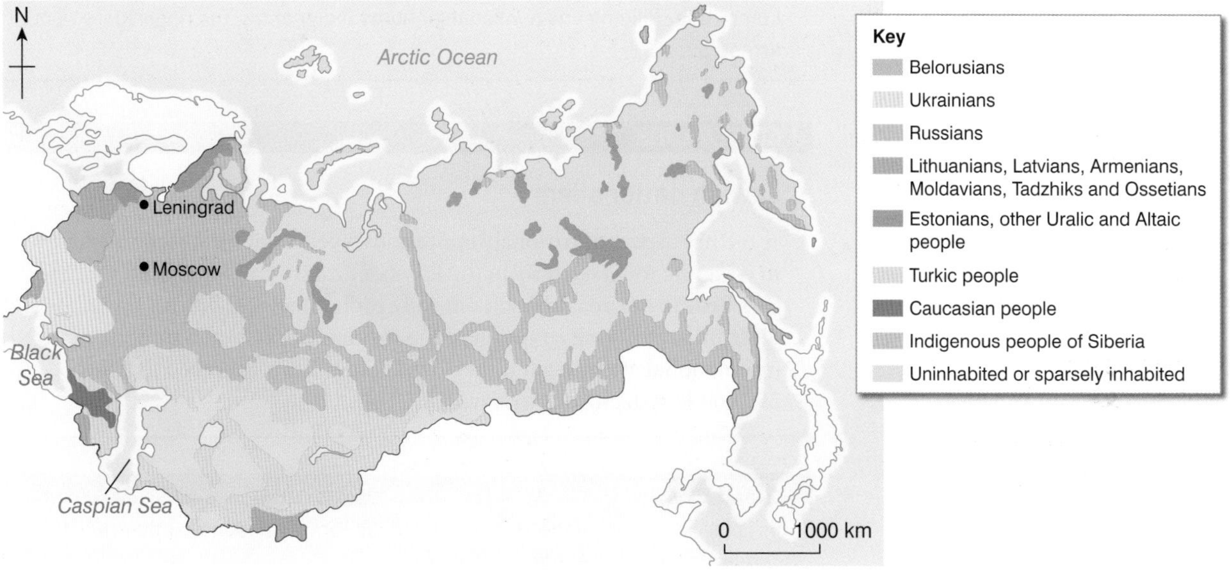

Fig. 3 *A map of nationalities in the USSR*

A CLOSER LOOK

Nationalities policy in the USSR

The Union of Soviet Socialist Republics (USSR) was not a country, but a federation of different nationalities: 15 major republics, the largest of which was the Russian Soviet Federalist Socialist Republic (RSFSR) was itself a federation of some 30 different ethnic territories. USSR policy was that all nationalities were equal. The Party did a lot to promote national identities that were previously quite weak, for example by developing written forms of languages that were previously mainly oral. However, Russia was always the 'first among equals'.

SOURCE 1

From the CIA's national intelligence memorandum 'Dimensions of civil unrest in the Soviet Union', 1983. This report was collated from published incidents and intelligence sources:

1978: On 22 May a large-scale riot broke out between native residents and Russians in Dunshanbe, the capital of Tadzhikistan. Relations between the two nationalities had been outwardly calm for years. The incident erupted when a Russian man beat up a Tadzhik youth in the city's central park [. . .] Several accounts were reported to a Western visitor that as many as 10,000 Tadzhiks and 3,000 Russians had been involved.

1980: Tallinn, Estonia. On 8 October a crowd of about 4,000 to 5,000 students gathered at Voida Square and carried placards stating: "Where is bread and butter?" "Where is meat?" "Away with Brezhnev." Similar leaflets were distributed to passers-by and at some schools. Dissidents said this action closely followed the example of Polish workers.

In 1978, when taxi rates were doubled throughout the USSR, cabdrivers in Minsk protested. Fearing that higher rates would result in fewer fares, several hundred of them reportedly drove their taxis to the Belorussian Party Central Committee Building and honked their horns indignantly. The ringleaders were arrested.

ACTIVITY

Evaluating primary sources

1. Study Source 1. Which of the incidents would you say would be described as nationalist unrest? Explain your answer.
2. Look at the list of issues connected to nationalist unrest on page 63. Which of those would you say relate to the nationalist unrest incidents in Source 1?
3. The CIA report says that nationalist unrest was often combined with economic grievances. Do any of the extracts in Source 1 support this claim?
4. How reliable would the sources of information for the CIA's report be for an historian studying popular opposition to the Soviet regime in the early 1980s?

A CLOSER LOOK

Jewish nationalism

A further aspect of nationalist unrest involved Soviet Jews who wished to emigrate to Israel. Jews in the Russian Empire had long faced virulent anti-Semitism and, although officially prohibited, anti-Jewish prejudice and discrimination were common in the Brezhnev era. Jewish protests received international attention and the Soviet leadership was forced to allow 250,000 Jewish citizens to leave the USSR.

ACTIVITY

This is the first verse of the 'Hymn of the USSR' (Soviet 'national' anthem):

Unbreakable Union of freeborn Republics,
Great Russia has welded forever to stand.
Created in struggle by will of the people,
United and mighty, our Soviet land!

What does it indicate to you about the relationship between Russia and the other republics?

The effect of nationalist unrest

Nationalist unrest could sometimes be used to reinforce the commitment of Russian citizens to the Soviet Union. This was both because Russians felt that they were the targets of nationalist unrest and because Russians knew that the Soviet system usually favoured them over other nationalities. In regard to Jewish unrest, it was easy for the Soviet media to portray the desire to leave the USSR as treachery from an ethnic group that had, supposedly, never been fully committed to building communism.

New leaders and political developments

The end of the Brezhnev era

Brezhnev died on 10 November 1982. He was 75 and had been unwell for many years. The stagnation of the Brezhnev era was associated with the **gerontocracy** of his Politburo: in 1919, the average age of the Politburo was 39; by 1982, it was 68. The membership of the Central Committee and Council of Ministers also had a similar elderly profile. Brezhnev had come to power reassuring the bureaucracy that there would be stability, and stability is what he delivered – to the point of fossilisation. By 1982, half the Politburo had been in post for 15 years or longer. Brezhnev himself had outlasted five US presidents.

KEY TERM

gerontocracy: when a country is led by a group of elderly people

Brezhnev's most likely successor had once been **Konstantin Chernenko**, until **Yuri Andropov**, the head of the KGB, had made a grab for power based on exposing corruption within Brezhnev's own family. Those scandals, together with the economic decline under Brezhnev, meant that Chernenko's closeness to Brezhnev had become a concern to Politburo members. It was enough for Andropov to get the support he needed to be selected as the new General Secretary, the new leader of the USSR, two days after Brezhnev's death, on 12 November 1982.

Fig. 4 *Leonid Brezhnev's funeral on 15 November 1982. The first two pall-bearers on the left are Defense Minister Ustinov and Premier Tikhonov. The first two on the right are Yuri Andropov and Konstantin Chernenko*

Andropov: limited political and economic reform

Andropov was 68, with serious health problems, when he became General Secretary. Although he launched economic and political reforms that could have been significant, he died after 15 months in charge, in 1984.

Andropov's political attitudes had been shaped by his involvement in some key events of Soviet foreign policy. He was Soviet ambassador in Hungary during the 1956 Hungarian Revolution in which Hungarian secret police had been lynched in the streets. He had been instrumental in convincing Khrushchev that the Revolution must be suppressed by force. In 1968, as head of the KGB, Andropov had again pushed for the use of force in suppressing popular unrest against Soviet control. Yet against this picture of arch conservatism, Andropov clearly recognised the need for change at the end of Brezhnev's era of stagnation, as patron for the reformer **Mikhail Gorbachev**, for example.

Political reforms

- Andropov tackled political stagnation by promoting younger people in the government and Party. Hundreds of new people took over senior positions.
- He used his KGB influence to target corruption within the government and Party. This involved new penalties for those caught accepting bribes. However, corruption was hard to root out, especially as Andropov's rival, Chernenko, offered protection to officials suspected of offences in return for their support against Andropov.

KEY PROFILE

Yuri Andropov (1914–84) had started his leadership career thanks to Khrushchev, who appointed him to the Central Committee. His next job was as head of the KGB, a position he held for 15 years. He succeeded Brezhnev as General Secretary of the CPSU in 1982 and in his 15 months as leader he set about challenging the corruption and stagnation of Brezhnev's era. Relationships with the West deteriorated and it was Andropov's USSR that Reagan denounced as an 'evil empire'.

Konstantin Chernenko (1911–85) had been working his way up the Party hierarchy when, as Head of Propaganda in Moldova in the early 1950s, he worked with Moldovan First Secretary, Leonid Brezhnev. Brezhnev became his patron and promoted him to the Central Committee. After Andropov's death in 1985, Chernenko was General Secretary of the CPSU for 13 months, dying in 1985. His leadership saw a return to Brezhnev-era stagnation, and the USSR's decision to boycott the 1984 Olympics in Los Angeles was made under his leadership.

CROSS-REFERENCE

Read more about **Mikhail Gorbachev**, his career and personality, in Chapter 9, page 69.

KEY TERM

perestroika: restructuring (a word made famous by Gorbachev's reforms)

absenteeism: regularly staying away from work

A CLOSER LOOK

Alcoholism in the USSR

Alcoholism was very widespread in Soviet society, to the extent of lowering life expectancy, in the early 1980s in rural areas, to 61.4 years for men and 59.3 years for women – the lowest of any European country.

CROSS-REFERENCE

Molotov, one of the few remaining 'old Bolsheviks', had been a protégée of Stalin and had remained steadfastly loyal to his old boss. He had been one of the contenders for power after Stalin's death, and is profiled on page 4.

CROSS-REFERENCE

After the suppression of the Hungarian Revolution in 1956, Hungary's Communist Party had gradually introduced economic reforms that mixed elements of a market economy into the planned economy model. These reforms are covered in Chapter 13, pages 110–11.

ACTIVITY

On a scale of 1–5, with 1 as excellent and 5 as poor, discuss with a partner how you would rank the leaders of the USSR covered so far – Khrushchev, Brezhnev, Andropov, and Chernenko – for:

a) popularity with ordinary Russians
b) economic effectiveness
c) foreign policy success
d) leadership. As a group, consider your decisions.

- He continued the rigorous suppression of Soviet dissidents that he had conducted as KGB head: there was no move towards increased freedom of speech or any alternative voice to the Party in Soviet politics.

Economic reforms

Andropov highlighted the existence of serious economic problems that had to be tackled if socialism was to develop further. The term ***perestroika*** – restructuring – began to be used to describe the reform that was needed.

- Andropov's solution to low worker productivity was to tackle the chronic **absenteeism** in the workplace by strict worker discipline. The police visited factories to check on workers' whereabouts, and did spot checks of people on the street, demanding identification. In a Soviet Union led by an ex-KGB boss, that was bound to make people nervous. However, it took up a lot of resources in return for only modest improvements in productivity, and was hard to sustain.
- He invited his protégée Mikhail Gorbachev to head an economic policy unit that would report in detail on how the Soviet economy should be reformed. This report was limited, however, because Gorbachev was not allowed to see the detailed budget for the USSR – a state secret.
- He also cracked down on drunkenness in the workplace and in public.

Chernenko as leader, and stagnation

Chernenko was 73 when he succeeded Andropov in February 1984, and he was also already very ill – too ill even to speak at Andropov's funeral. His duties as General Secretary were often carried out by his deputy, Mikhail Gorbachev, during his 13 months in office before his death on 10 March 1985.

Chernenko's faction was deeply conservative: it included Ustinov, the Defence Minister, and Premier Tikhonov. Moves were made during 1984 to restore Stalin's reputation, while further condemning Khrushchev for the damage he had done to the USSR's reputation. Ustinov proposed that Volgograd be named Stalingrad again. Molotov, by then 93 years old, was readmitted to the Party.

Chernenko had risen through the Party hierarchy along with his patron Brezhnev, working on Party ideology and propaganda and serving on the Party secretariat, administering all high-level Party correspondence. He was a prolific author on Marxist–Leninist ideology and the role of the Party, much of which was solidly orthodox material. As with Andropov, though, his writings include the terms that later became internationally known – *perestroika* and *glasnost* – and he wrote about the need for administrative reform to make the bureaucracy more responsive to people's needs. His political attitudes were consensus-based; he was a career politician who sought compromise between factions. This, plus his age and illness, was therefore a recipe for continued stagnation.

The reformers and the position of Gorbachev

Throughout his career, Andropov supported economic reform and had been very impressed by Hungary's economic successes. The Hungarian model might possibly have been applied to the USSR, had Andropov survived for longer (or taken over sooner).

The Andropov faction, during Brezhnev's rule, was opposed by Chernenko's conservative faction, and Andropov hoped to ensure Gorbachev would succeed him to continue his reforms. Chernenko's faction prevented this from happening, but Gorbachev's position was strong enough to be chosen to act as Chernenko's deputy when he was unwell. Gorbachev trod careful during the year of Chernenko's 'leadership', so as not to upset any potential supporters, and Chernenko's old guard squashed any economic reforms that Gorbachev was able to propose.

The day Chernenko died, Gorbachev acted very quickly to ensure he took over the top job. There were no other candidates with his qualifications, and too many supporters of his leadership for the old guard to block his appointment. Gorbachev's position was potentially precarious, however. As a relatively young man, he had not had the opportunity to build up a solid body of supporters who owed their careers to him. However, as can be seen from previous discussion of conservatives Andropov and Chernenko, the Party realised that something new had to be tried. Gorbachev's loyal deputising for the ailing Chernenko counted for him too: this was a man that the Party elite had seen in action and who had shown no signs of dangerously radical tendencies. As Chapter 9 will discuss, Gorbachev continued to follow the reforms of Andropov in his first years in power. This was what was hoped for and expected of him by his Politburo colleagues.

A LEVEL PRACTICE QUESTION

'In the years 1982 to 1985 nothing changed in the USSR.' Assess the validity of this view.

STUDY TIP

You may wish to refer to the Timeline (on pages xx–xi) to establish what key events occurred in this period. Once you have established the areas that you need to look at – political, economic and social – you can start to shape your answer.

SOURCE 2

From a book of Chernenko's political speeches, written in 1982. At the time, Chernenko was still Brezhnev's deputy in the Party, with responsibility for ideology:

Contrary to our ill-wishers' talk about a 'decline of communism', we take a long stride forward every year. As far as its economic and intellectual potential is concerned, the Soviet Union of the eighties differs strikingly not only from the young revolutionary Russia of the twenties but even from what it was twenty or thirty years ago. This is not to say that we have no difficulties. They do exist and the Communist Party frankly admits them. This, incidentally, is what helps the Soviet Union to cope with them successfully and to scale one summit after another in its progress. My country is getting richer and more advanced culturally, and its people have a higher standard of living than ever before.

SOURCE 3

From a report made by Mikhail Gorbachev in 1985 on renewing the Soviet economy, presented to a Party meeting on 'Questions of scientific and technical progress':

To hope that the State Planning Committee will be able to look into all the links of the chain between all the suppliers and all the consumers in the USSR, and identify the most efficient ways of connecting them, means to indulge in illusion. Neither can the ministries cope with this work. All this places on the order of the day the question of creating bodies for the management of big economic complexes. The role and function of the ministries should change in the new conditions. They will be able to concentrate their maximum attention on long-term planning, large-scale use of innovations for raising the technical standard of production and products. The administrative staff in the branches of the economy must be reduced considerably and its redundant links removed. Profound faith in the creative energies of the workers, peasants and intellectuals, in the high moral spirit and determination of the people nourishes the Party's optimism. But optimism does not free anybody of the need to work. We will have to work a lot.

STUDY TIP

When comparing sources it is helpful to work through the five Ws – what, where, when, who, and why – for each source. Try to use this analysis of provenance, and comment on the content and tone, to make an assessment as to the value of the source. Consider your own contextual knowledge to explain the points you make.

AS LEVEL PRACTICE QUESTION

With reference to Sources 2 and 3 and your understanding of the historical context, which of these two sources is the more valuable in explaining why the USSR was in need of reform after Brezhnev's death in 1982?

Summary

There are very good reasons for seeing Brezhnev's leadership as an 'era of stagnation'. The causes of economic decline – for instance, plummeting worker productivity and the problems of the planned economy and collective farming – were not addressed. In foreign relations, the USSR sought to continue peaceful coexistence. Domestically, any dissent was harshly stamped out. Brezhnev himself, however, referred to an era of 'developed socialism': the USSR had gone from a predominantly undeveloped peasant economy in 1917 to the world's second superpower in 60 years. Living conditions were much improved, consumer goods were available, and everyone had a job. Perhaps 'stagnation' may not tell the complete story.

3 The Gorbachev revolution, 1985–2000

9 Gorbachev as leader

Gorbachev: personality, aims, and power base

KEY CHRONOLOGY

1985	Gorbachev becomes General Secretary of the Communist Party
	Gorbachev and Reagan first meet in Geneva
1986	*Perestroika* and *glasnost* begin
1988	Withdrawal of troops from Afghanistan begins
1988	Gorbachev's speech to the UN: the end of the Brezhnev Doctrine Gorbachev and Bush meet in Malta

ACTIVITY

Research reports about Gorbachev in the Western media from 1984 to 1986.

Fig. 1 *Gorbachev and his wife, Raisa, on a diplomatic trip to Paris in 1985. Abroad, the Gorbachevs appeared a cultivated, Western couple*

LEARNING OBJECTIVES

In this chapter you will learn about:

- Gorbachev: personality, aims, and power base
- the reasons for ***perestroika*, *glasnost***, and *demokratizatsiya*
- withdrawal from Afghanistan and readiness to end the Cold War
- summit meetings leading to the Malta Agreement.

KEY PROFILE

Mikhail Gorbachev (b. 1931) was born into a peasant Ukrainian–Russian family in the agricultural region of Stavropol Krai. He completed degrees in both law and agricultural economy before starting a Party career. He became First Secretary of Stavropol in 1970 and by the 1980s he was a full member of Brezhnev's Politburo, with responsibilities for agriculture. A protegee of Brezhnev's successor, Andropov, he then deputised for the elderly Chernenko before becoming General Secretary of the CPSU on 11 March 1985. His reforms led to the end of the Cold War, to the introduction of democracy into the USSR, and to the end of the USSR itself.

Gorbachev's aims and personality

Gorbachev's reforms began cautiously, then grew more radical as he and his allies battled against conservative opponents of reform. His aims remained the same:

- to reconstruct the Soviet economy so it ran efficiently, not wastefully
- to re-energise the USSR through engaging the Soviet people in politics: socialist democracy.

KEY TERM

teetotaller: someone who never drinks alcohol

ACTIVITY

Discussion

From what you know about the Soviet leadership so far, which of Gorbachev's personality traits listed here would you consider were his top three strengths for his leadership? Which would be his top three limitations for success in the job?

Key aspects of Gorbachev's personality:

- a strong believer in socialism and the future of the Soviet Union
- lastingly affected by Khrushchev's shocking revelations of Stalin's role in the purges in the Secret Speech
- cultured, humane, and Westernised; a **teetotaller**
- ambitious – he cultivated important patrons (e.g. Andropov) to advance his career
- open to the press: always keen to use the media to promote his policies
- weak at organising the practical steps needed to implement his ideas
- frustrated by the stagnation of the bureaucratic system
- a mediator: looked to achieve compromises between factions
- open to new thinking: did not have a 'Cold War mentality'
- indecisive; delayed making difficult decisions
- keen to meet ordinary people; tried to answer questions honestly
- could be naïve about the implications of his policies.

A CLOSER LOOK

Gorbachev's ideology

Although Gorbachev was a committed socialist, who believed that socialism would inevitably triumph for all peoples, he was keen to replace the idea of an ideological struggle between socialism and capitalism with a recognition that international concerns were greater than any individual ideological position. Environmental issues, global issues of poverty, human rights, and removing the threat of nuclear war were, for him, areas where socialists and capitalists should work together.

Gorbachev's power base

In Gorbachev's early years in power, he emphasised the challenge facing the USSR by referring to 'developing socialism' rather than Brezhnev's 'developed socialism', and the key term of these times was *uskorenie* – acceleration. The USSR needed to move ahead again, with renewed vigour.

Gorbachev resumed Andropov's initiatives against alcoholism (which proved very unpopular) and labour indiscipline, and against corruption, attacking these areas with a new energy and sense of urgency. To achieve the 'acceleration' he wanted, he appointed new economic advisers to help identify where *perestroika* was required, did a deal with long-serving foreign minister Andrei Gromyko to free foreign policy for a new direction, and turned his attention to securing his position by replacing conservative opponents with new people with fresh ideas.

Gorbachev was able to make changes quickly due to a general acceptance in the Politburo that reform was required and a trust that Gorbachev would continue the reform programmes of Andropov and Chernenko. Unusually, the people he promoted were chosen for their ability to support reform, not because they owed patronage to Gorbachev.

- **Yegor Ligachev**, **Nikolai Ryzhkov**, and **Viktor Chebrikov** were elected full Politburo members in April 1985.
- Long-standing foreign minister Andrei Gromyko moved aside in July 1985 (he retired completely in 1988) to allow **Eduard Shevardnadze** to take over.
- The 70-year-old traditionalist Victor Grishkin, a rival of Gorbachev's, was replaced by **Boris Yeltsin** as the Moscow Party chief, also in July 1985.
- **Alexander Yakovlev** was elected to the Politburo in January 1987.

Half the members of the Politburo and Secretariat, and the Central Committee itself, were new.

ACTIVITY

Pair discussion

Read the Key Profiles of Gorbachev's key appointees of 1985–87 on page 71. Discuss with a partner the following theme: 'What sort of men did Gorbachev rely on? Did their support strengthen or weaken his authority?'.

KEY PROFILE

Fig. 2 *Yegor Ligachev*

Yegor Ligachev (b. 1920) had worked with Andropov in the bid to make Gorbachev his successor. Gorbachev made him Secretary for Ideology, which came with the responsibility of weeding out Party members who opposed reform. Although supporting the aims of *perestroika*, Ligachev was concerned that reform was happening too fast and in a way that was dragging the USSR towards capitalism. He became the leading conservative critic of Gorbachev.

Fig. 3 *Alexander Yakovlev*

Alexander Yakovlev (1923–2005) was the 'godfather of *glasnost*'. He had studied in America and was the ambassador to Canada for ten years. Yakovlev was convinced that democracy was the missing ingredient that would allow Gorbachev's reforms to work where Khrushchev's had failed. His influence waned as the effects of *glasnost* started to pull the Soviet Union apart and Gorbachev turned to conservatives to try to counteract the disintegration of the USSR.

Fig. 4 *Boris Yeltsin*

Boris Yeltsin (1931–2007) had been a Party boss in provincial Sverdlovsk when Gorbachev and Ligachev brought him to Moscow as mayor. He was a popular politician, anti-corruption, and keen to improve life for Moscow's population. He worked hard to shift traditionalists out of the way of Gorbachev's reforms. However, he was also an outspoken critic of the Party and, in 1987, launched an attack on Ligachev for slowing down the pace of reform. Gorbachev forced him to resign, making a political enemy who would eventually remove him from power.

Fig. 5 *Nikolai Ryzhkov*

Nikolai Ryzhkov (b. 1929) had a government career in heavy industry and central planning, and worked with Gorbachev as part of the group investigating the USSR's economic problems under Andropov. Gorbachev made him head of the Council of Ministers (the Premier) from 1985 to 1991. He replaced the elderly Nikolai Tikhonov, a major block to economic reform under Brezhnev. Ryzhkov was a liberal reformer, who supported the idea of an end to central planning and its replacement with a regulated free market.

Fig. 6 *Viktor Chebrikov*

Viktor Chebrikov (1923–99) was Andropov's deputy in the KGB and worked with him in the drive to rid the Party of corruption. Gorbachev made him his KGB head, and Chebrikov was a supporter of *perestroika*, at least initially. He was never a supporter of *glasnost*, however, and expressed concern that the tolerance of so much discussion and debate in the USSR would lead to the end of the Soviet Union. In 1988, he was replaced with Vladimir Kryuchkov, who went on to be one of the coup plotters of 1991.

Fig. 7 *Eduard Shevardnadze*

Eduard Shevardnadze (1928–2014) had spoken out strongly against corruption as Party chief in Georgia and introduced effective economic reforms that brought him to Gorbachev's attention. His promotion to foreign minister was a surprise, as he had had no previous experience in foreign diplomacy. He was very effective, however, at promoting Gorbachev's reforms abroad. In 1990, he resigned in protest against Gorbachev's lack of action against his critics.

Reasons for *perestroika, glasnost*, and *demokratizatsiya*

The need for restructuring of the planned economy was evident to the Soviet leadership long before Gorbachev but previous attempts at reform of the system, under Khrushchev, and under Kosygin, had failed due to the opposition of the Soviet bureaucracy and the vested interests of the military and heavy industry complex. Declining economic growth rates had made the need to do something with the planned economy more pressing. But Gorbachev's aims were broader – he wanted restructuring throughout the Soviet system: the completion of Khrushchev's de-Stalinisation that would detoxify socialism and allow the Soviet people to reconnect to it rather than resentfully put up with it.

Glasnost and *demokratizatsiya* were both part of this 're-engagement' of socialism and a strategy to overcome opposition.

- Gorbachev and his reformers believed that if the Soviet people could be involved in restructuring Soviet economy, society and politics, then they would identify with socialism again.
- If the process of restructuring was open for all to see and all to take part in, then people would regain their trust in the Party and its role in making life better for all.
- The reformers also believed that the workers understood the problems of the Soviet economy better than anyone else, and if they were involved in finding solutions then restructuring would be more effective. *Demokratizatsiya* was as much about workplace democracy as it was about having more Soviet citizens involved in Party decision-making.
- Once public support for restructuring and reform was gained, and once Party decision-making processes and actions were made open to the public, it would be much harder, the reformers believed, for conservatives in the Party to block the reforms.

CROSS-REFERENCE

Perestroika, glasnost, and *demokratizatsiya* are defined in the introduction to this book, page xiv.

A CLOSER LOOK

The end of the Brezhnev Doctrine

Gorbachev's 1988 speech to the United Nations dramatically indicated his desire to remove obstacles to achieving an end to the Cold War: 'force and the threat of force can no longer be, and should not be, instruments of foreign policy.' When popular unrest against communist governments arose in Eastern Europe, Gorbachev, true to his word, did not intervene. The speech indicates his naïve hope that the satellite states would stay in the 'socialist commonwealth' once they saw how socialism had been renewed in the USSR. The loss of the satellite states damaged Gorbachev's status at home, though it made him a hero internationally: he received the 1990 Nobel Peace Prize.

Withdrawal from Afghanistan and readiness to end the Cold War

Gorbachev was keen to restore détente so as to give his reforms room to succeed. An economy dominated by military–industrial priorities meant investment that would not be available for reforms and more power to the conservatives who would resist radical changes to the system. Gorbachev had a real fear of the prospect of nuclear war – something he shared with President Reagan. He also wanted the Soviet Union to be open and democratic: a cultural change that would be impossible while the Soviet people remained locked in a Cold War psychology.

These priorities led to changes in Soviet foreign policy which directly led to momentous changes in world history:

- successful dialogues between Gorbachev and Reagan on nuclear disarmament (1985–88)
- withdrawal from Afghanistan (1988)
- end of the Brezhnev Doctrine in Eastern Europe (1988).

Withdrawal from Afghanistan

The war in Afghanistan was a military and economic disaster, and in order to provide a face-saving pretext for withdrawal, the leadership patched together a settlement between the Soviet-backed government led by President Najibullah and the different warring parties in Afghanistan. To achieve this, the USSR asked the USA for help; both sides signed agreements saying they would no longer intervene in the country.

CROSS-REFERENCE

There is an extract from the Brezhnev Doctrine in Chapter 7, page 53.

How real this settlement actually was is shown by the fact that Afghan fighters continued to attack Soviet forces during the withdrawal, killing another 500 of the 100,000 Soviet troops who left Afghanistan between 15 May 1988 and 15 February 1989. As part of *glasnost*, the numbers of Soviet troops killed in Afghanistan – officially 15,000 – were finally released to the Soviet public during the withdrawal.

Fig. 2 *Soviet troops withdrawing from Afghanistan in 1988*

A CLOSER LOOK

The legacy of the war in Afghanistan

Vast numbers of Soviet weapons were left in Afghanistan and the mujahideen, gaining control of them, were able to defeat the Afghan government in 1992, brutally murdering President Najibullah. The Taliban (the mujahideen who took power) stayed in control until the US invasion in 2001.

Summit meetings

Gorbachev launched a series of measures designed to convince the USA that he was serious about achieving a breakthrough in the arms race: cutting troop numbers in Afghanistan (this was before the withdrawal) and in the USSR itself; halting Soviet nuclear testing; cutting back on Soviet funding to communist and anti-Western groups around the world; ending the jamming of Western radio signals to the USSR; and speaking again and again about the unacceptable danger posed to the world by nuclear weapons.

Western reactions were at first suspicious to the point of paranoia. However, President Reagan's strong religious faith made him receptive to moral arguments about ending the threat of nuclear war, and he and Gorbachev forged a strong personal connection that persisted through a series of four summit meetings:

- Geneva (1985) – Gorbachev and Reagan first met and agreed to hold several more summits. Months of negotiations on arms reductions had resulted in the USSR rejecting most of the proposals, but both Gorbachev and Reagan believed in the importance of a personal relationship between themselves, as leaders, as the necessary first step to making progress.
- Reykjavik (1986) – promised huge progress in scaling back intermediate ballistic weapons, but reached a stalemate over **SDI**: the USA insisted on carrying out tests in space, while the USSR required agreement that tests should be restricted to laboratories. Both leaders left the summit very disappointed that the good relations established at Geneva had not enabled success at Reykjavik.
- Washington (1987) – achieved the INF (Intermediate-range Nuclear Forces) Treaty, which banned mid-range Soviet and US missiles. This agreement took place when Gorbachev was having domestic problems with his reforms and was facing a challenge for authority from Boris Yeltsin: making it important for Gorbachev's leadership that his international status

CROSS-REFERENCE

Reagan's **Strategic Defence Initiative (SDI)**, nicknamed 'Star Wars', is discussed on page pages 57–58.

remained high. As usual, most of the details on the INF treaty had been agreed long in advance of the summit, but Gorbachev's willingness at this summit to go further in reducing troop numbers and chemical weapon stocks has been recognised by historians as a major missed opportunity: the US negotiators were not prepared and the Reagan administration was struggling with its own domestic problems.

- Moscow (1988) – signed the INF Treaty but made limited further progress on arms reductions as Reagan raised the issue of Soviet human rights abuses, which Gorbachev took as a sign of US stalling.

ACTIVITY

Research

The US National Security Archive website (**www.nsarchive.gwu.edu**) has a collection of source documents from the Washington summit (search for the 'INF Treaty'). Research the reasons why Gorbachev was anxious to make progress at Washington in 1987.

The Malta Agreement

In 1989, Gorbachev met with the new US President, **George H. Bush.** It was only three weeks since the Berlin Wall had come down, and the pace of change in Europe was so fast as to be a real concern to America as well as to the Soviet Union. Historians often describe the summit in Malta as a missed opportunity because President Bush was too cautious to take up Gorbachev's offer of further arms reductions, and by the time he was ready, Gorbachev had lost too much influence at home to be able to continue the discussions.

KEY PROFILE

George H.W. Bush (b. 1924) was US president from 1989 to 1993. The fall of the Berlin Wall happened during his presidency, and the end of the Soviet Union in 1991. He described this as the end of the 'totalitarian era' and saw the USA as 'refreshed by freedom'. Although Bush saw through important strategic decision-making with the USSR, meeting with Gorbachev for the 1989 Malta Agreement and signing START I (Strategic Arms Reduction Treaty) in 1991, his main foreign policy preoccupation was not with the USSR but the 1991 Gulf War, which saw allied forces led by the USA attack Iraqi forces in Kuwait.

CROSS-REFERENCE

The fall of the Berlin Wall is covered in Chapter 23, page 190.

A CLOSER LOOK

1989

The events of 1989, in which revolutions in the Soviet Union's satellite states marked the end of Soviet control in Eastern and Central Europe, changed completely the Cold War dynamics that had been in place since the end of the Second World War. Internationally, Gorbachev was celebrated as the man who had set Eastern Europe free. Domestically, Gorbachev was seen by many as having given away the satellite states without getting anything in return.

A CLOSER LOOK

The debate about Western values

Gorbachev was frustrated by President Bush's repeated references to Western values, which he saw as ideological: an attempt to impose American values on other countries. Gorbachev thought they should instead talk of *universal* human values. At the root of this frustration was concern that the USA would bring Eastern Europe into the Western sphere of influence, while Gorbachev hoped the satellite states, by then free of coercion, would willingly stay close to the USSR.

SOURCE 1

From Anatoly Chernyaev's diary for October 1988, first published in 1997. Chernyaev was Gorbachev's foreign policy adviser:

And then I came to realise how brave and farsighted M.S. [Gorbachev] is. He declared a "new thinking" [not tied to orthodox Marxist–Leninist theory] and began to act according to common sense. His ideas are: freedom of choice, mutual respect of each other's values, renunciation of force in politics, liquidation of nuclear armaments etc. All this, each by itself, is not original or new. What is new is that a person – who came out of Soviet Marxism–Leninism, Soviet society conditioned from top to bottom by Stalinism – began to carry out these ideas with all earnestness and sincerity when he became the head of state. No wonder that the world is stunned and full of admiration. And our public still cannot appreciate that he has already transferred all of them from one state to another.

SOURCE 2

From a 1996 book about Reagan's 'secret strategy' to put pressure on the Soviet Union through its economic problems. The book was written by an American academic, Peter Schweizer, from the Hoover Institution following interviews with Reagan's administrative team:

The 'resource crisis' that the Soviet leadership faced in the 1980s was not caused by American policy; it was inherent in the system [i.e. the problems of the Soviet economy were caused by the Soviet system itself]. But what is only now emerging is the fact that the United States had a comprehensive policy to exacerbate this crisis. That policy took many forms: hidden diplomacy, covert operations, a technologically intense and sustained defense buildup, as well as a series of actions designed to throw sand in the gears of the Soviet economy. At the same time, Washington was involved in a number of high-stakes efforts to eat away at the **Soviet periphery**, in effect to roll back Soviet communism not only in the third world but at the heart of the empire.

KEY TERM

Soviet periphery: Cold War thinking was originally characterised by the idea of 'spheres of influence'; the Soviet periphery referred to developing countries that had followed the Soviet model of development

gross national product: the income of a country in one year; actually, Soviet statisticians used a different measure of development from GNP, which had to be adjusted for comparisons

command economy: another term for the Soviet planned economy – instead of market forces deciding what was produced and in what quantity, a command economy sees these decisions being made centrally by the State

AS LEVEL PRACTICE QUESTION

Evaluating primary sources

With reference to Sources 1 and 2 and your understanding of the historical context, which of these sources is more valuable to an historian studying why Gorbachev was ready to end the Cold War?

STUDY TIP

There is a saying that 'history is written by the victors', but as historians we should take care not to be influenced in source analysis by hindsight. Compare provenance and content and apply your own knowledge of conditions at the time to evaluate these sources.

SOURCE 3

From a 1994 book by two North American political scientists, *We All Lost the Cold War,* that sets out to question the standard explanations for its beginning, continuation, and ending:

If American defense spending bankrupted the Soviet economy and led Gorbachev to end the Cold War, a sharp decline in defense spending should have occurred under Gorbachev. Despite his rejection of military competition with the United States, CIA statistics show that Soviet defense spending remained relatively constant as a proportion of Soviet **gross national product** during the first four years of Gorbachev's tenure. The critical factor in the Soviet economic decline was the rigid '**command economy**' imposed by Stalin in the early 1930s.

STUDY TIP

Why the Cold War came to an end is a major historical debate with many different viewpoints, arguments, and counter-arguments. That means there are various possible answers to this type of question. Try to evaluate the strengths and weaknesses of different viewpoints , in order to assess the significance of Gorbachev's beliefs.

A LEVEL PRACTICE QUESTION

'The Cold War ended because of the fundamental weaknesses of the Soviet Union's economy.' Assess the validity of this view.

ACTIVITY

Summary

Search YouTube for news clips about Gorbachev and Reagan's summits, which provide interesting insights into contemporary Western views of Gorbachev's leadership. Select one that you consider to be of most value to an historian and use it in a class presentation and discussion.

Summary

Internationally, Gorbachev's achievements seem as significant as any leader in history, and commentators at the time of the end of the Cold War and the fall of the Berlin Wall could see a clear connection between Gorbachev's outgoing, Westernised personality and the freedoms that his leadership permitted the Soviet peoples and the peoples of the Soviet satellite states. Within the USSR and within Russia in particular, his achievements were seen differently and they were linked to a different assessment of his character: that he was naïve, that his decisions were ill-judged, and that he had been over-influenced by the West to the degree that he sacrificed everything that the Soviet people had built and defended without getting anything in return.

10 Economic, political, and social policies under Gorbachev

The impact of Chernobyl

LEARNING OBJECTIVES

In this chapter you will learn about:

- the impact of Chernobyl
- economic restructuring and the outcome
- the attempt to democratise the Soviet political system and its outcome; main political reforms.

KEY CHRONOLOGY

1986 Chernobyl disaster
Campaign against alcohol begins

1987 Laws on joint enterprise and state enterprise

1988 Party Conference: announcement of contested elections
Law on cooperatives

1989
March Elections to the Congress of People's Deputies

A CLOSER LOOK

The Chernobyl disaster, 26 April 1986

- The Chernobyl power complex is in Ukraine, 130km north of Kiev.
- The accident happened when an explosion in a reactor threw a huge cloud of radionuclides into the air that then drifted over large areas of Russia, Ukraine, and Belarus.
- Two workers died on site.
- 28 people died from radiation poisoning within the next few weeks.
- Around 120,000 people living in a 30km radius of the site were evacuated.
- By 2000, some 4000 children in areas affected by radiation had thyroid cancer, most of which was most probably caused by the radiation. 60 have since died.
- UN estimates suggest the accident will eventually contribute to several thousand cancer deaths.

Fig. 1 *The Chernobyl nuclear power plant three days after the explosion of 26 April 1986*

ACTIVITY

Pair discussion

Why do you think that Gorbachev said, 20 years after the Chernobyl disaster, that Chernobyl 'was perhaps the real cause of the collapse of the Soviet Union'?

The nuclear meltdown at Chernobyl nuclear power plant in Ukraine, USSR was a significant turning point for Gorbachev's leadership because, put to the test, the government's commitment to *glasnost* proved shaky. Although Gorbachev later explained that the leadership was unsure of what exactly had happened in Ukraine for the first day after the disaster, its reaction was to impose a news blackout after 26 April in classic Soviet authoritarian style. Twenty years after the disaster, Gorbachev stated that Chernobyl 'was perhaps the real cause of the collapse of the Soviet Union five years later', explaining that the accident and the regime's response to it clarified for him 'how important it was to continue the policy of *glasnost*': in fact, to remove all obstacles to *glasnost* and make everything open.

Economic restructuring and the outcome

At first, Gorbachev's economic restructuring was usually referred to as 'acceleration' (*uskorenie*) rather than *perestroika.*

Acceleration

'Acceleration' had been a term used in Andropov's reforms. The idea was that the Soviet system was not broken, just inefficient. By streamlining processes and removing obstacles, problems could be solved and stagnation left behind.

One aspect of 'acceleration' was a renewed campaign against alcoholism. A decree of 4 April 1985 pushed up prices for vodka and strong wine, and cut production of other alcoholic drinks. At first, the Soviet press reported remarkable improvements in worker productivity and general health. Then, the USSR's many heavy drinkers turned to *samogen* (home-brewed alcohol) which had a disastrous effect on both the economy and health. The State lost its revenues from selling alcohol (which accounted for 17 per cent of revenues in 1985) and many people were poisoned by home-brewed spirits. By September 1988, the campaign was wound down.

External pressures

Problems from outside the Soviet Union made economic restructuring very difficult.

- A big fall in the international price of oil in 1986 meant that the USSR's foreign earnings dropped.
- Poor harvests meant that more foreign currency had to be spent on food imports.
- The USSR's international debt increased, which made the USSR's economic performance look even worse. The government printed more money to cover its debts, which increased **inflation** within the USSR. Officially, the USSR did not have a **budget deficit**, though in reality it had grown to over $30 billion by 1987.
- Reforms were funded by state investment; external economic problems meant investment was harder to justify.

KEY TERM

inflation: happens when prices increase, reducing the value of the money people have to spend or in savings

budget deficit: the amount a government has to borrow to fill the gap between what it spends and what it earns from taxes and other income

Reform from above

Gorbachev increased the Plan targets for a 20 per cent growth in national income by 1990 and to double it by 2000. Unfortunately, although the economy recovered a little in 1986 (following a good harvest), by 1987 it had declined. Gorbachev travelled around the USSR and everywhere heard the same story: nothing had changed because the local bosses kept things how they wanted them – except now there were more shortages.

Gorbachev and his advisers decided the answer was to impose more reform. There were many different laws and schemes in this direction, but three are particularly important:

- A law on **joint enterprises** (January 1987) allowed foreign companies to own up to 49 per cent of a Soviet company.
- A law on state enterprise (June 1987) gave factory managers more freedom from central control and the opportunity to keep profits.
- A law on **cooperatives** (June 1988) allowed people to set up their own private businesses, buy necessary materials from the wholesale market, employ people, sell their products at wages and prices they set, and keep profits.

Outcomes

The reforms ran into serious problems, as they clashed with the planned economy.

- The ministries and the central planners still had high plan targets to meet, so they found ways to ensure that state enterprises kept working for them, not for themselves.
- For any enterprises that did have some spare capacity, the easiest thing was to produce the same shoddy products as before but put the price up.
- While joint ventures were a good way in theory of bringing in foreign know-how, technology, and investment, and for Soviet firms to earn foreign currency from exports, it was very difficult for foreign businesses to operate in the USSR, where resources were allocated from the centre, prices were all fixed, and corruption was rife.
- The number of cooperatives grew very fast and they proved to be often much more productive than state enterprises. But corruption caused huge problems for those running cooperatives: state officials demanded bribes to cut through masses of **red tape**, while the Russian mafia demanded **protection money** from cooperatives.

Fig. 2 *A market scene in Moscow, 1988; prices at this market were at least three times higher than state prices*

ACTIVITY

Discussion

1. How would allowing foreign companies to own a large share of Soviet companies have helped accelerate the Soviet economy? What possible problems could you foresee happening with joint enterprises?
2. Compare the law on state enterprise with Kosygin's reforms of 1965. What similarities and differences can you identify?

CROSS-REFERENCE

Kosygin's attempted economic reforms are discussed in Chapter 6, pages 43–44.

KEY TERM

joint enterprise: when two different companies combine together, often one from the home country and one from a foreign country

cooperatives: owned and run by their members; for example, by workerstheir businesses

red tape: describes overly complex bureaucratic requirements

protection money: a mafia speciality – business owners are told that they need to pay money to the mafia in order to prevent any 'accidents' happening to them or their businesses

A CLOSER LOOK

The Russian mafia

Organised crime in the USSR began in the Gulags, spread into society with the release of prisoners under Khrushchev, and was boosted under Brezhnev by the growth of the black market and the widespread corruption of the *nomenklatura* system. After the collapse of the Soviet Union, mafia groups were heavily involved in asset stripping Soviet-era businesses.

ACTIVITY

Analyse the figures in Table 1. To what extent is it true to say that it was successes or failures in the USSR's agricultural output that had the biggest impact on national income?

Table 1 *Official Soviet economic data showing percentage growth for selected indicators, 1986–91*

	1986–90 average	1986	1987	1988	1989	1990	1991
National income produced	4.2	2.3	1.6	4.4	2.4	−4.0	−15.0
Industrial output	4.6	4.4	3.8	3.9	1.7	−1.2	−7.8
Agricultural output	2.7	5.3	-0.6	1.7	1.3	−2.3	−7.0

The attempt to democratise the Soviet political system and its outcome; main political reforms

Gorbachev saw enterprises like cooperatives as being a force for democracy: he wanted management to be elected and accountable to the workers for their decisions. This was accompanied by moves to make politics more democratic, with elections of local deputies who would supervise the running of local soviets which ran local affairs. The biggest changes to the political system were elections to a new Congress of People's Deputies, and more democracy in the Party itself.

KEY TERM

legislature: an elected group of people who make, change, or repeal the laws of a state

constituency: a particular area whose voters elect a representative to the legislature

ratify: to make something official

The Congress of People's Deputies and the Supreme Soviet

Under the old system, the **legislature**, the Supreme Soviet, was elected – but there was only ever one candidate in each **constituency** and the Supreme Soviet voted exactly as directed by the Party leadership: a rubber stamp. Candidates were all selected by the Party and met twice a year for two or three days.

At the Nineteenth Party Conference in June 1988, Gorbachev announced that a new two-tier legislature based on contested elections would be created.

- The Soviet people would vote for candidates to a new Congress of People's Deputies of the USSR and this body would then vote for the new Supreme Soviet.
- The Supreme Soviet would make the laws of the USSR, **ratify** ministerial appointments (including the president's choice of prime minister), question ministers, and set up commissions and committees to investigate political issues. Congress could vote to amend or reject those laws.
- The way the 1500 constituencies were organised ensured that population size was not the only thing determining representation.

Fig. 3 *The Congress of People's Deputies of the USSR*

The new legislative system was not fully democratic:

- 'Public organisations' had a third of all seats to be voted on, including a share of 100 seats controlled by the Communist Party.
- The local electoral system, which approved the selection of candidates, was controlled by the Communist Party.
- In some areas, Party candidates put pressure on other candidates to withdraw from the Congress elections, making them the only name on the ballot.
- Party politics and processes were not very clear. Congress deputies who were Party members were often not sure whether they should vote for the Party line or vote for what their **electorate** wanted.

Elections for the USSR's Congress of People's Deputies took place in March 1989, with its first session opening in May 1989. A year later, in 1990, elections for similar legislatures happened in the Union republics. Resistance to guaranteeing votes for the Communist Party meant the republics were allowed to set up their regional parliaments in different ways.

ACTIVITY

Write a speech either as Gorbachev might have given at the Nineteenth Party Conference of 1988, or as a Party member might have given to defend the traditional ways.

KEY TERM

electorate: the people who can vote in an election

Reform of the Party

At the Nineteenth Party Conference, Gorbachev also announced that the Party itself would change, to become more accountable and democratic:

- Party officials would be elected from competing Party candidates – a challenge to the ***nomenklatura*** system.
- Positions could not be held for more than two consecutive terms of five years.
- The Central Committee was to take a more active role in the highest levels of policy decision-making.
- Records of high-level Party meetings and Party budgets would be made public.
- The number of Central Committee departments was reduced from 20 to just nine.
- The Party lost its control of economic policy and the Politburo would only deal with Party issues (a body of Party leaders from the republics would take over its other functions).
- Nobody was allowed to hold both a Party and state position at the highest level (though Gorbachev did).

CROSS-REFERENCE

The ***nomenklatura*** system is discussed in Chapter 5, page 38.

Outcomes

- Some Party leaders were defeated in the Congress elections: for example, the mayors of Moscow and Kiev, the First Secretaries of Kiev and Minsk, and many of the senior Party members of Leningrad's administration. However, nearly 90 per cent of deputies were Party members.
- Pro-reform and conservative factions began to form. It became difficult to get laws passed.
- As part of *glasnost*, the new legislature was televised live. Between 90 and 100 million people watched as deputies criticised Party leaders.
- A big winner from the changes was Boris Yeltsin, who Gorbachev had sacked from an important Party post: enough usually to consign a politician to the scrapheap. Yeltsin stood against a Party candidate for the Moscow seat, campaigned hard, and won 89 per cent of the popular vote.

Changes within the Party did not answer the big question raised by *demokratizatsiya* – by what right did the Party govern the Soviet people, and especially those people who did not want to be part of the USSR?

Gorbachev's political reforms exposed real problems for the future of the USSR and his own leadership. While Gorbachev hoped that socialist democracy would re-energise the relationship between the Soviet people and their Communist Party, *demokratizatsiya* meant that alternatives to the Party were now allowed, that the Party no longer had control over key aspects of the State (such as the legal system), and that any failure in Gorbachev's reforms could now be directly criticised, to his face and on national TV.

A CLOSER LOOK

The Inter-Regional Group of Deputies

This radical reformist group within the Congress of People's Deputies put pressure on Gorbachev to go further with his changes. Both Sakharov and Yeltsin were members. A key campaigning issue was to remove the Communist Party's monopoly of power in the USSR. This group started the formation of what would become different political parties.

CROSS-REFERENCE

Andrei Sakharov was a leading dissident under Brezhnev's regime. There is more information about him in Chapter 8, page 60.

SOURCE 1

From an article by Radio Free Europe on the twentieth anniversary of the 1989 revolutions across Europe. Radio Free Europe was set up at the start of the Cold War to broadcast news and information from a Western perspective to audiences in Eastern Europe:

Some stayed home and sat glued to their television sets for hours. Some went about their daily business with transistor radios pressed tightly against their ears. They gasped in shock, awe, glee, and indignation at what they heard. They hung on every single word. It was the spring of 1989, the Soviet Union's first democratically elected legislature was in session. The daily sessions were filled with passionate speeches and heated disagreements. The Soviet public had never seen anything like it – and couldn't get enough. And what they heard was – for the time – revolutionary. Gone were the empty, scripted platitudes and numbing cadence that previously dominated official Soviet life. Instead, newly elected representatives were boldly chastising once-untouchable Politburo members, criticising their failures and shortcomings as the television cameras rolled.

SOURCE 2

From a book of interviews with Soviet public figures (politicians, journalists) who were engaged in implementing Gorbachev's reforms in the 1980s. In this interview, from 1989, Aleksandr Yakovlev, an ardent reformer in Gorbachev's Politburo, discusses the difficulties of democratisation:

We must learn the political culture of discussion, of tolerating the widest possible range of conflicting views, within the context of socialism. Over the years, we have developed habits of rejecting each other's opinions and tastes, This has caused harm. We still have too much autocratic, totalitarian thinking.

One goal of socialism is to allow different views so that multiple interests can be unified and harmonised. Unfortunately, some of these groups go to extremes. We welcome expressions of national feelings, but we condemn arrogant forms of nationalism, which turn one nationality against another. Some of this has also arisen.

ACTIVITY

In 1988, Reagan visited Moscow. A reporter asked if he still thought the USSR was an 'evil empire'. Reagan replied, 'No, I was talking about another time, another era.' Was 1988 a different era from 1983?

AS LEVEL PRACTICE QUESTION

Evaluating primary sources

With reference to Sources 1 and 2 and your understanding of the historical context, which of these sources is more valuable to an historian studying the impact of Gorbachev's attempt to democratise Soviet politics in the 1980s?

STUDY TIP

You will need to plan your points of comparison and should note the similarities and differences between the sources before you begin. You should consider both what they say about the issue and their provenance.

A LEVEL **PRACTICE QUESTION**

'Gorbachev's democratic reforms were a failure.' Assess the validity of this view.

STUDY TIP

Before composing your answer to a question like this, consider all the possible arguments for and against the statement, and the evidence to support each one. In your final answer, to make sure you explain clearly what it is you are agreeing or disagreeing with.

ACTIVITY

Summary

Imagine you were a Soviet citizen born in 1970, writing in 1989 about the changes you had seen since Gorbachev became General Secretary. What would be the most significant changes socially, economically, and politically that you would record?

Summary

Gorbachev's leadership has clear parallels with Khrushchev's leadership: the Party had agreed that reform was needed, but again the Party's hopes for reform turned out to be completely different from the actual consequences. Both Khrushchev and Gorbachev were socialist idealists who believed that the Party had to loosen its grip on power, and allow the Soviet people more of a role in making the system work. Gorbachev, looking back on his leadership, mourned the fact that his political reforms succeeded before his economic reforms had time to deliver.

11 Revolution and counter-revolution in the USSR

Opposition to Gorbachev's policies; nationalist unrest

Resistance to reform had been growing within conservative factions of the Party, but Gorbachev found himself increasingly isolated as his reformist supporters also started to criticise his methods.

- Conservatives thought *perestroika* was moving the USSR to a market economy, that *glasnost* was corrupting the USSR's view of its own history, and that *demokratizatsiya* was undermining the authority of the Party and risked the break-up of the USSR.
- Radical reformers thought *perestroika* was not going far enough, that the Party should renounce its constitutional leading role, that the republics should have more power, and that the USSR should move to a full market economy.
- The bureaucracy was directly threatened by the Party reforms, so there was considerable opposition from those whom Gorbachev relied on to implement his plans.
- Some non-Russians saw the opportunity for more power for their republics, or even independence from the USSR; other ethnic minority groups within the Union were concerned that their interests would no longer be protected if the USSR was weakened.
- Russian nationalists argued that Russia had given too much to the other republics, and also worried that Western influences were corrupting Russia's ancient collective culture.
- Popular support for Gorbachev's leadership weakened as his economic reforms led only to shortages and his political reforms unleashed criticism of his leadership and the USSR.

The presidency and changes to the role of the CPSU

The Congress of People's Deputies and its Supreme Soviet did pass some significant reformist laws, for example on freedom of speech and of religious belief. Gorbachev had hoped for 'socialist pluralism' – different opinions on how best to take socialism forward – which would be led by the Party. Instead, he faced the rapid growth and fragmentation of political opposition.

The role of president of the USSR was brought in in March 1990 to impose political stability. Gorbachev stood as the only candidate for election by Congress. The presidency had important powers (outranking the Politburo), but since Gorbachev had not been elected by the people, many feared that these powers could easily turn a president into a dictator.

In March 1990, the CPSU's 'leading role' in the USSR came to an end, following a sustained campaign by the Inter-Regional Group of Deputies. Soviet politics embraced a multi-party system.

A CLOSER LOOK

The Party's leading role

The USSR's 1977 constitution guaranteed its citizens freedom of speech and other key human rights which were, however, overruled in practice by Article 6 of the constitution, which said: 'The leading and guiding force of the Soviet society and the nucleus of its political system, of all state organisations and public organisations, is the Communist Party of the Soviet Union. The CPSU exists for the people and serves the people.' The Party was therefore, until March 1990, the only legitimate political party, a foolproof guide to every decision in the USSR.

LEARNING OBJECTIVES

In this chapter you will learn about:

- opposition to Gorbachev's policies; nationalist unrest
- deepening economic and political crises; the coup of August 1991 and Yeltsin's counter-attack; Gorbachev's resignation as president
- the collapse of the USSR; reasons for Gorbachev's apparent failure.

KEY CHRONOLOGY

1990 Gorbachev appointed President of the USSR

1990 Supreme Soviet votes to end CPSU's leading role in the USSR
Yeltsin elected Chairman of Russian Congress of People's Deputies
Yeltsin leaves Communist Party of Soviet Union

1991 Seventeen demonstrators killed in Latvia and Lithuania
Yeltsin elected President of RSFSR
Gorbachev proposes Union Treaty
August coup against Gorbachev
Collapse of the USSR
Gorbachev's resignation

CROSS-REFERENCE

Find out more about the Inter-Regional Group of Deputies in Chapter 10, page 82.

ACTIVITY

Draw a diagram to show the difference between the democracy Gorbachev had been hoping to achieve (socialist democracy, both in the Party and in the workplace) and the multi-party democracy that he was forced to accept.

Yeltsin's opposition

In 1990 and 1991, opposition began to clearly divide into democrats and what observers in the West characterised as the 'Communist old guard' (left-wing conservatives who wanted to preserve the USSR, socialism, and the Party's leading role – and their jobs).

Boris Yeltsin was a focus for the democrats, and during 1990 and 1991 he drove forward a startling sequence of events to challenge Gorbachev's leadership:

- In May 1990, Yeltsin was narrowly elected Chairman of the Russian Congress of People's Deputies.
- In June 1990, Yeltsin resigned from the Communist Party.
- On 12 June 1990, Russia's Congress voted in a Declaration of State Sovereignty for the RSFSR. This was not a declaration of independence from the USSR, but said that Russia was a **sovereign state** and the USSR only had such powers over Russia as Russia decided it could have. So if a law agreed by the Russian Congress contradicted a Soviet law, then the Russian law took precedence.
- On 15 June 1990, Russia's Congress voted to amend the RSFSR constitution to allow different political parties.
- On 12 June 1991, a Russian presidential election was held, which Yeltsin won with 57 per cent of Russians' votes. As the elected president of the Union's biggest republic, Yeltsin called on (unelected) Gorbachev to share power.

KEY TERM

sovereign state: a state that is run by its own government alone

Fig. 1 *Gorbachev watching Boris Yeltsin, as leader of the RSFSF, on TV. With Gorbachev are members of the Soviet press, presidential advisers, and a KGB director*

ACTIVITY

Write three essay titles, following the exam style for AS or A Level, about opposition to Gorbachev's policies. For example: *'It was personal ambition that motivated Yeltsin's opposition to Gorbachev's policies'. Explain why you agree or disagree with this view.* You could even try writing an answer to one of them!

Gorbachev's move to the right

In August 1990, the Soviet economist Stanislav Shatalin proposed a radical plan to move the USSR to a market economy in 500 days. Yeltsin supported the '500 days' plan but Gorbachev, under pressure from conservatives, finally decided against adopting the programme. Gorbachev feared popular unrest or even revolution from rapid privatisation.

In 1990, as Gorbachev's reformist allies began to split from him over arguments about the direction and pace of reform, he became increasingly reliant on conservatives, and replaced reformers with conservatives in some key positions. The power of the KGB was strengthened, a law on press freedoms was passed in June 1990 (which made it a criminal offence to abuse freedom of speech), and a law was passed that allowed Gorbachev to declare a state of emergency.

Nationalist unrest

Six main factors contributed to the rapid growth of nationalist unrest as Gorbachev's leadership weakened.

- *Glasnost* publicised historic Soviet injustices against many different nationalities and ethnicities within the USSR.
- The end of Communist control in Eastern Europe in 1989 inspired national movements within the USSR.
- *Demokratizatsiya* allowed nationalist politicians to gain influence, and to push for sovereign status or independence.
- Gorbachev's decision to create the role of president of the USSR in March 1990 was mirrored in the creation of presidencies in the republics also. These presidents now had their own power base.
- The decline in the influence of the CPSU meant it no longer mattered as much to the leaders of the republics what Moscow wanted: what kept them in power was listening to the needs of their own people.
- Gorbachev's leadership cracked down on nationalist unrest in the Baltic republics and in Georgia; 19 demonstrators were killed in Tbilisi, Georgia, in April 1989 and 17 were killed in Latvia and Lithuania in January 1991, with hundreds wounded. Fear of old-style Soviet repression spurred on the independence movements.

Fig. 2 *In August 1989, a human chain of two million people stretched over 400 miles through Latvia, Estonia, and Lithuania, in an amazing demonstration of popular protest against continued Soviet rule*

Gorbachev, desperate to keep the USSR together, proposed a Union Treaty in April 1991 that would have created a voluntary **federation** of independent states, to be called the Union of Socialist Sovereign Republics. Nine of the fifteen Union republics attended talks (not the three Baltic states, Georgia, Armenia, or Moldova). Gorbachev was forced into agreeing to transfer almost all Union powers to the individual states. Conservatives were deeply worried.

CROSS-REFERENCE

The end of communist control in Eastern Europe had, in many cases, direct parallels with the end of Communist control in the USSR. Chapter 23 provides details of this extraordinary process.

A CLOSER LOOK

Independence in the Baltics

The three Baltic SSRs (Latvia, Estonia, and Lithuania) had been independent countries before being 'incorporated' into the USSR in 1940. *Glasnost* allowed dissatisfaction against the USSR to be expressed openly. Lithuania was the first to declare independence, on 11 March 1990. The USSR's leadership sent tanks into Lithuania on 22 March. The hard-line conservatives within the leadership who ordered it hoped violence in the Baltics could be used as an excuse to impose a state of emergency across the USSR, keeping the Union together through repression.

KEY TERM

federation: a union of states that accepts a federal government

Deepening economic and political crises

The coup of August 1991 and Yeltsin's counter-attack

A date of 20 August 1991 was set for the Union Treaty to be signed. On 18 August, Gorbachev was preparing to leave his holiday home in the Crimea when he was put under house arrest there; on 19 August, a state of emergency was declared. Hard-line conservatives had decided that they must act to save the USSR. A return to authoritarian rule, with harsh repression of nationalist movements, would certainly have followed this **coup** attempt.

Four main factors prevented the coup:

- Gorbachev refused to be intimidated into handing over his powers.
- Hundreds of thousands of people demonstrated against the coup.
- Boris Yeltsin joined the demonstrators and became the public face of resistance to the coup.
- The coup was not well organised and the troops involved in Moscow were not committed to repressing the demonstrators.

Fig. 3 *Boris Yeltsin climbed onto a tank threatening the Russian government building, the White House, and rallied demonstrators against the coup*

Faced with these pressures, the coup attempt fell apart, ending on 21 August. Gorbachev returned to Moscow amid celebrations, but Yeltsin was the hero of the hour, while Gorbachev's authority was in tatters. Hope of signing the Union Treaty disappeared. The republics took the coup attempt as a warning: the three Baltic states – Armenia, Georgia, and Moldova – declared independence.

After another round of Union negotiations failed, Yeltsin, Kravchuk (leader of Ukraine), and Shushkevich (leader of Belarus) met on 8 December 1991 and drew up their own agreement for a Commonwealth of Independent States (CIS). Then, without any democratic involvement in the decision at all, they announced that the Soviet Union would end.

Gorbachev's resignation as president

As Yeltsin had planned, Gorbachev recognised that if the USSR ended, so did his leadership. He resigned on 25 December 1991. On the same day he made an announcement on television about his resignation. In it he referred to the

A CLOSER LOOK

The referendum on the Union, 1991

In a referendum of 17 March 1991, people in Russia, Ukraine, and Kazakhstan were asked whether they supported the preservation of the Union: 73 per cent of voters said that they did. Opinion polls in four major cities – Moscow, Kiev, Alma Ata, and Krasnoyarsk – in October, showed 75 per cent in favour, with 81 per cent of Muscovites wanting to keep the Union.

ACTIVITY

Discussion

What reasons might Soviet citizens in the republics have had to vote for the Union, rather than against it?
Try to think of five reasons (or more).

CROSS-REFERENCE

Turn to page 37 for explanation of what 'coup' means.

ACTIVITY

Using your knowledge of the Brezhnev era, put together a plan for returning Gorbachev's USSR to the sort of state the conservative coup-plotters would have imagined. The first step would be to declare a state of emergency (giving your leadership the power to take whatever actions were necessary). What would your three next steps be? You can assume that you have the backing of the Soviet Army and the KGB.

formation of the Commonwealth of Independent States, as 'disuniting the State', and something he could not 'subscribe to'.

While he admitted that the task of renovating the State and bringing about drastic changes with the international community had been a challenge, he highlighted positive achievements of his political career. He insisted that society in the USSR was more free than ever, free from the threats of the Cold War, with free elections, a free press, and greater human rights.

'All this change had taken a lot of strain,' he admitted, 'The old system fell apart even before the new system began to work. [But] I am positive that sooner or later, some day our common efforts will bear fruit and our nations will live in a prosperous, democratic society.'

ACTIVITY

1. Explain why Gorbachev resigned in December 1991.
2. How far do you agree with Gorbachev's list of achievements? What would you include in a list of his failures?
3. Outline the steps by which Yeltsin got the better of Gorbachev.

The collapse of the USSR and reasons for Gorbachev's apparent failure

Reasons for the collapse of the USSR

The following are general points of agreement about why the collapse of the USSR happened when it did:

- Although some republics would never have stayed in a new USSR, the Union Treaty probably would have been signed if the August coup had not happened. The coup plotters achieved exactly the opposite of what they intended.
- Yeltsin was also able to neutralise any further conservative actions to defend the USSR by linking any opposition to him to support for the disgraced August plotters.
- Yeltsin's decision to sign the CIS agreement instead of Gorbachev's Union Treaty was done to remove Gorbachev as president; preventing the USSR continuing as a voluntary Union was a strategy to achieve that aim.
- The end of the USSR was a political collapse, not a revolution brought about by a wave of popular unrest. The role of individuals was key to why it happened when it did.

Reasons for Gorbachev's apparent failure

Historians agree that if Gorbachev had chosen just to 'reign', like Brezhnev, then the USSR could have continued into the twenty-first century. Despite its problems, there was no sign of building pressure 'from below' to change the system.

The following were crucial in leading to Gorbachev's apparent failure:

- The lack of a definite goal: it was never clear what the Soviet Union and socialism would be like once the reforms had done their work.
- Gorbachev's charismatic personality had helped him to sell the idea of reform to the Soviet people, but his desire to find a middle path meant he became seen as indecisive. As problems mounted, calls began for a 'firm hand' in leadership.
- Preserving key elements of the Soviet system alongside the introduction of market economics and democratic politics made for huge difficulties: the problems of the planned economy were integral to that system.
- Gorbachev's reforms created strong opposition. The Party and government bureaucracy had little reason to support the reforms, especially once they became directly threatened by them.
- Gorbachev's reluctance to abandon the planned economy and the leading role of the Party, and his failure to endorse the '500 days' plan, meant that reformists also turned away from him and left him isolated.

ACTIVITY

Pair discussion

Choose one (or more) of the following three viewpoints to discuss. What arguments can you make for or against them?

1. Gorbachev tried to steer a middle course between the Party bureaucrats, who had no incentive to share power, and the people, who had no prior experience of democracy.
2. It was naïve to think that making the Communist Party more democratic would be enough. It was inevitable that opposition to the Party would mean the development of independent political parties.
3. Instead of *glasnost* strengthening socialism, as Gorbachev intended, it released an outpouring of evidence that the USSR was built on murder, torture, and forced labour, totally eroding the legitimacy of the system.

- In his resignation speech Gorbachev claimed that the old system was dismantled before there was anything to replace it. The economy foundered as no one knew whether to continue supplying according to Plan targets, or to start producing for themselves.
- Although Gorbachev received a huge amount of praise internationally, the fall in global oil prices stripped the Soviet economy of any cushion that could have made reforms less painful for consumers.

Gorbachev surely was right when he said in his resignation that change in so vast a system 'could not have been carried out without difficulties, shock and pain'.

SOURCE 1

From a book written in 1993 in which Stephen White, a Professor of Politics with a specialism in Soviet studies, sums up the reasons for Gorbachev's failures:

Gorbachev, it was clear, had personally and courageously initiated a search for a combination of plan and market, and of popular government and party rule, that was still expected to remain within the bounds of socialism. As his administration came to an end after more than six turbulent years, it was also clear that he had found no coherent framework for reconciling these often incompatible objectives and that a solution to the problems he had identified was likely to require a reconsideration of the bases of the Soviet system and not simply an attempt to manage that system more effectively.

SOURCE 2

From a memoir written in 1993 by Yegor Ligachev, by then a severe critic of Gorbachev from the conservative faction of the Party. In this passage, Ligachev describes his take on events in 1987 as Gorbachev moved from cautious reforms to more radical approaches:

Gorbachev truly displayed his character that time. Apparently he was absolutely convinced that he was right, that all economic problems would be solved as soon as we implemented a radical reform, the sooner the better. To get a full picture, we need to recall what was taking place outside the Kremlin walls. The radicals' star was rising. Having cranked public opinion into high gear, they directed it against the central government, accusing it of conservatism, deceleration, attempting to return to the period of stagnation. The right-wing radicals of the mass media beat into the national consciousness each day that only government and ministerial offices stood in the way of a new life. If they were removed, the gates to paradise on earth would immediately be thrown open.

SOURCE 3

From a TV interview given by Boris Yeltsin in 1991 as part of his campaign for the Russian presidency, in which he was strongly critical of Gorbachev:

As recently as a month ago [Gorbachev] was saying everywhere that he is only for socialism, only for socialism, we cannot do otherwise. Just as for over seventy years we have been marching to a bright future, that is how [he says] we will continue, and somehow we will arrive. Our country has not been lucky. It was decided to carry out this Marxist experiment on us – fate pushed us in precisely this direction. Instead of some country in Africa, they began this experiment with us. In the end, we proved that there is no place for this idea. It has simply pushed us off the road the world's civilised countries have taken. This is reflected today, when 40 per cent of people are living below the poverty line and in constant humiliation when they receive produce upon the presentation of ration cards. This is a constant humiliation, a reminder every hour that you are a slave in this country.

AS LEVEL **PRACTICE QUESTION**

Evaluating primary sources

With reference to Sources 2 and 3 and your understanding of the historical context, which of the two sources is more valuable in explaining criticism of Gorbachev's policies?

STUDY TIP

Consider the tone, vocabulary, and use of language in sources. This will help you assess their value.

AS LEVEL **PRACTICE QUESTION**

'Gorbachev's domestic policies were a failure.' Explain why you agree or disagree with this view.

STUDY TIP

With this type of question try to identify the possible explanations for and against the view. Look for supporting evidence for these explanations. Aim to keep your answer balanced; you do not necessarily have to totally agree or disagree.

ACTIVITY

Summary

Storyboard the main scenes for a documentary about the collapse of the USSR. You will need to include pointers for the narration that include evidence to back up the claims made. Consider:

a) background to Gorbachev's reforms
b) economic problems
c) political changes
d) opposition
e) the coup and Yeltsin's counter-attack
f) the breakup of the USSR and Gorbachev's resignation.

Look on YouTube for existing documentaries on this period to help your planning.

12 Yeltsin as leader

Fig. 1 *Yeltsin dancing during an election campaign event in June 1996*

LEARNING OBJECTIVES

In this chapter you will learn about:

- Yeltsin's personality, aims, and style of rule
- economic and political problems and policies
- political unrest; Yeltsin's re-election and resignation
- Putin as leader; the state of Russia politically, economically, and socially by 2000.

KEY CHRONOLOGY

1992	Price controls lifted on most products as part of Gaidar's reforms
	Inflation reaches 2500 per cent
	Chernomyrdin replaces Gaidar as Prime Minister
1993	Attack on White House – more than 140 people killed
	New constitution approved that widens Yeltsin's powers
1994	First Chechen War
1996	Yeltsin re-elected as president
	Yeltsin suffers heart attack, has bypass surgery, contracts pneumonia
1998	Collapse of Russian economy: financial crisis
1999	Yeltsin resigns, apologising for his mistakes
2000	Putin elected as leader

Yeltsin's personality, aims, and style of rule

Yeltsin's personality

After his role in defeating the August coup against Gorbachev and his reforms, Yeltsin was the most popular figure in Russia. Western observers sought to categorise him, but events kept on forcing a rethink – once a loyal communist who went on to bring down the Soviet Union; a defender of democracy at the White House in 1991 who turned his own tanks on the very same building in

ACTIVITY

Research

Compile a profile of the different aspects of Yeltsin's personality. A good place to start would be to read through obituaries in the Western media following his death on 23 April 2007.

1993; a market reformist who presided over the strip mining of his country's assets by mafia bosses; an international hero who embarrassed his country with periods of alcohol-linked incapacity. A study of his speeches in *Pravda* in 1991 said Yeltsin was 'predictable in only one aspect – his unpredictability'.

Yeltsin's aims

After the collapse of the Soviet Union in August 1991, Yeltsin chose to focus on the economy. In other areas, he seemed to aim at preserving the status quo.

- He did *not* start his leadership by dismantling the old structures of Soviet government, banning former Party leaders from political office, setting up a new constitution, or introducing genuine multi-party politics.
- Although he had banned the Communist Party in Russia, as part of his attack on the USSR, and accused it of being a criminal organisation, once in sole control of Russia, he did *not* begin a process to give victims under the USSR the chance to face their persecutors.
- The KGB was reformed in 1991, but it was an internal reform that the KGB itself carried out. In 1994, it rebranded itself the Federal Security Service (FSB), but remained a very similar organisation.
- In his personal life, too, Yeltsin seemed to aim for continuity with the Soviet past. He moved into the luxurious mansion that had been constructed for Gorbachev, and took frequent hunting trips, like Brezhnev, in the old Party retreats.

There were good reasons for this strategy: the 'old guard' of Party conservatives had not gone away and Yeltsin needed to tread carefully with the big ministries, the KGB/FSB, and the military. Also, most Russians had not resisted the Soviet system: there was national pride related to Russia's role in world events as the leading nation in the USSR. So much had been achieved already in regard to democratisation and the devolution of power from the old Soviet system, which left the economy as the all-important priority. However, it may also be possible that Yeltsin was overwhelmed by the scale of the task facing him. Getting to the top by removing Gorbachev had been his main aim. He did not come to power with clear aims about what to do next.

A CLOSER LOOK

The rise of the oligarchs

An oligarchy is when a small number of people have all the power in a country. Russian oligarchs do not always have political power (though some do); it is a term used to describe those who made vast profits during Yeltsin's privatisation process. This was done by buying state enterprises very cheaply whose products (especially oil and gas) were very valuable in international markets.

Yeltsin's style of rule

Yeltsin was a controlling ruler in office, demanding unswerving loyalty from the lower ranks and finding any criticism entirely unacceptable. Having reached the top through Congress elections, he then sought to concentrate executive powers in the presidency. Unlike Gorbachev, he did not have to worry about keeping the different factions of the Communist Party in balance. However, he was to a degree dependent on continuing media support and the support of the oligarchs who had become rich from his reforms.

Like Gorbachev, Yeltsin was not an economist and brought in experts to fill in the details of the plan, while he set out his 'vision' for Russia. His leadership alternated periods of hard work and rest: in fact, to the alarm of his supporters, he went on holiday for a month to recover from the strains of the August coup of 1991. He was also prone to depression and physical ill health. Like Brezhnev during his later rule, Yeltsin was sometimes confused and unclear.

ACTIVITY

Research

In groups, find out more about the following businessmen who benefited from privatisation under Yeltsin: Roman Abramovich, Boris Berezovsky, and Mikhail Khordorkovsky. What was their background, how did they make their vast fortunes, and to what extent was their success connected to Yeltsin? Prepare a short class presentation on your assigned personality.

Economic and political problems and policies

Shock therapy for the Russian economy

Russia's economy in 1991 was collapsing. Gross national product (GNP) fell by 17 per cent during 1991 as the Soviet system of production fell apart. Rationing was brought in for most areas of Russia, but ration cards were often useless as there were no supplies to be rationed. Russia's production of oil and gas had dipped due to low international oil prices and strikes; its foreign trade fell by 39 per cent and its budget deficit grew from 6 per cent in 1990 to as much as 26 per cent of GDP in 1991. Foreign debt was $80 billion – Russia had agreed to take on all of the USSR's debts.

Faced with economic crisis, Yeltsin reached first for the '**500 days' plan**, only to reject that in favour of a more radical plan still – the 'shock therapy' route to a market economy provided by Yeltsin's deputy prime minister for the economy, **Yegor Gaidar**.

A CLOSER LOOK

'Shock therapy' and the International Monetary Fund (IMF)

The IMF is an international organisation made up of (currently) 188 countries who contribute money to a fund worth hundreds of billions of dollars. Countries facing financial troubles can apply for loans. In return for the loans are conditions which, in the 1990s, required countries to follow a strict process of privatisation called 'shock therapy' by its critics (referring to the fast pace of reform demanded by the IMF and its often drastic consequences for living standards).

Gaidar's policies and their impact

In 1991 and 1992, Gaidar introduced a series of free market reforms. The state planning organisations were dismantled; the ministries lost their roles in organising production. State-owned enterprises were privatised: small and medium enterprises were transferred to collectives of their current workers and managers, while Russian citizens were offered the chance to purchase shares (vouchers) in the larger state companies. Soviet-era restrictions on trade were dropped: now anyone could start selling (almost) anything.

In January 1992, Gaidar's reforms lifted price controls on most food and consumer products in Russia. Controls remained on energy prices. As a result, prices rose very rapidly – on average, by 1200 per cent compared with 1991. Yeltsin prophesied that 'the liberalisation of prices will put everything in its right place'.

This was not to be, however. Inflation rocketed to 2500 per cent in 1992. With inflation this high, people stopped using the Russian rouble and switched to a currency (particularly US dollars) that would hold its value. This boosted the black market, crime, and corruption. Companies were forced to close as the government cut back on its contracts and as people put off buying things while prices continued to rise. Bills were paid as late as possible, since the amount demanded would have halved in value after a few weeks.

Table 1 *Official data showing percentage change on previous year for selected indicators of the Russian economy, 1989–93*

	1989	1990	1991	1992	1993
National income produced	1.9	4.0	-11.0	-22.0	-13.0
Industrial production	1.4	-0.1	-8.0	-18.0	-16.2
Agricultural production	1.7	-3.6	-4.5	-8.0	-4.0
Housing construction	-2.6	-12.4	-20.0	-23.0	1.0
Retail trade turnover	8.4	10.0	-7.2	-35.3	-0.1
Paid services	6.6	10.2	-20.8	-41.0	-30.0

CROSS-REFERENCE

Details of the **'500 days' plan** are in Chapter 11, pages 86 and 89.

KEY PROFILE

Yegor Gaidar (1956–2009) had trained as an economist and was a long-time member of the Communist Party before leaving it in 1991 to work with Yeltsin. He was Yeltsin's minister of finance and minister of economics before becoming Russia's prime minister in 1992.

A CLOSER LOOK

Price controls in the USSR

Price controls – deliberately keeping products cheap – had long been a major problem for the Soviet system. They reduced incentives for producers to deliver, innovate, or improve quality, and contributed to shortages because, when wages were increased, people had more money to spend on the same limited supply of cheap products. However, price controls were naturally popular with Soviet consumers.

ACTIVITY

1. Look back through this book to find similar economic data for previous years. How do the data presented in Table 1 compare with the years under Khrushchev, Brezhnev, Andropov, Chernenko, or Gorbachev?

KEY PROFILE

Viktor Chernomyrdin (1938–2010) had run Gazprom, the huge gas company that was the first state enterprise in the USSR (1989). He went on to be Russia's longest-serving prime minister to date, saying, when he came to office, 'I am for the market, not the bazaar' – a criticism of the free-for-all of Gaidar's reforms.

Viktor Gerashchenko (b. 1937) had been the head of the USSR's state bank and was not in any way a radical reformer. He returned to giving subsidies and cheap credit to industry and agriculture, further fuelling inflation.

Political problems

As the impacts of shock therapy began, Yeltsin's popularity fell and political opposition to his reforms increased. In early 1992, conservative politicians in the Congress of People's Deputies combined together to block further reforms. This began a battle between Russia's parliament and its president.

By attacking the right of the president to keep his executive powers, the deputies forced Yeltsin to replace key reformists, including Gaidar, with less radical figures, including the new premier, **Viktor Chernomyrdin**, and the new chairman of the Central Bank of Russia, **Viktor Gerashchenko**. These appointments softened the liberalisation of prices.

The Congress of Deputies attacked the way privatisation was proceeding. Lobbied by the directors of state enterprises who objected to the public being able to gain control of 'their' companies, conservative deputies loaded the privatisation programme with amendments when it came to Congress for parliamentary approval. These amendments allowed directors to take control of their enterprises, which is what then duly happened in most cases.

Political unrest; Yeltsin's re-election and resignation

Political unrest

In October 1993, the campaign by Congress deputies, led by Ruslan Khasbulatov, to reduce or remove Yeltsin's executive powers, turned from a battle of words to an actual battle. Yeltsin had used these powers to dissolve Congress in September 1993, leading Congress to declare that Yeltsin had acted illegally. The deputies recognised Yeltsin's vice president as President Rutskoi. Yeltsin then used force to dissolve Congress, which involved the death of several hundred people during fighting around the White House.

Fig. 2 *Spectators watch the attack on the White House, 3–4 October 1993*

A new constitution

After defeating Congress in October 1993, Yeltsin brought forward a new constitution that included a new government system: the president, prime minister, and government, and a new parliament (the state Duma) and its upper house (the Federation Council). Yeltsin put his constitution to a public referendum vote in December 1993 and it was approved, although there were claims of fraud in the voting system.

In this new system, the Russian president gained very significant powers, including the power to appoint the prime minister (although the Duma had to agree with this choice), to nominate senior judges, and to issue decrees that have the force of law. As before, the president was directly elected by the Russian people and Yeltsin ensured that the Duma would now have little power without the president's approval (including approval for its budget). The president had key ministers report directly to him, was head of the armed forces, and decided both defence policy and foreign policy.

Yeltsin's re-election

Parliamentary elections in 1993 and 1995 showed voter disapproval of Yeltsin: the extreme nationalist Vladimir Zhirinovsky's Liberal Democratic Party of Russia (LDPR) and a resurgent Communist Party of the Russian Federation (CPRF), led by Gennady Zyuganov, won many votes. The reformist parties split into many different groups, including one led by Chernomyrdin and one led by Gaidar (that did very badly). Their poor results in both elections strongly suggested that Yeltsin's time as president would be up when he faced the voters in the 1996 presidential election. Economic meltdown, sending tanks against Congress, and starting a disastrous war in Chechnya did not seem a very promising election platform. At the start of his campaign early in 1996, polls gave him only 8 per cent of the vote, compared with 20 per cent for Zyuganov.

Yeltsin's campaign strategy

Yeltsin ran a successful campaign based on:

- an improved image: he appeared more in public and lost weight
- pay increases for government employees and the military, and pension rises
- the promise of an end to the war in Chechnya
- an IMF loan of $10.2 billion (this funded the pay increases) – only Yeltsin, his campaign said, was able to access such funds
- scare tactics against the communists and nationalists (the IMF said they would take back the loan if reformists lost)
- support from the oligarchs running Russia's media.

Yeltsin won the election, beating Zyuganov in the second round with 54 per cent. The support he got from the oligarchs, fearful of losing their fabulous wealth if the communists returned to power, was certainly an important factor.

Fig. 3 An elderly woman begging in the streets of Moscow during the financial crisis of 1998

ACTIVITY

Explain why each of the following groups had an interest in Yeltsin not losing the 1996 election:

a) the oligarchs
b) the media
c) the IMF.

A CLOSER LOOK

The war in Chechnya

The Russian Federation is made up of over 80 'federal subjects', one of which is the independent republic of Chechnya. Stalin ordered almost the entire Chechen population to be deported to Kazakhstan after the Great Patriotic War, causing thousands of Chechen deaths in the process. As soon as the August coup of 1991 was defeated, Chechnya declared independence from Russia. Yeltsin's 1993 constitution attempted to keep Chechnya in the federation, but following challenges and unrest in 1994, Yeltsin used military force to deal with opposition. However, his invasion of Chechnya was a disaster, with up to 50,000 Russians being killed by 1996.

KEY PROFILE

Vladimir Putin (b. 1952) served in the KGB for 16 years before going into politics, working for the St Petersburg mayor to attract foreign investment to the city before moving to Moscow to work for Yeltsin. In 1998, Yeltsin made him head of the FSB, although there were many more senior and experienced candidates for the role. He became the second President of Russia in May 2000 and oversaw a recovery in Russia's economy fuelled by high global oil prices.

Yeltsin's resignation

After his success in the 1996 presidential elections, Yeltsin underwent heart surgery that left him in hospital for several months. The economy appeared to be recovering in 1996 and 1997, boosted by a total of $40 billion in IMF loans. So it was a great shock in 1998 when Russia failed to make its loan repayments, triggering a financial crisis. It turned out that large amounts of IMF money had in fact been stolen, and that oligarch profits made in Russia had been taken out of the country and invested abroad, while ordinary Russians saw their banks failing and inflation spiralling upwards again. Forty per cent of Russians were living below the poverty line by the end of 1998. Yeltsin sacked Chernomyrdin and launched new reforms, which were blocked by the Duma, forcing Yeltsin to use his presidential decrees to rule. National strikes called on Yeltsin to resign.

Yeltsin, however, would not leave until he had ensured that the right man would succeed him. In a last masterful political move, he sacked the Duma's preferred prime minister, Primakov, and appointed **Vladimir Putin** as his new prime minister. At the time, Putin was not well known and had few supporters in government.

Some commentators believed that the price of Putin's rise to power was a promise that Yeltsin and his family would be protected from possible prosecution after his resignation. Whatever the reasons, on 31 December 1999, Yeltsin resigned.

STUDY TIP

Try to use your knowledge of the historical context of Russia's financial crisis in 1988, and similar financial crises during this period, when preparing your answer to this type of question.

A LEVEL PRACTICE QUESTION

To what extent was Yeltsin to blame for Russia's 1998 financial crisis?

Putin as leader; the state of Russia politically, economically, and socially by 2000

Putin as leader

Putin won the March 2000 presidential election in the first round, with 53 per cent of the vote against Zyuganov's 30 per cent. A few weeks before, the Unity bloc, which was pro-Putin, won control in the Duma.

Western observers of the 2000 presidential election made the following conclusions about factors that helped Putin's victory:

- He was already doing the job of president, which meant people were voting for someone they could already see in action.
- Although all candidates were allotted equal amounts of campaigning time in the media, Putin appeared much more often on screen as part of news items showing him acting presidentially.
- The Russian media depended on state support, and that support came with strings attached during the presidential election, meaning that the media was generally very pro-Putin.
- Regional governors threw their support behind Putin because of advance warning that he was intending to directly appoint governors to their jobs rather than them being elected (which happened in 2005).
- There was evidence of faults in the election process that may have favoured Putin.

Fig. 4 *Vladimir Putin and Boris Yeltsin in 1998*

Putin's appeal to the Russian voters was surely also related to him appearing to be a 'firm hand' in leading the country, shown in his success in the second war in Chechnya and his mission to restore some of the prestige that Russians had felt as part of the world's second superpower in the years before the end of the Cold War. Yeltsin himself stated that he was looking for someone as his successor who had a backbone of steel, with a firm manner, who could strengthen political authority, but respect the democratic system. He found these qualities in Putin.

The state of Russia politically, economically, and socially by 2000

The economic and social state of Russia in 2000

Putin's electoral success was helped by a significant improvement in Russia's economy by 2000, fuelled by the results of the rouble's **devaluation** in 1998 and, slightly later, by a rise in global oil prices (from around 12 dollars per barrel in 1998 to 27 dollars per barrel in 2000). Russia's GDP growth went from minus 5 per cent in 1998 to plus 10 per cent in 2000.

SOURCE 1

From data on Russia in 2000 collected by Alpha Bank, Russia's largest commercial bank, founded in 1990:

- Economic growth (GNP) rose from 0.5 per cent growth in 1999 to 10 per cent in 2000.
- 50 per cent of Russia's export earnings came from oil in 2000, compared to 37 per cent in 1995.
- Inflation dropped from 9 per cent in 1999 to 5 per cent in 2000.
- Unemployment fell from 13 per cent of those able to work in 1999 to 9 per cent in 2000.
- Disposable income went up 12 per cent from 1999, but was still half what it had been in 1991.
- Avoidable deaths continued to rise due to reduced spending on state healthcare.
- Public sector employment remained high: 17 per cent of the population were employed by the State (it was 9 per cent in the UK in 2000).
- Half the population were still living in poverty in 2000, yet a few Russians had become extremely rich. Almost half (47 per cent) of all the country's wealth was in the hands of just 20 per cent of its population.

KEY TERM

devaluation: when the international value of a currency is set lower than previously; in Russia, in 1998, the exchange rate went from being 6 roubles to the dollar to 21 roubles to the dollar

A CLOSER LOOK

The impact of devaluation

When the rouble's value was cut compared to other currencies, Russian exports became a lot cheaper, while imports became too expensive for most Russians to afford, forcing them to buy Russian-made alternatives. This boosted export production and domestic production at the same time.

ACTIVITY

1. Study the data in Source 2. Which of these statistics relate to the economic state of Russia in 2000, and which relate to the social state?
2. Using Source 2 and your own research, identify the main economic and social factors affecting Russia in 2000.

- Most Russians worked for large enterprises: only 15 per cent worked in small to medium sized enterprises, compared with 54 per cent in the USA.
- The country had a huge foreign debt: $128 billion (51 per cent of GDP).

The political state of Russia in 2000

Putin continued the economically liberal approaches favoured by Gorbachev and Yeltsin, but sought to reduce the democratic element in Russian life that had caused so much friction over economic reform between President Yeltsin and Congress in the 1990s. Putin's political priorities in 2000 included:

- Calming political relations: pro-Putin parties occupied two-thirds of the Duma's seats in 2000 and Putin aimed to continue that dominance through voting changes and restrictions on the political parties allowed into the Duma, as well as by reducing the influence of regional governors who had often challenged Yeltsin's authority.
- Restoring the authority of the State: the oligarchs running many of Russia's biggest businesses were put under pressure to act in line with Kremlin wishes – or face the consequences. There was increased nationalisation of key Russian industries.
- Increasing public trust in the State: reporting of public opinion surveys was made less frequent, while state propaganda became more frequent. National TV stations and newspapers were to be closed down or taken over if they were overly critical of Putin's leadership.
- Restoring national pride, including pride in Soviet achievements: access to KGB and other archives containing information about historic crimes was made more difficult to obtain. Western observers in 2001 started to note a 'personality cult' developing around Putin.

SOURCE 2

Results from two market research questions from a survey of 1600 Russians carried out in January 2000 by the Russian Public Opinion Research Centre, first established in 1987. It is owned by the State and its methods and results are rated as very reliable in the West:

Q1 What good things did the years of Yeltsin's rule bring?

	All replies (%)
Democracy, political rights and freedom	23
Getting rid of shortages, coupons and queues	16
Ending Communist rule	10
Improved relations with the West	7
Improved quality of goods and services	4
Removing the threat of a new world war	3
Can't name anything good	46

Q2 What bad things did the years of Yeltsin's rule bring? (Replies of 15% or more)

	All replies (%)
Economic crisis, fall in production	40
Closures of enterprises, mass unemployment	36
Chechen war of 1993–96	34
Collapse of the USSR	31
Rising crime and penetration of state by organised crime	28
Collapse of system of education, health and social security	19
Political instability, conflicts in the leadership	16

Source: Nationwide VCIOM survey, 8–10 January 2000

SOURCE 3

From an oral history of the post-Stalin generation. The author, an American academic called Donald Raleigh, who has spent many years in post-Soviet Saratov, asked people about their memories of life under Yeltsin:

Most educated Russians of their [post war] generation spoke ill of Yeltsin. Leonid Volodarsky vehemently opposed Yeltsin's economic policies: 'I believe that he's probably the person who, in the entire history of Russia, brought his country the most harm. It's hard to imagine anyone doing something worse for his country.' Critical of Gorbachev, Larisa Petrova likewise scolded Yeltsin: 'For one thing, he's dishonest. Because of him, crime has begun to strangle Russia. I believe that the years he ruled were unlucky ones for Russia. These were years when much that was started and could have been nurtured got squandered.' 'He's only for himself,' opined Aleksandr Ivanov. 'He did nothing sensible for Russia.' Ivanov regretted that Putin granted Yeltsin and his family immunity. 'Just as the leadership was all for itself back then, the leadership is all for itself now.'

Summary

Putin's leadership of Russia has been compared to Brezhnev's, because of the way it has produced rising living standards in return for public acceptance of an authoritarian style of rule, and also to Stalin's, because of Putin's suspicion of Western intentions towards his country and his hard-line public persona. His actions have provided the 'steel backbone' that Yeltsin felt was required to push through economic reform in Russia. Although he has undone much of the *glasnost* and *demokratizatsiya* of Gorbachev's leadership, he has completed much of the *perestroika* of Russia's economy that Gorbachev hoped to see, combining it with a strong economic role for the State that preserves just a few of the socialist elements that dominated the ideology of his predecessors.

Russian society under Putin shows significant change from Soviet society, especially in the high degree of inequality between the very rich and the very poor (a structure typical of resource-rich countries). There is continuity from Soviet times, though. Russian society has retained a cautious view towards the West, helped by Western gloating in having 'won' the Cold War. Putin's administration has reinvested heavily in the military, with foreign policy seeking to restore Russia's global influence and recover its control over former Soviet republics. Some aspects of Russian life, such as the return to prominence of religious belief, reach back to pre-revolutionary times for inspiration, especially in Muslim areas of the country where the USSR tried hardest to encourage a rejection of traditional religious beliefs.

AS LEVEL PRACTICE QUESTION

Evaluating primary sources

With reference to Sources 2 and 3 and your understanding of the historical context, which of these two sources is more valuable for explaining the impact of Yeltsin's economic reforms on Russian society?

STUDY TIP

Sources 3 and 4 show quantitative/qualitative differences. These are a challenge to compare: quantitative data provide objective information, but lack the insights into people's feelings that qualitative sources show.

STUDY TIP

While an economic recovery is something that can be measured using indices like the growth in GDP of a country, the concept of a political recovery is explored by considering in what ways Russia had political problems before Putin and in what ways, and with what success, those problems were tackled.

A LEVEL PRACTICE QUESTION

To what extent did Putin bring about the economic and political recovery of Russia?

ACTIVITY

Summary

Create your own chart for comparing Gorbachev, Yeltsin, and Putin as leaders. You could consider setting up something like this:

Leader	Economic policy	Social policy	Political developments	Key successes and failures
Gorbachev				
Yeltsin				
Putin				

4 Soviet satellites, 1953–68

13 The political and economic condition of the satellite states of Central Europe

Fig. 1 *The Soviet Union, its satellite states, and other socialist states in Europe no longer aligned to the USSR by 1960*

LEARNING OBJECTIVES

In this chapter you will learn about:

- the leadership of the Central European satellite states of Poland, Czechoslovakia, Hungary, and East Germany
- the political organisation and influence of the Communist Party; economic organisation, state of collectivisation and the centrally planned economy; political and economic strengths and weaknesses of each of those satellite states.

The satellite states of Central Europe

The satellite states of Central Europe and their dates of formation and collapse were (or split from the USSR in the case of Albania):

- Czechoslovak Socialist Republic (1948–89)
- German Democratic Republic (1948–89)
- Hungarian People's Republic (1949–89)
- Polish People's Republic (1944–89)
- People's Republic of Bulgaria (1946–90)
- People's Republic of Romania (1947–89)
- People's Socialist Republic of Albania (1944–60)

KEY CHRONOLOGY

1953	Death of Stalin
	Strikes in the GDR suppressed by Soviet Army and GDR police
	Imre Nagy becomes Premier in Hungary
1955	Warsaw Pact is signed
	Khrushchev apologises to Yugoslavia for Stalin's split
1956	Khrushchev's Secret Speech denounces Stalin
	Workers riot in Poland
	Kádár forms new pro-Soviet government in Hungary
1961	Berlin crisis results in construction of Berlin Wall
1968	Dubček replaces Novotny as First Secretary of the Czechoslovak Communist Party
	Warsaw Pact forces invade Czechoslovakia to suppress 'Prague Spring

A CLOSER LOOK

The significance of Yugoslavia

Most of the **satellite states** were ruled by Communist Parties that answered to the USSR. This had come about following their occupation by the Red Army as it advanced towards Berlin in 1945. Yugoslavia was different: its Communist Party was 'home grown'. Stalin had put pressure on Yugoslavia to follow the USSR, but in 1948 Yugoslavia refused, causing huge concerns in the USSR that its satellite states would 'deviate' from the Soviet approach to socialism and seek to leave the USSR's sphere of influence.

Poland

Poland and the leadership of Gomułka

Leaders in the satellite states of Poland, Czechoslovakia, Hungary, and the German Democratic Republic (GDR) had modelled themselves on Stalin, including carrying out purges of suspected political opponents. Stalin's death in 1953 left them unsure how to position themselves – especially once Khrushchev began his process of de-Stalinisation.

The Polish Communist Party (the PUWP – Polish United Workers' Party) was created as a Party that fully supported the Soviet Union being closely involved in Poland's transition to a socialist state. Once this had been achieved, Sovietisation proceeded: the rapid industrialisation of Poland according to the Stalinist model and an attempt to collectivise Polish peasant agriculture (which had to be halted following strong peasant resistance).

By 1956, industrialisation had failed to deliver what the workers had been promised: they were made to work long hours in often unsafe conditions; they lived in crowded, insanitary conditions; and food was poor and often in short supply. In June 1956, there were strikes and riots by 100,000 Polish workers, protesting for better working conditions. These events shook Soviet confidence in the wisdom of hard-line leadership in Poland.

Władysław Gomułka was elected First Party Secretary of the Polish Communist Party (PUWP) in 1956. Although he was a committed believer in Marxism–Leninism (see page 1), Gomułka was not the leader the USSR would ideally have wanted because he believed that Poland should follow its own path to socialism rather than the Soviet one. However, in the context of the threat of further unrest and Khrushchev's programme of de-Stalinisation, change was required.

- The PUWP selected Gomułka as a popular, moderate choice after the death in 1956 of its 'little Stalin' leader, Bolesław Bierut.
- Gomułka agreed, on condition that he be allowed to make reforms.
- He convinced a worried Soviet Union that his leadership would not threaten Poland's alliance with the USSR or its membership of the Warsaw Pact.
- Khrushchev felt Gomułka would toe the line, which he proceeded to do.

CROSS-REFERENCE

Remind yourself of the 1955 Warsaw Pact by returning to Chapter 4, page 27.

The 1956 riots in Poland are discussed in Chapter pages 131–32.

De-Stalinisation is explained in Chapter 1, page 1.

A CLOSER LOOK

Comintern, Cominform, Comecon

Comintern was the Communist international organisation that bound all Communist Parties together in ruthlessly policed conformity. All members of Comintern had to follow the Stalinist model of the planned economy. In 1943, Comintern was shut down because the differences between the satellite states made a single approach to implementing socialism too complex.

Cominform (Communist Information Bureau) was set up in 1947 to coordinate the different Communist Parties under the leadership of the CPSU (Communist Party of the Soviet Union). It lasted until 1956. It was Cominform that, in 1948, denounced Yugoslavia's deviation from the socialist path and announced that all satellite states were to follow the USSR's route to socialism. Comecon (Council for Mutual Economic Assistance) was set up in 1949, under the leadership of the USSR, to coordinate the economies of socialist states. The USSR's hope of implementing a single Five Year Plan for all Comecon members was resisted by the satellite states. Instead, favourable trading relations were set up (e.g. cheap Soviet oil for cheap manufactured products from the GDR) and technological knowledge shared.

The political organisation and influence of the Communist Party in Poland

Communist Parties took different routes to power in the satellite states, but once in power, they followed the Soviet model in organisation, purpose (taking control of all political, judicial, social, economic, and cultural aspects of life in the State), and influence. There was also usually a regional version of the Party structure, including a regional First Secretary.

The Party had full authority over government actions. Senior government officials were often Politburo members. The same was true of the legal system and of the centrally planned economy. As in the USSR, the basis of this approach was that the Party ran the country for the benefit of the workers, until communism was achieved, when the need for a state would, as Marx had predicted, 'wither away'.

Poland's Communist Party, the PUWP, was organised in a generally similar manner to the CPSU (see Fig. 3), but with one key difference: the legislature – the Sejm – included representatives from more than one party. Instead of having one approved Communist Party candidate, in Polish elections the electorate had a list of candidates to choose from. However, this was not democracy as it was understood in the West. The parties all belonged to the Front of National Unity (renamed this in 1956): a collection of parties and trade unions allied to the PUWP. The Front of National Unity controlled the lists of candidates, ensuring that no one would be chosen who would oppose the PUWP in any way.

Local Party organisations elected delegates to the Party Congress

↓

Party Congresses elected members to the Central Committee

↓

The Central Committee met several times a year to pass resolutions (which the government made into law), and elected the members of the Politburo, following a list decided by the Politburo

↓

The Politburo / Presidium of the Central Committee met frequently and made all the Party's key decisions; the Secretariat of the Central Committee oversaw these decisions

Fig. 3 *Communist Parties in the satellite states followed the model of the CPSU*

Fig. 2 *Władysław Gomułka speaking at a large demonstration in Warsaw in October 1956 in support of his becoming leader*

KEY PROFILE

Władysław Gomułka (1905–82) came from a poor family, joined what was then a tiny Polish Communist Party in his early twenties, took part in strikes, went to prison, and then travelled to Moscow to attend the Comintern's official training school (the International Lenin School). Returning to Poland during the war, he then led the rebuilt Communist Party to victory in the elections of 1947. However, Stalin had been developing his own leader for Poland, Bolesław Bierut. Gomułka's resistance to Stalinist methods (e.g. collectivisation) saw him expelled from the Party and imprisoned until 1954.

A CLOSER LOOK

Communist Parties of the satellite states

These had various names:

- CPCz Communist Party of Czechoslovakia
- SED Socialist Unity Party of Germany
- MSzP Hungarian Socialist Workers' Party (from 1956)
- PUWP Polish United Workers' Party

CROSS-REFERENCE

Read about **Khrushchev's Secret Speech** in Chapter 2, page 10.

A CLOSER LOOK

The **'New Course'** was a term used to describe changing Soviet policies after Stalin's death, including and principally comprising what we now call de-Stalinisation.

A CLOSER LOOK

The centrally planned economy

The Stalinist model of central planning was applied to the satellite states, too. The process was broadly the same everywhere:

- Industries were nationalised, at first leaving small firms and shops in private hands, but then extending state ownership to those also.
- Central planning agencies were established, which came under Communist Party control. Five Year Plans (Six Year Plans for Poland) were drawn up.
- Investment was stripped from agriculture and ploughed into heavy industry.
- Workers were urged to meet punishing production targets through propaganda or coercion, rather than by paying them more.
- Foreign trade was re-routed, on very favourable terms, from capitalist countries to the USSR and other satellite states, coordinated by Comecon.

But in other ways, the PUWP in 1956 was very different from the CPSU and Parties in other satellite states: its reformist agenda predated both **Khrushchev's Secret Speech** and Gomułka's election to the leadership, putting it at odds with the other satellite states where 'little Stalin' leaders viewed the **'New Course'** with suspicion and sought to minimise the impact of de-Stalinisation. Reasons for the PUWP's differences included:

- Purges of the Party had been much less severe than in the USSR and some other satellite states. The PUWP tolerated a wider range of options.
- Related to this, intellectuals had a strong presence and influence inside the PUWP and pushed for liberalisation.
- The Roman Catholic Church was hugely important in Poland. This not only reduced the influence of the PUWP in Poland, as Church leaders and the Pope were alternate leadership figures, but it also had a moderating effect on PUWP policy.
- Although Polish people supported socialism, the Soviet Union was not popular because of its role in Poland before and at the close of the war. Poles were nationalistic. The Party knew that any attempt to 'Sovietise' the population would be resisted. To have influence and legitimacy, the PUWP had to establish its independence from the USSR as markedly as possible.

Economic organisation, state of collectivisation, and the centrally planned economy in Poland

Economic organisation

Poland's economy post-war had required extensive rebuilding and reorganisation, not just because of war damage and altered economic functions under the Nazis, but because new territories had been integrated into the State. Following the Stalinist model, investment was focused on heavy industry and on steel production in particular. Pre-war, Poland had exported its coal and manufactured goods to Western Europe. Post-war, this trade was directed solely towards the USSR and other satellite states, with the USSR dictating that Poland should also expand production of copper and sulphur. In return, the USSR became Poland's supplier for oil, natural gas, and iron ore (a raw material for steel production).

The state of collectivisation

Prior to 1956, collectivisation had proceeded slowly in Poland, fiercely resisted in most areas by peasant farmers. While similar resistance in the USSR had failed in the face of Stalin's genocidal purges, repression in Poland, although severe for those involved, was mostly in the form of harassment by the authorities and financial penalties. In 1953, with the death of Stalin, the Party switched to financial rewards for collectivisation, which had a more positive response from poor peasants. As a result, by 1955, collective farms had covered around 9 per cent of Poland's farmland. Productivity on collective farms was lower than on private farms.

The move towards the collectivisation of agriculture was stopped completely by Gomułka, after the unrest of 1956. He also allowed peasants to leave collective farms. By 1959, only 1 per cent of arable land in Poland was collective farm land. Polish farming remained dominated by small, individually owned farms.

The centrally planned economy in Poland

After Stalin's death, the PUWP decided to reduce investment in heavy industry and increase it in agriculture, housing, and consumer goods industries, and to raise wages, in response to growing worker discontent. A Second Congress of

Economists in June 1956 openly criticised the Stalinist model and called for decentralisation, introduction of market pricing rather than state-controlled pricing, and for private businesses to be allowed again. But early hopes among the intellectuals in Gomułka's leadership slipped away as he reverted to the familiar Soviet model. Plan targets were increased, work norms were raised, and wages failed to keep pace with increased production.

Poland: strengths and weaknesses

From the point of view of the USSR, 1950s Poland was a problematic satellite state. Although it had valuable raw materials and much industrial potential, its long history of dislike towards Russia and, more recently, to the Soviet Union, and its intense sense of itself as a nation, made it difficult to manage. Polish communists sought the maximum possible independence from the USSR, which was deeply troubling: Poland's strategic position in Europe was of the utmost importance to the USSR. Also, the PUWP was weak: it was internally divided, had to share authority with the Catholic Church, and proved unable to push through the Soviet model in the effective manner of other satellite states.

ACTIVITY

Extension

Find out more about Gomułka's relationship with Cardinal Wyszyński. Why did Gomułka release him from internment in 1956, and what does that say about Gomułka's leadership and the influence of the PUWP in Poland?

Czechoslovakia

Czechoslovakia and the leadership of Novotný

Antonín Novotný, First Secretary of the Communist Party of Czechoslovakia (CPCz), was a **hard-line** Stalinist with the full backing of the Soviet leadership. This backing enabled him to largely resist pressures for reform from within the Czechoslovak Communist Party following Stalin's death.

KEY PROFILE

Antonín Novotný (1904–75) came from a working-class background, had joined the CPCz at its start, and, like Gomułka, had been selected by Comintern for development as a potential Communist Party leader. In the war, he was arrested and sent to a Nazi concentration camp. He played a leading part in the coup that brought the CPCz to power in 1948, and became General Secretary in Czechoslovakia in 1953.

KEY TERM

hard-line: unbending; so a hard-line Stalinist would not accept any deviation from Stalinist teachings, regardless of context; a hardliner would criticise those who suggested compromise or a different approach as deviationists or revisionists

show trial: a court trial where the objective is to influence public opinion rather than achieve justice

Fig. 4 *Antonín Novotný with Young Pioneers. The Pioneers was a Marxist–Leninist youth organisation across the satellite states and in the USSR. Uniforms were the same in Poland, East Germany, Hungary, and Czechoslovakia, and Pioneers all swore to 'defend socialism'*

Novotný had been involved in organising **show trials** and purges in the CPCz during the 1950s, so he was reluctant to pursue de-Stalinisation despite it becoming the official party of the CPSU. By 1960, there were still 9000 political prisoners in Czechoslovakia. Dislike of his rigid and authoritarian leadership in

CROSS-REFERENCE

The **Young Pioneers** are mentioned again in Chapter 14, page 121.

both Czechoslovakia and in Khrushchev's USSR meant Novotný had to allow investigation of the trials and rehabilitation of their victims, many of whom were then freed. One of those investigating the trials was **Alexander Dubček**.

KEY PROFILE

Alexander Dubček (1921–92) was born in Czechoslovakia but moved with his strongly socialist family to the USSR when he was three. He fought the Nazis as part of the Slovak resistance and joined the Slovak Communist Party, which became part of the CPCz in 1948. Working his way up through Party ranks, he became the leader of the Slovak branch of the CPCz and was responsible for bringing in liberal reforms to Slovakia.

The political organisation and influence of the Communist Party in Czechoslovakia

The Czechs and the Slovaks had a long and turbulent history and experienced the Second World War quite differently – the Slovaks had backed the Nazis in return for independence. Their differences were not resolved by the creation of Czechoslovakia in 1945: the CPCz ruled over the entire country, with the separate Slovak Communist Party subordinate to it. Czech and Slovak experiences as satellites of the USSR varied considerably.

As in Poland, the CPCz shared power, in theory, with five other political parties, united under the National Front organisation which arranged candidate lists and elections as the Front of National Unity did in Poland. As in Poland, the other parties were completely submissive to the CPCz, elections were set up to provide the right candidates, and all parties followed CPCz policies.

Unlike in Poland, reformists did not make up an influential faction within the Party after Stalin's death as these 'deviationists' had been purged in 1952, following Stalin's split with Yugoslavia and Soviet concerns over satellite states straying from the proper path to socialism. Eleven reformists from the CPCz, including its General Secretary Rudolf Slansky, were executed in 1952 after a show trial. Widespread arrests and interrogations led to many people being executed or imprisoned. The CPCz's influence by 1956 was, therefore, characterised by fear and repression. The Catholic Church – the largest religious group in pre-Communist Czechoslovakia – had its activities severely restricted, for example.

Economic organisation, state of collectivisation, and the centrally planned economy in Czechoslovakia

Economic organisation

Even more so than Poland, the pre-war economy of Czechoslovakia had been highly dependent on exports of high-quality metalwork, machinery, and consumer products. It was one of the world's largest manufacturing economies, despite its relatively small size and low level of natural resources. In fact, this industrial success was also geographically limited within Czechoslovakia to the former countries of Bohemia and Moravia in the Czech half of the country, the rest of the country being mostly peasant agriculture.

When Czechoslovakia turned to the USSR after the end of the Second World War and a Communist Party coup established the CPCz's rule over the country, industries were nationalised, management was replaced with Party appointees, and all production began to operate according to central plans. Trade to other satellite states and the USSR increased, with the USSR requiring favourable prices. But trade with the West, the basis of Czechoslovak economic success, was drastically cut.

ACTIVITY

Research

Skoda was a successful pre-war Czechoslovak company. Research its history in Czechoslovakia under communism. When was the company taken into state ownership, and production moved from international export markets to serving the domestic needs of the USSR and its satellite states?

The state of collectivisation

Czechoslovakia was relatively quick to adopt collectivisation, with 43 per cent of farmland collectivised by 1953 (compared with just 7 per cent in Poland and none at all in the GDR). A second wave, beginning in 1957, achieved full collectivisation by 1960. Czechoslovakia was Eastern Europe's most industrialised country and had a long history of farming collectives; its industries were already geared up for supplying the fertilisers that made collective farming more productive.

The centrally planned economy in Czechoslovakia

Growth was initially promising (7 per cent on average between 1956 and 1960), but by the end of the 1950s stagnation had set in: national income actually declined in 1963.

Czechoslovakia's previous industrial success depended on foreign trade, specialisation, and highly skilled workers. The centrally planned approach did not fit well with this legacy. With production linked to supplying the USSR at a heavily subsidised rate, there was no incentive to innovate. With planning devoted to quantity rather than quality, what mattered was more workers, not a skilled workforce. Without access to Western markets, Czechoslovak industries fell behind technologically. By the late 1960s, economists in Czechoslovakia were pushing for decentralising reform.

Czechoslovakia: strengths and weaknesses

As a more industrially developed state than the USSR, Czechoslovakia had many strengths from the Soviet perspective. Having broadly chosen the USSR as its partner in development, the population, or at least part of it, did not resent the Soviet model. In the post-war period, the Soviet model was proving itself year after year in its growth rates, cultural achievements, and progress in science and technology. Czechoslovakia fitted very well into the successful brotherhood of socialist states. It also had an efficient Party that had weeded out unsuitable elements and was developing impressive security powers over the population – again, from the Soviet point of view.

One weakness was that pre-war Czechoslovakia was geared towards West European export markets, and the complete change of focus towards Comecon and the needs of the USSR and other satellite states was costly.

Another potential weakness was the nature of the state itself: industrialisation was concentrated in the Czech lands, while Slovakia was relatively underdeveloped. According to Marxist theory, however, this tension could have creative and positive results. Socialism certainly had a better track record than capitalism for reducing inequality between regions, and the semi-independence of the Slovak Party meant it could try out new ideas and approaches.

Hungary

Hungary and the leadership of Nagy; Rákosi, Gerő, and Kádár

Mátyás Rákosi was selected by the USSR as the first General Secretary of the Hungarian Communist Party following the Red Army's occupation of Hungary in 1945. His leadership was modelled on Stalin: he described himself as 'Stalin's best pupil'. Once he had consolidated one-Party rule in Hungary, in 1948, he set about purging possible political opponents. By 1956, some 350,000 Hungarians had been imprisoned and over 2000 executed.

The death of Stalin in 1953 meant problems for 'Stalin's best pupil'. The new Soviet leadership was concerned that Rákosi's harsh rule would lead to unrest and insisted that he appoint the reformist **Imre Nagy** as premier in a collective leadership. Rákosi complied but then did his utmost to undermine Nagy's calls for more economic and political freedom. He succeeded in getting Nagy replaced by fellow hardliner **Ernő Gerő**.

Following Khrushchev's Secret Speech in 1956, the USSR put pressure on the Hungarian Communist Party (MKP) to replace Rákosi, as leader, with Gerő. Rákosi was taken to the USSR for 'health reasons' and kept there until 1970. Gerő's leadership only lasted three months, with the Soviet leadership forcing him to resign after he made an ill-judged hard-line speech on the second day of the Hungarian Revolution of October 1956.

KEY PROFILE

Mátyás Rákosi (1892–1971) was taken prisoner by the Red Army in the First World War and became a committed communist. He was a founder member of the Hungarian Communist Party, escaping abroad as Hungary was taken over by the fascist Horthy regime. In the USSR, he worked as Secretary for Comintern; returning to Hungary, he was arrested and imprisoned (Stalin suspecting that Rákosi then betrayed Comintern secrets to the fascists). Perhaps because of the hold he had over him, Stalin still felt that Rakosi was the right man to turn Hungary into a model of the Soviet system.

Ernő Gerő (1898–1980) was a life-long communist who lived in the USSR for 20 years and was closely linked there to both Comintern and the KGB. A hardliner, he was kept in government after Rákosi was ordered to bring Nagy into the leadership as a way to counteract Nagy's reformism.

Imre Nagy (1896–1958) was captured by the Russians during the First World War and became a communist while being held as a prisoner of war. From a peasant family, he fled Hungary during the Second World War and became an expert in socialist agriculture. After the war, he was favoured by the USSR for a leadership role in the Hungarian Communist Party. He introduced extensive land reforms in Hungary, but these brought him into conflict with Rákosi, and he was purged. His role in the Hungarian Revolution of 1956 means he is now considered a national hero in Hungary.

CROSS-REFERENCE

The **Warsaw Pact** is discussed in Chapter Chapter 4, page 27.

KEY PROFILE

János Kádár (1912–1989) was General Secretary from 1956 until his retirement in 1988. His leadership, from a difficult start, charted a successful course through the 1960s and 1970s.

Fig. 5 *Imre Nagy in 1955; seated next to him is Rákosi*

CROSS-REFERENCE

Stalin's purges are mentioned in Chapter 1, page 2.

The **Hungarian Revolution** is covered in Chapter 16, pages 132–33.

Nagy first attempted to restore order, but then backed the uprising, calling for Hungary to leave the **Warsaw Pact**. The implications of Nagy's decision are discussed in Chapter 16. He was executed after a secret trial in June 1958.

Once Hungary was back under Soviet control, **János Kádár** was chosen by the Party leadership to be the new General Secretary and premier. Kádár had been a victim of Rákosi's purges and in prison until 1954. Kádár's economic reforms, known as 'goulash communism', were an important model for Soviet economic reformers, including Gorbachev.

The political organisation and influence of the Communist Party in Hungary

The MSzP, the Hungarian Socialist Workers' Party (the name of Hungary's Communist Party from 1956) was organised in a similar fashion to Communist Parties in all the other satellite states, with a National Front-style organisation called the Independent Democratic Front (not at all independent and controlled by the Communist Party).

One key problem for the MSzP was that Hungary had been an ally of Germany during the Second World War and, therefore, the Soviet Union had defeated Hungary and treated it accordingly. This meant there was little enthusiasm for the Communist Party. In free elections in 1945, the Communists got only 17 per cent of the vote. Elimination of the opposition (called 'salami tactics' by Rákosi, as he removed the opposition 'slice by slice') brought the Party to power, at which point it set about drastic purges of itself, based on Stalin's model. By 1956, popular discontent with the Communists fuelled the **Hungarian Revolution**.

Economic organisation, state of collectivisation, and the centrally planned economy in Hungary

Economic organisation

Hungary had been a primarily agricultural country, with little heavy industry, before the war. Its relative lack of natural resources made it reliant on foreign trade. Soviet-style nationalisation utterly transformed Hungary's economy. In return, the USSR supplied Hungary with around half of its energy supplies, which led to the building of a 2700km-long pipeline to supply Hungary with natural gas. However, the war had done a huge amount of damage to Hungary: its capital city, Budapest, was in ruins, and the country had lost 40 per cent of its pre-war GDP. The Soviet Union also demanded reparations from Hungary for its part in the USSR's enormous wartime losses, and a million Hungarians were prisoners of war in the USSR for many years after the war, all of which had an impact on Hungary's economic recovery and on the way in which Hungarians viewed the USSR and its Soviet-exported Communist Party.

The state of collectivisation

Land reform after the war had changed Hungary from a society in which 1 per cent of the population owned 50 per cent of the arable land, to a situation where no single landowner was allowed to own more than 115 hectares (a highly popular reform conducted by Imre Nagy). Three years later, in 1948, collectivisation took all this away, and was strongly resisted by the peasantry. Collective farms were forced to sell their produce at very low prices. Raids regularly took place to find where people were hiding their grain. Thousands of peasants were labelled 'kulaks' and sent to labour camps. Widespread famine resulted.

By 1956, a third of the farming area of Hungary had been collectivised when the 1956 Hungarian Revolution nearly derailed collectivisation. However, a second wave after 1959 resulted in complete collectivisation by 1960.

Central planning in Hungary

In the years before Stalin's death, Rákosi imposed the Stalinist model on Hungary's economy with utter dedication. Rákosi and Gerő aimed to turn this agricultural economy into a 'land of coal and steel'. Five Year Plan targets were constantly being adjusted upwards, setting punishingly high production norms and harsh penalties for absenteeism – 15,000 workers were jailed for work discipline offences between 1951 and 1952, for example. Product quality tumbled as worker resentment grew. While living conditions in the other satellite states improved, in Hungary, they got worse.

Central planning in Hungary also resulted in the creation of enormous heavy industry facilities that made no economic sense. An example is the town of Sztálinváros, a huge steel factory and town for steelworkers, which required vast quantities of raw materials that did not exist in Hungary and had to be imported from Soviet Central Asia. At the same time, resources that Hungary did have were sold off to the USSR at knock-down prices (principally uranium) when they could have gained Hungary much-needed foreign currency.

The Soviet leadership after Stalin's death criticised Rákosi harshly for his economic incompetence (even though he had just been following the Soviet model) and promoted Nagy. Nagy's 'New Course' of 1953 included:

- more investment in light industry and agriculture, less stress on heavy industry
- a reduction in work norms and increases in wages (up 15 per cent)
- an end to persecution of kulaks; people could leave the kolkhozes to set up their own farms (200,000 new small farms appeared between 1953 and 1954)
- some small private businesses were allowed.

The USSR's (then factionalised) leadership approved the plan in principle, but then did nothing to support it as Rákosi set to work undermining his rival. Nagy's experiment was soon judged a failure and he was expelled from the Party.

Hungary: strengths and weaknesses

From the Soviet perspective, Hungarians had attacked the USSR in the war and were therefore in line for a rougher move to socialism than other states. Rákosi was a brutal leader who proved unable to soften his approach even when the USSR, under Khrushchev's leadership, recognised the damage he was doing to the security of the USSR's stake in the country. In light of the 1956 Hungarian Revolution, this concern was well-placed. In terms of strengths, Hungary was a hothouse for new ideas in economic and political socialist policy, with Nagy's reforms prefiguring later reforms in the USSR.

CROSS-REFERENCE

For the 1953 uprising in the GDR, see Chapter 16, page 131.

East Germany

East Germany and the leadership of Ulbricht

Walter Ulbricht became Party Secretary in 1950 and dominated politics in the German Democratic Republic (GDR) until 1971. In the early years of the GDR's existence, his position was far from certain. He not only had the USSR watching his every move and regarding the East Germans as an inferior and 'defeated' people, there were also internal disputes within his own party. A mass purge of the GDR's Communist Party, the SED (the Socialist Unity Party of Germany), took place in 1948, followed up again in 1951. Factionalist challenges were finally resolved in Ulbricht's favour following his suppression of the 1953 uprising.

KEY PROFILE

Walter Ulbricht (1893–1973) was born in Leipzig. As a promising young Communist Party leader, he was trained in Moscow at Comintern's International Lenin School. When Hitler came to power, Ulbricht stayed abroad, living in the USSR from 1937 to 1945. He returned to Germany in 1945 and helped form the SED. Stalin thought highly of him and made him General Secretary of the SED in 1950.

Fig. 6 *By the time of this photo (1970) Walter Ulbricht was an ill man. Brezhnev, with whom he did not get on well, and his former protégée, Erich Honecker, were both undermining his leadership*

ACTIVITY

Collect photos of the satellite leaders in this chapter and make a picture gallery. You could include a brief summary of each leader below his photos.

By the 1960s, and with the coming of the 1961 Berlin Wall, the greater security of Ulbricht's personal position led him to widen the scope of his Party's Central Committee and allow more discussion with 'technical experts'; yet the centralisation of power continued and the final decision-making remained in Ulbricht's hands as the 'supreme father figure'.

The political organisation and influence of the Communist Party in East Germany

The SED was organised on the model of the CPSU. As with the other satellite states, but unlike the USSR, the GDR's legislature, the *Volkskammer*, was made up of elected representatives from several different parties, including the SED. These parties had to give full support to the SED, voting as the SED directed. As elsewhere in the satellite states, there was the appearance of multi-party politics, but it was not genuine.

A CLOSER LOOK

Democratic centralism

The elections within the Party were described as democratic centralism, in which there was a 'chain of authority' carrying the views of ordinary workers up to the Party leadership, who made the correct decisions about them on the basis of Marxist–Leninist theory, and then passed those decisions down to the people again.

Ulbricht's purges of the SED continued in the aftermath of the 1953 unrest: over 60 per cent of SED members were forced out of the Party by 1954. So while in Poland unrest signalled reform, in the GDR the opposite occurred: reformists were excluded from the Party. Some historians have suggested that the chance to leave the GDR meant that dissatisfaction there was lower than in other satellite states, where purges that excluded large numbers of reform-minded people created a social group with a grudge against the Party, which worked to lessen Party influence. Ulbricht felt secure enough to pay little attention to Khrushchev's de-Stalinisation programme, pushing ahead with collectivisation and the industrialisation programme.

Economic organisation, state of collectivisation, and the centrally planned economy in East Germany

Economic organisation

East Germany had been largely agricultural before the war, so, as well as repairing the devastation of the war, the SED's commitment was to create a modern industrial, socialist state in the GDR. This was made difficult by the following factors:

- The USSR demanded 25 per cent of industrial products in the GDR as reparations for the damage done by Germany to the Soviet Union. The Soviets also dismantled over a thousand East German industrial plants and took them to the USSR.
- East German industry had always got its supplies of coal and steel from the Ruhr, now in West Germany; it had limited supplies of its own.
- Before the building of the Berlin Wall (1961), very large numbers of East Germans were able to leave the GDR for West Germany, especially through the border that ran through Berlin. The numbers leaving reached just under 200,000 in 1960 and 150,000 in the first half of 1961. The loss of labour, especially skilled labour, to the West proved a drain which continued and grew as change spread.

ACTIVITY

Divide the class into four groups representing Poland, Czechoslovakia, Hungary and East Germany. Each group should present a picture of their country's strengths and weaknesses using a PowerPoint presentation. At the end, vote as a class to decide which is the strongest and which the weakest country.

The state of collectivisation

In the GDR, a wave of collectivisation had begun in 1952, but the resulting food shortages and price increases fed directly into the unrest in 1953 and so collectivisation was halted. A second wave of collectivisation was more successful, so by 1960, 85 per cent of farmland was collectivised.

Central planning in East Germany

Industries were nationalised and Five Year Plans launched. The 1950 plan promised to double the output of 1936. Its emphasis was on heavy industry: metalwork and machine-building in particular. The GDR joined Comecon in 1950. By 1951, 76 per cent of its trade was directed to the Soviet bloc.

By the 1960s, the GDR's economy was growing at about 3 per cent a year, but West Germany was averaging 8 per cent. The Seven Year Plan that began in 1959 had seen Ulbricht promise that, by 1961, the socialist economy would overtake the Federal Republic of Germany (FRG) with higher per capita (for each person) consumption of foodstuffs and most consumer goods. This was totally unrealistic.

Economic reforms were brought in in 1963 – the **New Economic System**. This permitted some decentralisation. Profit incentives and greater decision-making powers were granted to middle-level managers, and a move away from the emphasis on quantity ensured that the profitability of goods was taken into account in industrial planning. However, the system proved incompatible with the continuation of centrally fixed prices, and in the wake of the '**Prague Spring**' in Czechoslovakia in 1968, the system was abandoned in favour of increased centralisation.

CROSS-REFERENCE

Read about the **'Prague Spring'** in Chapter 16, page 135.

East Germany: strengths and weaknesses

The GDR was the front line of the Cold War and so it was very important to the USSR that it was both secure and also reflected the achievements of socialism to the West. Before 1961 and the building of the Berlin Wall, the massive exodus of East Germans was an enormous propaganda gift for the West. The GDR was neither secure nor a compelling advertisement for socialist development at this time. The unrest of 1953 was also deeply concerning for the USSR for security and propaganda reasons, and because of the fear that unrest could spread, as it did to Poland and to Hungary.

These weaknesses were lessened significantly after the border controls of 1961 stopped the flight of GDR citizens to the FRG. After that, it was possible for the politically astute Ulbricht to build socialism in East Germany so successfully that it soon had the highest growth rate among the satellite states, the highest standards of living, and the highest worker productivity. Politically, it was very stable, with lessons learned after 1953: Party purges and the Eastern bloc's most extensive Secret Police making sure of that.

ACTIVITY

1. In pairs, decide which of the leaders described in this chapter you would categorise as 'hard-line' Stalinists, and what that meant in practice. [Think about political, economic, and social measures.]
2. Which of the leaders you have just read about would you categorise as reformers, and what did that mean in practice?
3. Make a note of the events that prompted Soviet concerns about leaders in the satellite states. Were these concerns more about too much reform or too little?

SOURCE 1

From a speech made by Władysław Gomułka on 20 October 1956 to announce his leadership of the PUWP. He made the speech to the PUWP's Central Committee, and it was also broadcast live on Polish radio:

Recently the working class gave a painful lesson to the Party leadership and government. The workers of Poznań were not protesting against People's Poland, against socialism, when they came out into their city streets. They were protesting against the evil that has become so widespread in our social system and which touched them so painfully, against distortions of the basic rules of socialism, which is their ideal.

There can be different kinds of socialism. It can be the socialism that was created in the Soviet Union, or it can be formed as we see it now in Yugoslavia, or it can be some other type still. Only by experience and by studying the achievements of the different countries that are building socialism can the best model arise in given circumstances [i.e. in the particular context of one country].

SOURCE 2

From an article written by Imre Nagy in November 1956, in which he described the Rákosi regime:

They destroy the most noble human virtues, virtues that, in a socialist society, should be cultivated with love: I speak of courage, of steadiness, of sincerity, of fidelity to principles, of constancy. Instead of these cowardice, hypocrisy, servility, falsehood and opportunism are praised as virtues. Lies proliferate; careerism spreads destroying honour and honesty, an atmosphere of distrust, suspicion and vengeance weighs on the minds; humanism, which should be the characteristic trait of socialism, is repressed and its opposite, a cold inhumanity, reigns in public relations. Our social life presents an astonishing picture.

The degeneration and corruption of public life lead to the corruption of hearts and the degradation of character. The debasement of the soul to be observed in society is one of the gravest manifestations of the ethical and moral crisis taking place at this moment.

SOURCE 3

From a resolution for approval presented by Malenkov to the Council of Ministers of the USSR on 2 June 1956. The resolution was titled 'On measures to improve the health of the political situation in the GDR in the context of 600,000 East Germans leaving the GDR between 1951 and June 1953':

It must be recognised that the chief reason for the situation that has been created is that a mistaken course was adopted [by the SED] in accelerating the construction of socialism in East Germany. In particular, the hasty creation of agricultural cooperatives in the absence of the foundations [necessary] for them in the countryside led to: serious difficulties in the area of supplying the population with manufactured goods and food stuffs; a sharp fall in the mark's exchange rate; the ruin of a large number of small entrepreneurs-artisans, workers in domestic industries, and others. It also set a significant stratum of the populace against the existing authorities. The matter has gone so far that at present more than 500,000 hectares of land have been abandoned and neglected, and the thrifty German peasants, usually strongly tied to their plots, have begun to abandon their land and move to West Germany en masse.

A LEVEL PRACTICE QUESTION

Evaluating primary sources

With reference to Sources 1, 2, and 3 and your understanding of the historical context, assess the value of these sources to an historian studying the impact of Stalin's death on the satellite states of Poland, Hungary and East Germany.

STUDY TIP

One approach would be to evaluate the sources by comparing them, linking what they each say as you work through your evaluation. Alternatively you could deal with each source in turn.

A LEVEL PRACTICE QUESTION

'In the years between 1953 and 1964 the satellite states were politically strong.' Assess the validity of this view.

STUDY TIP

You will need to establish exactly what you understand by 'politically strong' and should examine each state in turn, evaluating its political strengths and weaknesses. You may want to offer some overall observations in your conclusion.

Summary: political and economic strengths and weaknesses of states

Table 1 *Annual percentage increase in wages in four of the satellite states, sourced from official statistics*

	1956–60	1961–65	1966–70	1971–75
Czechoslovakia	4.6	1.2	3.5	3.4
GDR	7.4	2.5	3.7	3.8
Hungary	8.0	1.7	3.5	3.4
Poland	5.1	1.5	1.9	7.3

ACTIVITY

Study Table 1. Explain how it could be used to compare the four satellite states in terms of economic strengths and weaknesses.

ACTIVITY

Summary

Copy and complete the table to record key political and economic details about the satellite states.

	Poland	Czechoslovakia	Hungary	GDR
Leadership and organisation				
The Communist Party and political control				
Economic organisation and industry				
Agriculture and collectivisation				
Other factors				

STUDY TIP

Economic statistics from the satellite states were no more reliable than those from the USSR, with those from the GDR particularly suspect due to the pressure of comparisons with the FGR. However, historians have some confidence in the consistency of data from one year to another.

14 Life in the Soviet satellite states

Enforced Sovietisation and the use of propaganda

From 1948, there was a move towards Sovietisation – the attempt to make all aspects of life in the satellite states match the Soviet model (in politics, economics, society and its institutions, and culture). In 1947, US President Harry S. Truman described the Soviet way of life as one that was enforced, with 'the will of a minority forcibly imposed upon the majority', relying on 'terror and oppression, a controlled press and radio, fixed elections and the suppression of personal freedoms'. However, the USSR was convinced that its ideology was superior and Sovietisation was the spread of a society that benefited the working people and offered opportunities for all. The satellite states were taught to look to the USSR, like children to a father, and learn from their parent state.

LEARNING OBJECTIVES

In this chapter you will learn about:

- enforced Sovietisation and the use of propaganda
- living standards; education; state organisations
- benefits and problems of life in the satellite states.

Propaganda

Propaganda in the satellite states had two functions: influencing opinions within a state and reinforcing solidarity against other countries, especially the West. These were often blurred. For example, sporting prowess was a key means of promoting the values of socialism (as seen in Czechoslovakia's ice hockey team; East Germany's weightlifters) These were impressive achievements of socialism that national audiences could feel pride in and Western audiences could be impressed by. But propaganda was also potentially an arena for resistance, too, as in the famous 'blood in the water' water polo match between Hungary and the USSR in the 1956 Olympics (after the suppression of the Hungarian uprising), where an epic battle between the two teams ended in Hungarian victory.

Propaganda for domestic consumers had very similar themes throughout the satellite states.

- The Party controlled all media within each state (though radio broadcasts from the West were often outside this control), and used them for propaganda, with views that conflicted with the Party line being suppressed (or permitted in periods of 'thaw').
- Propaganda praised the achievements of socialism and the USSR, promoted campaigns or requirements, or criticised the West. For example, at the end of each day's broadcast, Czechoslovak radio and TV played the Soviet national anthem alongside the Czechoslovak anthem.
- Because of its position on the front line of the Cold War (plus the problem of GDR citizens leaving for the West before 1961), propaganda was most intense in the GDR.

ACTIVITY

What message or messages is Fig. 1 seeking to convey?

Fig. 1 *This satirical poster from the GDR (1953) attacks RIAS (Radio in the American Sector) broadcasts from Berlin across much of East Germany. The radio programme is listed as: '1. Lies and propaganda, 2. Murder and sabotage, 3. American Boogie Woogie and Culture'*

A CLOSER LOOK

Jamming

Jamming of foreign radio broadcasts began with the Nazis' attempt to prevent British radio broadcasts reaching German listeners. It continued throughout the Cold War, with attempts to block the satellite states from broadcasting from radio stations like Radio Free Europe, Radio Liberty, Voice of America, and the BBC World Service.

Fig. 2 *In September 1960, Czechoslovak factory workers in Prague read about a speech by Khrushchev at the United Nations in* Rudé Právo, *the official newspaper of the Czechoslovak Communist Party, with a circulation of one million. The Party made sure it was widely read by occasionally stopping other newspapers being printed, preventing other papers being sold before 10am, and preventing kiosks from selling any papers but* Rudé Právo

ACTIVITY

Research

Find examples of propaganda from each of the four satellite states – Poland, Czechoslovakia, Hungary, and East Germany – which express the concept of friendship between the State and the USSR. How does the way friendship is symbolised link to Marxist–Leninist ideology?

Living standards; education; state organisations

Living standards

As in the USSR, after the end of Stalinist coercion the satellite states needed to convince their citizens that socialism was delivering ever-better living conditions that would soon surpass those in the West. Some key points to consider are:

- Living conditions and working conditions (norms and wages) were key factors in triggering unrest against the Soviet model of economic development, and in prompting resistance to Sovietisation.
- There was widespread resentment that the *nomenklatura* were able to access a wider range of high-quality consumer goods than the rest of the population.
- Standards of healthcare were high across the satellite states, education was free, and there was virtually no unemployment or homelessness.
- For those who benefited from socialism – in general terms, working-class people and women – living standards might still be regarded as an improvement on life before the war, or as not so significant compared to other goals in life.
- Living standards differed between the satellite states: the GDR had the highest standards – by 1970, nearly 70 per cent of GDR households had TVs, 56 per cent had refrigerators, and 16 per cent even had cars.

CROSS-REFERENCE

The *nomenklatura* – the elite bureaucrats who controlled appointments to desirable and influential jobs – are discussed in Chapter 5, page 38.

- Source analysis concerning living standards should also recognise that differences in living standards between East and West were seized upon as proof of the superiority of capitalism by Western commentators: there are issues of bias on both sides.
- Living standards in the satellite states did not only include individuals' private, domestic living conditions: the public sphere was also important. Therefore access to leisure and culture should be considered.

Fig. 3 *This massive monument to Stalin was unveiled in Prague, Czechoslovakia, on 1 May 1955. As de-Stalinisation progressed, it was seen as an embarrassment and was removed in 1962. The statue was nicknamed 'the meat queue' in Czechoslovakia*

ACTIVITY

Why was it subversive to call the Stalin monument in Figure 3 'the meat queue'? What does this reveal about attitudes to socialism and living standards in the satellite states?

Table 1 *Estimates (in US dollars) of gross domestic product (GDP) per capita per year figures for selected European countries and the USA*

	1950	1973	1990
Czechoslovakia	3429	7000	8464
West Germany	4429	12,981	18,537
East Germany	3127	8559	5704
Hungary	2481	5596	6454
Poland	2447	5334	5113
USA	9561	16,689	23,221
USSR	2827	6101	6888

(Per capita figures divide GDP (the economic output of a country) by its population: a measure that does not record disparities in income)

SOURCE 1

Information collected by Radio Free Europe, as part of its regular monitoring of information from Poland, on 'Poland's Absenteeism Problem', 26 August 1957:

Complaints of mass absenteeism in Polish industry continue to be reported by the Polish press and radio. The Chairman of the Central Council of Trade Unions revealed recently that during the first six months of 1957, the number of hours lost due to unexcused absences had more than doubled compared with the corresponding period of 1956. Causes of the mass absenteeism now afflicting the Polish industrial sector are, according to the Polish press, a general 'demoralisation' of the self-discipline of the Polish worker due to 12 years of exploitation under 'Stalinism', better wages being paid in the so-called 'private sector', the improvements in the agricultural sector, an attitude of disrespect towards established authority and a genuine disillusionment with the economic measures of the Gomułka regime in the matter of wages and the standard of living.

SOURCE 2

An East German woman talks about her life in the GDR in the 1950s:

There were special classes for women. After work I went to school, the kids were in the weekday nursery, and for the quarter of a year I had full-time practical formation. At the time we also worked on Saturdays. After one and a half years I passed the test to be a skilled worker in mechanics, and the party appointed me to a department which was just being built up and for which skilled workers were sought. Actually I did not want to leave the girls from the previous collective but then I also understood it to be necessary and went. We always said: work socialistic, learn and live. And that's how we did it. We worked a lot and we worked well.

SOURCE 3

From a report written in June 1968 by a delegation of Soviet workers to Czechoslovakia. The report expresses concern about the lack of respect for the Soviet Union and Marxist–Leninist ideology in Czechoslovakia, and the lack of action taken by the Communist Party of Czechoslovakia to address this:

At some of the enterprises, new trade union committees are being selected without Communist participants; unjustified changes in management are under way; unrealistic demands are being voiced for increases in pay; and discipline is sharply deteriorating. Workers at the factories are restless and are often expressing dissatisfaction, which in a number of cases is justified. Some of the workers at the Pešok machine building factory declared: "Earlier they said to us that the working class is in charge of the country, but now only the intellectuals appear on television and radio. We ourselves have no such opportunity." No party slogans and exhortations can be heard at the factory. On the walls in the factory sections they have put up photographs of half-naked women, rather than agitational posters. [One speaker from the factory at a discussion session] declared that Marxism is obsolete [and] that the USSR did a lot of harm to Czechoslovakia and is not able to serve as a model of socialism because people's living standards in the USSR are inadequate and salaries are low.

ACTIVITY

Research examples of Sovietisation through education for the other satellite states. There are documentaries about life under communism available online.

STUDY TIP

Try to consider provenance, content and argument, tone and emphasis when answering this type of question.

A LEVEL PRACTICE QUESTION

Evaluating primary sources

With reference to Sources 1, 2 and 3 and your understanding of the historical context, assess the value of these sources to an historian studying the impact of Sovietisation on living standards in the satellite states.

Education

Education in the satellite states followed the Soviet system, which had the following main characteristics:

- Provided for free by the State; private schools were abolished
- Highly centralised: all schools taught the same curriculum in the same way
- Secular: no religious instruction or religious education
- Egalitarian: designed to be open and relevant to all, so less of the 'academic' (classics) and more of the 'technical' (mathematics, science)
- Communist: teaching and textbooks followed approved ideological requirements, and Marxism–Leninism was a compulsory subject for all

- Specialist: students were channelled towards productive careers through technical specialisms and a focus on learning about work
- Soviet-led: most textbooks in the satellite states were translations of Soviet textbooks; Russian was the principal foreign language taught.

By extending education to all groups in society, especially those who had previously had little access to it – the poor, people in rural areas, women – the Soviet education model achieved among the highest participation and literacy rates in the world. Young people across the satellite states were exposed to full-intensity Sovietisation, which undoubtedly left its mark. However, this education system had further key consequences:

- It produced an educated population who could often clearly see the gap between what socialism promised and what it delivered.
- It created generations of students for whom Marxism–Leninism was an exceptionally dull subject that had to be endured in order to complete their courses.

State organisations

The satellite states each had a wide range of state-controlled social organisations, such as trade unions, sports clubs, youth organisations, professional organisations, and women's organisations. Any of these could potentially become areas of challenge to Party control, which meant that the Party ensured it had sufficient oversight. In many cases this was done by just having the Party run the organisation directly, but this was not always possible, in which case the Party would carefully monitor the organisation, as shown in the following example from the GDR.

Youth organisations in the GDR

Youth activities were strictly controlled and monitored by SED party officials. Only officially sanctioned youth organisations were permitted, and of these, the most important was the Free German Youth (FDJ). This was established in 1946 as a vehicle for educating young people in the principles of the State.

Membership was open to all between the ages of 14 and 25, but although membership was voluntary, it became essential for anyone who wanted to advance themselves educationally or in seeking jobs. Another organisation, the Ernst Thälmann Pioneers or Young Pioneers (named after a former Communist Party leader murdered by the Nazis in Buchenwald Concentration Camp) was for children of 6 to 14 years and, by the 1960s, nearly all children of that age group were members.

ACTIVITY

Extension

Find out more about other youth organisations in the satellite states and create a spider diagram detailing key features of each one.

Benefits and problems of life in the satellite states

Benefits to life in the Soviet satellite states included the impressive achievements with regard to education, health, and employment; there were also extensive cultural and leisure opportunities that were far more accessible to the population as a whole than in the West. For those willing to accept its requirements, toeing the Party line brought openings, especially for working people and women, that were not available pre-war, and not available to the same extent in Western countries either.

Problems were significant, however, and included:

- economic problems: boring work, poorly paid, poorly motivated; shortages of consumer goods, poor-quality goods; cramped housing, poor-quality housing
- social problems: high degree of conformity expected and enforced; conflicts between religious affiliations and Party requirements
- political problems: limited freedom of expression; limited freedom of movement (foreign travel heavily restricted, for example); limited career opportunities without Party membership.

ACTIVITY

Study the sources provided in this chapter and note from them as many signs of the benefits and problems of life in the satellite states as you can. Compare your list with a partner's.

STUDY TIP

This quotation invites you to challenge it, but it is also possible to agree with the view to a certain extent. Try to provide an answer balanced between the positive aspects of life for young people, particularly in regard to education and youth groups, and the downside of life in a controlled Soviet regime. Ensure that each side of the argument is supported with carefully selected evidence.

A LEVEL PRACTICE QUESTION

'There were more advantages than disadvantages for those living in the satellite states in the years to 1968.' Assess the validity of this view.

Summary

Sovietisation was denounced as equivalent to brainwashing by Western leaderships; it is possible now for historians to take a more nuanced view: people in the satellite states were required to conform outwardly with expectations set out by the Soviet model, but in some cases people did this because it worked for them rather than because they had no other choice.
In other cases, people did not conform. Not all children joined Party youth organisations. Far from all adults were Party members. However, these choices were made in the knowledge that a lack of conformity could be pushed only so far before consequences would become serious.

15 Repression in the Soviet satellite states

State security; secret police systems; censorship

State security

In 1955, the **Warsaw Pact** was signed between the USSR and its seven satellite states, in response to West Germany joining NATO. As part of the Warsaw Pact, the satellite states put their armed forces under Soviet high command, and also had Soviet troops stationed in their countries. These troops were used to suppress unrest, although this was not the expressed intention of the Warsaw Pact when it was created.

KEY CHRONOLOGY

1945	Formation of the StB (*Statni Bezpecnost* – State Security), Czechoslovakia's secret police
1945	Formation of the AVH (*Allamvedelmi Hatosag* – State Protection Authority), Hungary's secret police
1950	Formation of the Stasi (*Ministerium fur Staatssicherheit*) – Ministry for State Security, the GDR's secret police
1952	GDR's inner border sealed
1955	Warsaw Pact signed
1956	Formation of the SB (*Sluzba Bezpieczenstwa* – Security Service), Poland's secret police
1956	Hungary becomes only satellite state without a formal secret police force

LEARNING OBJECTIVES

In this chapter you will learn about:

- state security; secret police systems; censorship
- repression by the legal system; repression of the Church
- emigration restrictions and defections.

CROSS-REFERENCE

A Closer Look at the **Warsaw Pact** can be found in Chapter 4, page 28.

Secret police systems

The secret police in each of the satellite states followed the same model. During the war, Soviet administrators started to recruit reliable men to attend an NKVD (People's Commissariat for Internal Affairs) training school. After the war, it was these Soviet-trained men who then set up security police training in their own countries, and Soviet advisers always remained inside each state's secret police systems.

Fig. 1 *This spy camera was designed to fit into the lining of a coat, with the camera lens behind the button*

The secret police in Poland

The SB was set up in 1956 and gradually developed an extensive network of informants throughout Polish society – around 81,000 by 1981, when the Solidarity movement was directly threatening the PUWP's hold on power. The Catholic Church was drawn into this network too: historian Jan Zaryn estimates that perhaps 15 per cent of priests were informants for the SB. During the period of Gomułka's reforms, the SB was much less active than after 1968, when it took on a much greater role in monitoring and suppressing the actions of potential political opponents of the Party.

The secret police in Czechoslovakia

The StB was very influential in the rise to power of the Communist Party of Czechoslovakia. The StB worked in both the Czech and Slovak regions, but was supervised by each region's own Ministry of the Interior. As in the other satellite states, vast amounts of information were kept on the daily activities of citizens under surveillance. In the Czech Republic today, archives hold an estimated 280 million pages of StB reports, even after the StB destroyed many of its files in 1989. Analysis of files suggests that many agents and informers were themselves spied on.

The secret police in Hungary

The secret police were feared and resented across the satellite states, but in Hungary the AVH was particularly detested. Since the Communist Party had very little support after the war, the AVO, as it was then called, was tasked with removing opposition from other more popular parties, which it did through accusing leaders of other parties of Nazi collaboration and torturing confessions out of them. Once in power, Rákosi used the AVO to purge the Party. In 1950, the organisation changed its name to AVH. Known AVO/AVH operatives were a target in the 1956 Hungarian Revolution, and Imre Nagy announced that the AVH would be shut down as part of the Revolution. After 1956, the USSR decided that it would be impossible to re-establish another secret police force in Hungary and it remained the only Warsaw Pact satellite state without one, although many of the same functions of counter-intelligence were carried out by the Ministry of the Interior.

The secret police in East Germany

The Stasi is generally agreed to have been the most far-reaching and effective of all the secret police forces in the satellite states, through its vast network of informers and its effective repression of any significant protest in East Germany. The Stasi was also very successful in infiltrating West German political and business organisations. The KGB was closely involved with all satellite states' secret police forces, but particularly so with the Stasi because of the chance to spy on the West and the propaganda potential to the USSR of East Germany remaining staunchly socialist. The number of people on the Stasi's pay list is estimated at 274,000, the vast majority being informers. It is thought that 2.5 per cent of East Germany's adult population were acting as informers at some point after 1950.

A secret police service is distinguished from other police by its ability to act without answering to the public, the legal system, or government. The secret police in the satellite states owed their allegiance to the Party. Their role was to identify possible enemies of the State, both from outside (spies for the West or for renegade socialist states like Yugoslavia) and from within. The secret police systems took from the USSR the belief that socialism was under threat from all sides, and that no one was above suspicion. On this basis, the key to secret police success was to gain as much information as possible about as many people as possible. Methods included:

A CLOSER LOOK

After Khrushchev's censure of the secret police's role in Stalin's Party purges, the KGB and the secret police in the satellite states switched to psychological harassment of dissidents and other suspected enemies. The aim was to 'decompose' people's ability to damage the State by wrecking their reputations, careers, and relationships in ways that could not be conclusively linked to the secret police.

- intercepting and reading letters; tapping telephone conversations; bugging homes, hotel rooms, workplaces, schools, universities, hospitals, and public places
- surveillance of people's movements; house searches; searches of household rubbish (for incriminating Western products)
- infiltration by secret police agents of organisations, workplaces, apartment block maintenance staff
- paying, blackmailing, intimidating people to inform on others: people with a lot of contact with others (e.g. teachers, doctors) were especially valuable as informants
- arrests, detentions, psychological harassment, torture, murder.

Reports from the different secret police systems, including those of Soviet officials stationed within them, were the main way in which the USSR's leadership gauged the progress, or otherwise, of Sovietisation in the satellite states.

Fig. 2 *An exhibition at the Terror Haza (House of Terror) Museum in Budapest, Hungary; each person shown on the wall was a victim of the secret police*

SOURCE 1

From a report to Yuri Andropov, head of the KGB, written by a Hungarian university student informing on conversations with his fellow students in November 1968:

Students' attitudes toward the ongoing situation in Czechoslovakia are of two main types. On the one hand, indignation is expressed toward the [Czechoslovak] 'brothers' whom we [the Hungarians] 'have been subsidising for so many years' and who are now responding with vile ingratitude. However, this group is small in number. The rest of the students, who generally take pleasure in anything that causes problems for or conflicts with the official line, are watching the ongoing situation in Czechoslovakia with benevolent curiosity. Some even contemplate (albeit hypothetically) the possibility of repeating the Czech experience in our own country. In discussion with the author of this review, a third-year student said: 'It's interesting to think whether such events could take place here. I personally would take part if they did.'

ACTIVITY

Extension

The Lives of Others, a German-language film released in 2006, depicts numerous Stasi techniques for monitoring and controlling the GDR's population. View clips from the film, identify the techniques used, and consider their likely effectiveness.

ACTIVITY

Imagine you were asked to write a report for the security services on your fellow students, following information on an imminent terrorist attack. Would you agree or not, and what would your reasons be?

ACTIVITY

Research

The OSA's digital repository (www.osaarchivum.org) includes a collection of reports on state media by Radio Free Europe and Radio Liberty (RFE/RL Situation Reports, 1959–89), which provide detailed accounts of the use of censorship and propaganda to provide news and information that met the needs of the Communist Party. The archive can be filtered by country and year.

a) Working in groups on each of the four satellite states, find three pieces of source material about censorship or propaganda for your state for the period 1953–68.

b) Swap source materials with another group and use their materials to assess the value of the sources for a study of how information was controlled by governments of the satellite states in this period.

A CLOSER LOOK

Socialist legality was a law in a socialist state that was designed to protect the State's interests rather than private property. It often featured tribunals made up of ordinary people who decided on 'revolutionary justice' for certain types of crimes.

ACTIVITY

Explain the message of Source 2 in your own words. Why is it important for judges to be independent and show integrity?

KEY TERM

imperialist: someone who supports other countries being subordinated as part of an empire

Censorship

Government institutions in the satellite states controlled the information that was, and was not, allowed to reach the public. Libraries were purged of books containing material deemed unsuitable for a socialist state and of writers considered unreliable. The states also jammed particular radio and TV broadcasts and had control over the press, publishers, and broadcasters. Usually, a Party official within the organisation would judge whether or not material was permissible for publication, broadcast, or performance within a state.

The censors' list of unacceptable topics changed over time and included any criticism of communism, of the leadership of the State and of the USSR, of living standards or working conditions; praise for the enemies of communism; and topics that might have a bad influence on people (like discussions of homosexuality).

Repression by the legal system; repression of the Church

The legal system

Khrushchev announced his determination to return the USSR to **socialist legality**, in which the courts would determine sentences according to law, not the arbitrary decisions of the secret police. However, socialist legal systems were, like everything else, still a tool of the Party because the Party's leading role in building socialism could not be challenged by other organisations in society. The legal system had concern for the individual's rights and liberties, but only within the framework of obedience to the State and the tenets of Marxist–Leninist ideology.

This way of thinking influenced legal systems throughout the satellite states. Since the law was subservient to the Party, ordinary people who were having problems (perhaps were in trouble with the police) would try to find someone of influence within the Party who might be able to help solve their problems, usually for an appropriate fee. Judges were not respected in society because their low pay encouraged corruption. Ordinary people used courts almost entirely for family issues only: judging paternity, maintenance payments, and so on. The Party, however, used the legal system extensively to ensure that the population behaved correctly. As in the USSR, socialist laws were introduced against, for example, worker absenteeism and 'parasitism' (where people were judged to be taking more from the system than they were putting in).

SOURCE 2

Statement by a judge from Czechoslovakia in the 1950s, after the death of Stalin:

In about ninety per cent of the court's agenda, there was not the slightest sign of interference in our decision-making. This observation, however, does not warrant the conclusion that some sort of 'ninety per cent juridical independence and integrity' existed. Both the sorry experience with the remaining ten per cent and the awareness that someone might at any time inflict his 'suggestion' upon us, conditioned all our adjudication.

The Church

Religion was a problem for Sovietisation as it meant a second set of ideological beliefs in conflict with Marxism–Leninism, and a second set of leaders within society to whom people owed their allegiance.

The Church in Czechoslovakia

Czechoslovakia was an overwhelmingly Catholic country. The CPCz launched a huge campaign after the war to discredit the Church as a foreign institution that was seeking to destroy the state of Czechoslovakia. The StB arrested thousands of priests, monks, and nuns, while elaborate show trials were arranged with Church leaders tortured into confessing to **imperialist** plots to overthrow the State. After that, with all Church property seized by the State, the Church operated entirely under the Party's control. In the 1950s and 1960s, religious education was removed from schools, propaganda spread scandalous tales about immoral priests, only one seminary for training priests was allowed to stay open, individual priests were harassed and restricted from giving services, and pressure was put on collective farmers to stay away from church. All the same, church attendance in the towns stayed high.

The Church in the GDR

Catholics were a minority in East Germany, but the Protestant Church provided a potential forum for opposition. Ulbricht tried to weaken the Churches in the 1950s, removing their influence in education, making the *Junge Gemeinde* (Young Christian) organisation illegal, introducing the *Jugendweihe*, (a dedication ceremony for 14-year-olds) and promoting secularism. This all had limited effect, however, since the Churches continued to run old people's homes, childcare facilities, hospitals, and other essential services on which the State relied.

In 1969, some German Protestants decided to form their own separate East German Church and work 'within' (rather than against or alongside) the State. This paved the way for better relations, but while the Church learned to accommodate socialist rule, individual Christians kept their thoughts private. Those who spoke out, such as Otto Dibelius, Bishop of Berlin, found themselves subjected to repeated harassment.

Fig. 3 *This photo, taken around 1957, shows East Berliners going into the Marienkirche Church to attend mass given by Bishop Dibelius*

The Church in Hungary

In post-war Hungary, about 70 per cent of the population was Catholic, and once all political opposition had been removed, the Church was the only organisation standing in the way of Rákosi's take-over. The leader of the Catholic Church was Cardinal **József Mindszenty**, a fierce opponent of communism. When the MSZP announced that all church schools would be nationalised (and secularised), Mindszenty declared that he would **excommunicate** all those involved in this programme, and forbade Catholic teachers to work in these schools. He was arrested and tortured, and confessed to ridiculous crimes that saw him convicted in a show trial of trying to overthrow the regime, of starting a Third World War with American help, and taking control of Hungary himself. Other prominent religious leaders in the Catholic and Lutheran faiths, and then all priests of every religion, were made to swear allegiance to the State, with those who refused being imprisoned. As in Czechoslovakia, the Church was only allowed to continue under complete State control.

KEY PROFILE

József Mindszenty (1892–1975) was arrested for opposition to Hungarian Nazis, and then arrested and sentenced to life imprisonment in 1949 for his opposition to the Communist Party. There was international outcry at his treatment, with the Pope calling on all Catholics to never submit to obedience to the State instead of God. Mindszenty was released following the Hungarian uprising in 1956, and when Soviet armed forces suppressed the uprising, he took political asylum in the American embassy in Budapest, where he lived for 15 years..He was allowed to leave Hungary in 1971 and died in Austria in 1975.

The Church in Poland

The Church in Poland, an overwhelmingly Catholic country (95 per cent of the population were Catholic after the war), enjoyed more freedom and influence than in the other satellite states. There were no persecutions of religious leaders leading to show trials. However, the PUWP could not simply allow the Church to provide an opposing ideology to socialism (not just in churches but in all the thousands of Catholic schools and social care institutions that the Church ran). The Party seized Church property and attempted to portray Church leaders as Nazi sympathisers, imprisoning many for opposing socialist legislation. The leader of the Polish Catholics, Cardinal Stefan Wyszyński, was imprisoned from 1953 to 1956 for criticising the Party leadership. When he was released in 1956, with the return to leadership of Gomułka, a less tense relationship was worked out between the Party and the Church which gave the latter more freedom in its educational role and its control over Church property.

KEY TERM

excommunicate: a process by which people are excluded from the Church communion. It is designed to persuade people to amend their behaviour so they can return to the Church communion.

Fig. 4 *This photo from 1957 shows nuns in Warsaw presenting their documents at a polling station after the Church called on everyone to vote in Party elections*

SOURCE 3

From an article in *The Tablet* (a weekly Catholic newspaper from the UK) from 9 June 1962, titled 'Communism and the Church in Czechoslovakia':

It would not have been possible to carry out the collectivisation programme without formidable pressure to discredit the clergy and minimise their influence. Personal attacks at them were poured forth in the press and on the radio. In the towns, however, the opposite is true, since it is not possible to keep so strict a control on those who would go to the churches as it is in the villages, and they are frequently crammed with worshippers. In spite of all the efforts of the regime, such as threats and persuasion to give up church-going, fear induced for the future of their children whose openings for higher education may be reduced or even abolished, severe limitations to careers, even transfer to another and worse job with no prospects, the majority of the Czechoslovak population remains faithful still. It can even be said that the present spiritual vacuum has led a great proportion of the Czech intelligentsia back to the Church, in which they find consolation and comfort in their present tribulations.

SOURCE 4

From a report from 1958 by Radio Free Europe, as part of its regular monitoring of information from the satellite states. This report summarises an article in a Yugoslav daily newspaper, *Borba*, about the impact of Catholicism in Poland:

Catholic fanaticism has never been so great in Poland as today, said the Belgrade daily *Borba* of July 6. After returning from a visit to Poland, the paper's special correspondent, Duško Jovanović, wrote a report dealing with the great difficulties which the Polish authorities face in trying to get dead Communists buried in Catholic cemeteries. Jovanović gave details about what had happened in an unnamed Polish village recently. The president of the local village committee had died. Because he was a Communist, the inhabitants of the village organised themselves so as to forcibly prevent his burial in the common 'Christian' cemetery. Armed with stones, a 'silent group of several hundred men and women' surrounded the burial processions. Only 'thanks to the cleverness of the priest', who made a half hour speech to the rioters, did they allow the dead Communist functionary to be buried in the cemetery.

SOURCE 5

From an anthology of complaints about the treatment of Catholics in the satellite states titled *The Persecuted Church Appeals to the Pope*, written in Rome in 1955. This document was used in broadcasts by Radio Free Europe:

From another persecuted nation [the name of the satellite state it is from is not recorded] a child of ten years of age cast at the feet of the Holy Father [the Pope] this homage smuggled across the frontier by some refugees.

"Praise to Jesus Christ! Holy Father I send to you my kindest greetings and wish You good health. I hope that this Communism will finish as soon as possible because I want to go as a missionary to the Indians.

"I am now in the fourth class at elementary school, but we are only taught Communist subjects, and those of us who are the best in these subjects have to become 'pioneers.' Nowadays, on the birthday of the President of the Republic we have to take the oath of the pioneers.

"I act as server at the Holy Mass very often. Who is Your server when You celebrate the Mass, Holy Father?"

A LEVEL PRACTICE QUESTION

Evaluating primary sources

With reference to Sources 3, 4, and 5 and your understanding of the historical context, assess the value of these sources to an historian studying the position of the Church in the satellite states.

STUDY TIP

Study the provenance carefully. Sources about the Church which come from religious organisations. are likely to have a strong viewpoint. Remember a full analysis of the provenance is as important as a detailed consideration of content, argument and tone when responding to this type of question.

Emigration restrictions and defections

The satellite states kept a tight hold on their populations through stringent restrictions on the numbers allowed to emigrate and very significant investment in border security. The argument was that people gained so much from socialism that it was not fair if people chose then to take all these gifts to a Western country, instead of repaying the debt they owed to their own state.

Emigration was not illegal in the satellite states, but it was almost impossible to achieve permission to emigrate due to deliberately impassable bureaucratic restrictions. People only managed to leave in any numbers during times of upheaval: for example, 200,000 people fled Hungary as refugees during the 1956 uprising, and a similar number left Czechoslovakia during the Soviet repression of 1968. The exception to all this, before the building of the Berlin Wall in 1961, was East Germany.

Emigration restrictions in the GDR

Until 1961, Berliners were still able to move freely through the entire city: 53,000 East Berliners worked in the western sector. This was an 'escape' route for unhappy East German citizens who were otherwise unable to travel to the West after the 1381km inner-German border had been sealed in 1952. They had only to walk or take a train across the open border into West Berlin and declare their intentions and from there, they could be flown or taken by road to the FRG.

Between 1949 and 1961, 2.5 million people had left the GDR (from a total population of approximately 17 million). This drain of workers proved insufferable to Ulbricht. It was both economically and psychologically damaging his country and he was determined to halt the flow. The result of this was the Berlin Wall.

Defections

In the satellite states, **defection** was treated as treason and those caught trying to leave the State illegally were punished very harshly. Cold War propaganda included the arts and sport, and it boosted the reputation of the USSR and the satellite states when their artists and sportspeople (e.g. ballet dancers, writers, classical musicians, competitors in the Olympic Games) travelled abroad. When such high-profile people defected on such tours, it was a considerable propaganda victory for the West. Even more valuable were the defections of state security personnel – secret policemen and spies with inside information about the operations and resources of the 'other side'. However, there were many attempts by ordinary people to leave the satellite states, in violation of emigration restrictions and sometimes with tragic consequences.

A CLOSER LOOK

Sealing the border, 1952

A 10 metre strip was ploughed along the entire length of the inner border, with an adjoining 500 metre-wide zone (the *Schutzstreifen*) and a further 5km-wide zone (the *Sperrzone*) in which only those holding a special permit could live or work. Trees, vegetation, and even houses were destroyed to enable border guards to keep watch over the border, and the farming of fields along the border was only allowed in daylight hours and under the watch of armed border guards.

CROSS-REFERENCE

Additional information about the construction of the Berlin Wall is provided in Chapter 16, pages 134–35.

KEY TERM

defection: leaving one state to live in another one, in violation of emigration restrictions

ACTIVITY

Research

Undertake some research about Soviet and Eastern Bloc defectors during the period 1953 to 1968. Try to find some interesting cases to share with your group.

Fig. 5 *East German border guard Conrad Schumann, defects to the French Sector of West Berlin during the construction of the Berlin Wall in 15 August 1961*

STUDY TIP

Try to provide a balanced response, but maintain a clear view that you can argue for consistently. There is a lot of evidence which can be offered either in support of the significance of Church control or against it. Select your evidence carefully, state your argument clearly in the introduction and repeat it in the conclusion.

A LEVEL PRACTICE QUESTION

How significant was control of the Church in maintaining Communist regimes in the satellite states?

ACTIVITY

Summary

Use a table like the following to determine which satellite state was the most repressive. Use information from this book, plus the results of the research activities in this chapter, to complete the table. For each category, give the degree of repression a score out of 10, and add some supporting evidence.

	Poland	**Czechoslovakia**	**Hungary**	**East Germany**
Repression by the State/secret police				
Repression by censorship				
Repression by the legal system				
Repression of the Church				
Repression by emigration restrictions				

16 Threats to stability in the Soviet satellite states

Risings in East Germany, Poland, and Hungary

East Germany: the riots of June 1953

On 16 June, building workers in the *Stalinallee* in East Berlin, where a massive construction programme was under way to transform the street into a Stalinist memorial, went on strike against new increased work norms, protesting at the Trades Union (FDGB) headquarters. Other workers joined them and when no one from the SED leadership came to talk to them, they moved on to the Haus der Ministerien (the government building). Here, conflicting messages were received. Minister Selbman said the new work norms would be abandoned, but another Politburo message said they would be 'reconsidered'. As the crowd became increasingly restless, they called for the resignation of the SED leaders, more political freedom, and more consumer goods. A general strike was called but only around 6 per cent of the total workforce took part, with no participation from the intellectuals or the peasants.

Ulbricht was forced to back down on the work norms, but the USSR was horrified at the way the situation was escalating out of control and sent in 20,000 Soviet Army troops, with tanks, to help the 8000 GDR police crush the uprising. There was fierce fighting and between 20 and 125 people were killed.

Factors contributing to the uprising

- The death of Stalin was followed by signs of a relaxation of control from the USSR.
- Enforced socialism and collectivisation were causing masses of East Germans to leave the GDR: 447,000 between January 1951 and April 1953.
- Workers resented low wages, high taxation (which was used to pay for the new armed border guards), and rising food prices.

Consequences

Ulbricht had been reluctant to introduce the reforms the Soviet leadership thought were required in the GDR, and the uprising was seen as proving him right, and those in the Soviet leadership like Beria, who had pushed for a change in course, as being wrong. Ulbricht remained in his post, reforms were halted, and a crackdown began. Around 6000 people were arrested in the months following the uprising, and around 20,000 civil servants were sacked, along with 50,000 apparatchiks, as Ulbricht purged the SED of those with unreliable political backgrounds.

The Stasi was also reformed, ordered to compile daily reports for each district, and put under firmer Party control. Although the USSR insisted on some concessions – raising pensions, increasing the production of consumer goods, and lowering food prices – any chance of radical change passed as Ulbricht became more entrenched than ever.

Poland: the riots of June 1956

On 28 June, workers from the Stalin Works, which employed 15,000 people in Poznań, started demonstrations against an increase in production norms and a reduction in overtime payments. This followed Party refusal of a 20 per cent wage increase for workers. The demonstrators rioted, setting Party offices on fire, attacking the SB headquarters and city jail, and making political demands, including an end to Soviet occupation. Local troops could not contain the rioters and reinforcements were sent from Warsaw. Figures released in 1981 put the casualties at 75 dead and 900 wounded.

LEARNING OBJECTIVES

In this chapter you will learn about:

- risings in East Germany, Poland, and Hungary
- issues over Berlin and the Berlin Wall
- Dubček and the Prague Spring in Czechoslovakia
- reasons for the threats, their development and outcome for the State and for its relations with the USSR.

KEY CHRONOLOGY

1953	June	Riots in East Germany
1956	June	Riots in Poland
1956	October	Revolution in Hungary
	October	Suez Crisis
1958	November	Khrushchev's Berlin ultimatum
1961	August	East and West Berlin divided
1968	April	'Action Programme' in Czechoslovakia
	August	Warsaw Pact troops invade Czechoslovakia
	November	Brezhnev Doctrine is announced

Consequences

Soviet troops advanced to the outskirts of Warsaw and a hard-line minority within the PUWP began drawing up lists of people to arrest. However, in the months following the uprising, agreement developed within liberal parts of the PUWP and other organisations that the problem was the centralising Soviet model. Instead of a crackdown, the workers should get better pay and conditions, and more of a say in the way production was organised in their workplaces. By October, the movement for reform was able to bring back Gomułka, who, in turn, was able to convince Khrushchev that he would restore order in Poland. A series of reformist measures followed:

- Soviet advisers left the Polish security forces and the Soviet Army returned to its bases.
- Elections with a real choice between candidates (instead of an approved list) were reinstated.
- Political prisoners (including religious leaders, among them Cardinal Stefan Wyszyński) were freed from prison.

At the same time, an end was called to the collectivisation campaign, wages were increased by 30 per cent, and restrictions were placed on future raises to work norms. Hard-line elements within the Politburo were sacked. By December, the USSR had agreed that the movement of Soviet troops within Poland without prior agreement with the government was now banned.

ACTIVITY

Research

Find the Hungarian students' 16-point manifesto online Which of the 16 points would you include in each of the following categories:

a) anti-Soviet
b) economic
c) democratic
d) nationalistic/cultural
e) legal/relating to justice?

CROSS-REFERENCE

The appointment of Imre Nagy is discussed in Chapter 13, page 109.

Hungary: the Revolution of October 1956

On 13 October, 1956, the USSR leadership's concerns about Rákosi led to the return of Imre Nagy, a massively popular reformist figure (though also a Moscow-trained Party loyalist). This was accompanied by a significant 'thaw', and the freedom of speech that resulted grew more radical, especially in relation to the victims of Rákosi's savage purges. Student demonstrations followed the public reburial ceremony of one of the victims of the purges, László Rajk. By 22 October 1956, students had produced a manifesto of 16 points which they demanded be read out on national radio. A gigantic statue of Stalin was pulled down – one of the 16 points.

Fig. 1 *A statue of Stalin, constructed in 1949, was toppled during the Hungarian Revolution. Insulting remarks were scrawled on the broken bits, including the message 'Russians, when you run away, don't leave me behind'*

Nagy was put under pressure to sign a request to the USSR for help suppressing the unrest, which he refused to do. He did put a state of emergency into operation. Soviet troops already within Hungary and Hungarian forces fought with protestors in the streets of Budapest. Under pressure, Nagy changed into a defender of the reformers. He announced in a radio broadcast that he was to discuss the removal of all Soviet troops from Hungary and the introduction of multi-party democracy.

KEY PROFILE

Dwight D. Eisenhower (1890–1969), nicknamed 'Ike', was US president from 1953 to 1961. An Army careerist, Eisenhower was appointed as the Supreme Commander of the Allied Forces in Europe during the Second World War, and his victory in the war made him a national hero. Upon being elected president in 1953, he focused his foreign policy on containing the spread of communism and to combatting the influence of the USSR on developing nations around the world.

Reasons for the uprising

- Hungary's Revolution was anti-Soviet Union, but not anti-socialist. It was not the Catholic Church or the peasants who began the Revolution, but disaffected students desperate for reform.
- Hungarians believed that the USA would join their fight against the USSR, because the **Eisenhower** government had talked tough about 'rolling back communism', with Radio Free Europe encouraging Hungarians to push for freedom.
- The 'thaw' in Hungary's literary and political circles revealed how superficial the Sovietisation of Hungary really was, and how deeply many Hungarians resented it.

Consequences

The Soviet leadership was split on what to do. There was a growing acceptance of the need to make big concessions in Hungary to ensure it stayed part of the socialist bloc. But Nagy announced his intention for Hungary to withdraw from the Warsaw Pact, and lynchings of secret police personnel and Party leaders began in Budapest.

CROSS-REFERENCE

A Closer Look at the **Warsaw Pact** can be found in Chapter 4, page 27.

Fig. 2 *The body of an AVH (Allamvedelmi Hatosag – secret police) colonel is dragged through the streets of Budapest*

The Soviet decision was made on 31 October to use massive force to crush the Revolution. It was a favourable time to use force because the world's attention was focused on the **Suez Canal Crisis**. Between 4 and 7 November, fighting against the invasion force of Soviet troops led to 2500 Hungarian deaths and 20,000 people wounded. Following the attempted Revolution, 100,000 people were arrested, some 26,000 put in prison, and between 300 and 600 executed, including Imre Nagy himself.

A CLOSER LOOK

The Suez Crisis, 1956

Following nationalisation of the Suez Canal (the vital waterway between the Mediterranean and Indian Ocean) by Egypt in 1956, at the end of October, Britain and France invaded Egypt under the pretence of separating Egyptian and Israeli forces (Israel had actually helped put the plan together), while really aiming to overthrow the Egyptian leadership of Nasser. World opinion was scandalised by this invasion, and the USSR was able to portray it as imperialism at its worst.

ACTIVITY

Compare the risings in Germany, Poland, and Hungary in 1953 and 1956, considering the following factors:

a) External triggers – including the impacts of policy change in the USSR
b) Internal triggers – including responses to Sovietisation and repression
c) Demands – whether economic or political
d) Numbers involved – including social groups involved; people killed
e) Responses – government response and Soviet response
f) Consequences – including concessions, reforms, international significance.

You could prepare your comparisons in the form of a PowerPoint presentation.

Issues over Berlin and the Berlin Wall

The reasons for the building of the Berlin Wall

Berlin, deep within East Germany but divided into East and West, raised many key issues for the GDR, the USSR, and their international relations. It had been Stalin's intention to gradually make Western presence in Berlin (and Germany as a whole) unsustainable, which appeared easy to do considering the need for West Berlin to receive supplies from the FRG along East German roads and rail lines or through East German airspace. Berlin also clarified the difference in Soviet and Western aims for Germany: the USSR wanting to keep the country weak so that it would not again be a military threat; the West seeking to rebuild Germany as a strong economic power. Disputes between the USSR and the West over Germany had their flashpoints in Berlin, with heavily armed forces on both sides ready for rapid mobilisation.

Chief among the issues for the GDR, however, was the free movement of Germans across the border between East Germany and West Germany. Before 1953, this was relatively easy at many points along the border. After 1953, border control changes meant it was very difficult, except in Berlin, where the border was controlled by the Western powers as well as the USSR.

Until 1961, Berliners were still able to move freely through the entire city. Around 12,000 West Berliners worked in the eastern sector, while 53,000 East Berliners worked in the western sector. The freedom of movement in Berlin offered an ideal 'escape' route for dissatisfied East German citizens.

CROSS-REFERENCE

The Berlin Crisis is also discussed in Chapter 4, page 30.

The Berlin Crisis, 1958–61

Although in 1959, the Soviet Union withdrew its ultimatum for the Western Powers to quit Berlin, by the same year, the crisis had intensified flight from the GDR:

- in 1959, about 144,000 people fled the country
- in 1960, the figure rose to 199,000
- between January and August 1961, 181,007 people left. Of these emigrants, nearly half were under the age of 25.

It is not known who made the actual decision to erect the Berlin Wall, but the impetus undoubtedly came from Ulbricht, Honecker (the minister in charge of state security), and the SED, rather than the USSR. By the early summer of 1961. Khrushchev was persuaded that he would have to agree to Ulbricht's request for support to build a wall to plug the border gap, and so at least deal with the immediate problem.

The building of the wall

Overnight on Sunday, 13 August 1961, the border with West Berlin was closed. The underground and overground train network, as well as the streets that had connected East and West Berlin, were cut in two.

SOURCE 1

Miriam Flotow, a recent émigré to West Berlin from the GDR, describes going to look at the wall for herself on Sunday, 13 August 1961:

The atmosphere was oppressive. There were many people there, standing dumbfounded, looking at the barrier of barbed wire and soldiers. Many people were crying, waving to relatives. I, too, had an Aunt in the East. It never crossed my mind I wouldn't see her again for years. We were all very emotional on this evening. But we were still certain that the whole commotion would be over soon. Even now with the city divided in two, no one thought that the division would last almost three decades.

Initially, the border guards were ordered not to fire live bullets to prevent escapes. However on 22 August, the SED Politburo, tiring of the endless escapes, issued the order 'that any violation of the border to our German Democratic Republic, will be answered with the call of firearms'.

Dubček and the Prague Spring in Czechoslovakia

In January 1968, Alexander Dubček was elected First Secretary of the CPCz, after Party reformers forced Novotný to resign. Novotný's leadership team was too associated with the vicious purges of the 1950s to be able to fit in with de-Stalinisation and, from the early 1960s, Dubček had seen the chance to oust Novotný from power by becoming the leader of an anti-Novotný faction.

A key factor about the Czechoslovakian 'Prague Spring' of 1968 was that reform came from within the Communist Party itself. Dubček wanted to move away from the Soviet model and strengthen Czechoslovak socialism through making it democratic. This was known as 'socialism with a human face. He also wanted to reform the economy by reducing the inefficiencies of the centralised system. An 'Action Programme' of reforms was introduced in April 1968 to increase investment in consumer goods production, decentralise the planned economy, allow other parties to share some power, and rehabilitate victims of the purges. Censorship was almost completely abandoned, with the result that intellectuals began to challenge the authority of the Party through literature, art, and political discussion. Student demonstrations called for more change. Criticism of the USSR and the Soviet system appeared in the press. In June 1968, Czech intellectuals released *The Two Thousand Words* document, which called for more reform: hardliners saw it as the manifesto for a counter-revolution. The intellectuals said 'we have no choice but to complete our plan to humanise the regime. If we did not, the old forces would exact cruel revenge.'

This criticism concerned Brezhnev and leaders of other satellite states. The KGB chief, Andropov, who had been an ambassador in Hungary in

ACTIVITY

1. To what extent did the building of the Berlin Wall improve the stability of the GDR?
   Put together the following information to support an answer to this question:
   a) Evidence about numbers leaving the GDR through Berlin
   b) Detail about the consequences of emigration on the economy of the GDR
   c) Evidence about the cultural impact of the Wall for GDR citizens.
2. A counter-argument is that the ability of potential dissidents to leave the GDR through Berlin lessened the numbers of disaffected people in the GDR. Assess the significance of this counter-argument.

A CLOSER LOOK

On 24 August, 24-year-old Günter Liftin was the first to die trying to escape over the Berlin Wall. He had attempted to escape by swimming across the Humboldt Harbour which was on border territory. A guard had fired two warning shots, which he ignored; the third shot killed him. During the 28 years of the wall's existence, over 100 people were shot trying to escape. A further 3200 people were also caught trying to escape; they were arrested and given long prison sentences.

KEY CHRONOLOGY

1968	**5 January**	Alexander Dubček replaces Antonín Novotný
	5 April	The Party approves a package of reforms
	8 May	Dubček's reforms are discussed by the Warsaw Pact Five
	27 June	Czech intellectuals publish calls for more reform
	17 July	Warsaw Pact Five condemns reforms
	20 August	Invasion of Czechoslovakia by Warsaw Pact Five
	26 August	Brezhnev Doctrine declared
1969	**17 April**	Dubček replaced by Gustáv Husák

1956, noted how the protests in Czechoslovakia were very reminiscent of the Hungarian ones, saying 'This is how it began in Hungary.' Gomułka told Dubček he feared that if things got worse in Czechoslovakia, 'hostile elements' in Poland would rise up in sympathy, as intellectuals and students were already speaking out in support of the Czechoslovaks.

The Warsaw Pact Five (USSR, Bulgaria, GDR, Hungary and Poland) sent Dubček a letter on 17 July 1968 warning him of their concerns. Not only were they unable to stand by and watch 'hostile forces' push Czechoslovakia off the road to socialism, with the damage that would do to the community of socialist states, but they feared that the impact of the Czech reforms and protests would infect their own countries, too. This meant the events in Czechoslovakia were 'no longer only your concern', but were now the 'common concern of all Communists'.

Dubček repeatedly made the case that Czechoslovakia remained a loyal member of the Warsaw Pact, and took steps to reimpose censorship, but events were beyond his control. Huge demonstrations were dispersed by police violence; national strikes were called. The Warsaw Pact Five ran out of patience with Dubček's inability to restore control. On 20 August 1968, 120,000 Soviet troops, plus 80,000 from several Warsaw Pact countries (including Poland, Hungary, and the GDR), invaded Czechoslovakia and suppressed the uprising. The invasion was a great shock, not least to Dubček, who said, 'I, who have devoted my whole life to cooperation with the Soviet Union, now they do this to me! This is the tragedy of my life!'

Fig. 3 *Czech students in Prague, 1968. The banner reads 'Never Again with the Soviet Union', mocking a Communist Party slogan 'Forever with the Soviet Union'*

Martial law was declared and, in August, the Moscow Agreement required the Czechoslovak government to 'normalise' the situation, which meant reversing the reforms and agreeing to Soviet troops remaining in Czechoslovakia. Each step in reversing the political and economic reforms was met by demonstrations, now including workers. The Soviet leadership was furious with the slow pace of 'normalisation', and Brezhnev told Dubček that the Czechoslovaks should 'learn to do as they were told'. The CPCz was purged of unreliable elements (reformers) and Dubček was replaced (in 1969) with Gustáv Husák.

In November 1968, Brezhnev announced what became known as the **Brezhnev Doctrine**. The argument from the USSR was that any attack on socialism had to be countered. Little open resistance was seen again in the satellite states until the 1980s.

CROSS-REFERENCE

For more about the **Brezhnev Doctrine** see Chapter 7, page 53.

SOURCE 2

From a speech by Leonid Brezhnev at the Fifth Congress of the Polish United Workers' Party on 13 November 1968:

The peoples of the socialist countries and Communist parties certainly do have and should have freedom for determining the ways of advance of their respective countries. However, none of their decisions should damage either socialism in their country or the fundamental interests of other socialist countries, and the whole working-class movement, which is working for socialism.

This means that each Communist Party is responsible not only to its own people, but also to all the socialist countries, to the entire Communist movement. Whoever forgets this, in stressing only the independence of the Communist Party, becomes one-sided. He deviates from his international duty.

SOURCE 3

From a flyer called 'The Truth for Soviet Soldiers' produced by the Czechoslovak resistance in 1968:

As the mother of three sons, I pity those Soviet boys who don't even know what country they're in, and I condemn the cold-blooded undertaking of the leadership of all the occupying armies, who have summoned these boys here to kill, rob, and take away our freedom and peace. The defenders of this shameful act have shamed the honour and memory of Yuri Gagarin, who made the name of Soviet man famous throughout the whole world. But no planet is as high as our nation's contempt and scorn, and that of the whole world, are deep. In the future not one government will admire Soviet achievements, no matter what they might be.

SOURCE 4

From a report on the Czechoslovak crisis in June 1968, written by a Slovak Communist Party member, Miloš Krn, while visiting the First Secretary of the Ukrainian Communist Party, Petro Shelest, in Kiev, Ukraine:

Because of the rude leadership of Novotný and his cronies, an extremely tense situation emerged in the country . Overall, living conditions in Czechoslovakia aren't all that bad nowadays, but in neighbouring countries – the FRG and Austria – the standard of living is much higher. Enemies of the party are citing this and are now exploiting every mistake committed by the previous leadership, which was installed by Khrushchev. They say to the population: you see how socialism stultifies [smothers] the development of the country. If there were no Communist Party, thousands of innocent people would not have suffered, and all of us would be much better off materially.

A LEVEL PRACTICE QUESTION

Evaluating primary sources

With reference to Sources 2, 3, and 4 and your understanding of the historical context, assess the value of these sources to an historian studying the Prague Spring of 1968.

STUDY TIP

Try to evaluate the sources in terms of the insight they offer into the Prague Spring, as part of a wider historical context. Consider the particular strengths of each source by referring to the provenance and the information it provides, but also assess its limitations in relation to the topic.

Outcomes for the states and relations with the USSR

The move to reform that followed de-Stalinisation caused major problems for the leaders in the satellite states, most of whom were deeply implicated in the Stalinist purges of the 1950s that they were now supposed to criticise. After 1968, when the USSR showed the limits of its tolerance for political reform – and that it had no respect for national borders – there was a return to the dominant 'leading' role for the Communist Party in the satellite states. Any reform would be limited to economic reform without any political changes. Popular opinion was kept broadly satisfied by a drive to raise living standards, financed by loans from the West and very cheap energy resources from the USSR.

The Soviet leadership had portrayed the uprisings as being led by counter-revolutionary, Western-influenced hostile forces within the satellite states, but was privately very relieved that the West had not intervened in what was recognised as the USSR's sphere of influence. In the satellite states and in the USSR itself, however, those who had hoped that the Prague Spring would bring about 'socialism with a human face' saw the end of their dreams of reform.

ACTIVITY

Summary

Re-read the outlines in this chapter of the uprisings in East Germany, Poland, Hungary, and Czechoslovakia. Use the information to complete a table like the following, which you could use in answering the practice question.

State and uprising	Reasons for the uprising	How was the uprising dealt with?	Outcomes of the uprising
East Germany, 1953			
Poland, 1956			
Hungary, 1956			
Czechoslovakia, 1968			

Summary

Brezhnev's doctrine accepted that the satellite states should be able to make their own path to socialism. However, this had strict limits. Any action deemed to damage socialism in their own country, or socialism as an international movement, had to be opposed by all true socialists. The brutal Soviet reaction to the risings in Hungary and Czechoslovakia was the way that the Soviet leaderships in 1956 and 1968 decided to deal with the two most serious political challenges to Soviet control, and the consequences of these decisions were very far reaching.

STUDY TIP

Consider other factors involved in each of the uprisings, and try to weigh these up against the impacts of de-Stalinisation. Your answer could identify the 'conservative' reasons behind worker strikes and riots in the GDR and Poland.

A LEVEL PRACTICE QUESTION

Khrushchev's 'De-Stalinisation was responsible for the uprisings of 1953 and 1956 in the satellite states.'

Assess the validity of this view.

5 'Real existing socialism', 1968–80

17 Political developments in the satellite states of Central Europe

The year 1968 was an important year for the satellite states, as the leadership in each one was forced to respond to the implications of the Soviet-led invasion of Czechoslovakia. The leaderships sought to improve living standards for their citizens as a means of showing them that socialism was no longer a future dream but something real and existing.

Poland and the leadership of Gierek

Food price increases in December 1970 sparked worker strikes and riots in the Polish shipyards of Gdańsk and Gdynia. Gomułka responded with repression which proved so unpopular with the Polish people that he was forced to resign.

Edward Gierek took over the leadership. Gierek had been in charge of the enquiry into the 1956 Poznań riots, concluding then that the government had lost touch with the workers. In 1970, Gierek seemed to have the answers that Gomułka lacked. He slashed food prices, increased wages, negotiated an end to the strikes, boosted press freedom, and called for a modernisation programme linked to the West, especially large loans from Western countries and imports of Western technology. These loans paid for rapid rises in living standards (socialist consumerism), but created a foreign debt of nearly $30 billion by 1980 (bigger than the USSR's foreign debt), without creating the economic framework for growth. Having raised expectations regarding living standards, Gierek's leadership found itself under intense pressure from its international creditors to make reforms that went against Communist ideas. These were unpopular, because they caused price rises for food products that had traditionally been heavily subsidised as part of the socialist state's commitment to the needs of its workers. Not only were these price rises unpopular in themselves, but their sudden imposition, without consultation or prior announcement, infuriated workers. In 1976 there were price increases of 60 per cent, which prompted massive strikes in Gdańsk and the beginnings of calls for more worker involvement in the way the PUWP was running Poland.

KEY PROFILE

Edward Gierek (1913–2001) grew up in France after the death of his father in Poland in a mining accident. He joined the French Communist Party but was deported from France, worked as a miner in Belgium, and fought in the resistance during the war. He returned to Poland after the war and worked his way up through the PUWP. He became a popular regional governor and was elected because of his popularity and reformist credentials. Gierek was the first leader of the Eastern bloc who had not been trained in the Soviet Union.

LEARNING OBJECTIVES

In this chapter you will learn about:

- Poland and the leadership of Gierek
- Czechoslovakia and the leadership of Husák
- Hungary and the leadership of Kádár
- the GDR and the leadership of Honecker
- policy changes and the extent of reform.

KEY CHRONOLOGY

1956	János Kádár seeks Soviet assistance to suppress the Hungarian Revolution
1969	Gustáv Husák takes control in Czechoslovakia
1970	Gomułka is replaced by Edward Gierek in Poland
1971	Erich Honecker becomes leader in the GDR
1972	East and West Germany sign the 'Basic Treaty'

CROSS-REFERENCE

Socialist consumerism is discussed in Chapter 6, page 48.

Fig. 1 *The 'Lenin' shipyard in Gdańsk in 1972. This enormous shipyard is now known as 'the crucible of modern Europe' as it was here that strike demands grew into the formation of a political pressure group that went on to break the PUWP's monopoly on political power – Solidarity*

At the same time, an upsurge in workers' demands for real representation through trade unions coincided with the election of Karol Wojtyła as Pope John Paul II, the first ever Polish pope, rousing Poles' religious and national identity.

Policy changes and the extent of reform

Gierek came to power promising to improve the 'material situation' of Polish workers and their families, and did more than any other satellite state leader to open his country up to Western investment and Western products – economic reforms with a social purpose. There were also reforms to reduce corruption within the *nomenklatura* which, together with the considerable improvement in living conditions in the first years of his rule, made him a very popular leader. However, his reforms proved to be superficial because he did not use Western investment to reform the centralised Polish economy; in fact, reforms increased that centralisation (with more emphasis on heavy industry at a time of falling demand and increasing global competition in this sector) and failed to improve Poland's inefficient agricultural sector. Anti-corruption policies proved hollow.

ACTIVITY

Pair discussion

Gierek later justified his leadership by saying that no Polish worker had ever been shot under his rule. Was this a significant achievement in its historical context?

Czechoslovakia and the leadership of Husák

The slow pace of Dubček's 'normalisation' programme led to an ultimatum from Brezhnev – bring back censorship, stop any further discussions about the Party sharing power, restore order, or expect another invasion. This was enough to prompt the Party into demoting Dubček and replacing him with **Gustáv Husák** in April 1969. Although a victim of the earlier Party purges himself, Husák showed no hesitation in implementing a crackdown on dissent. Over the next few years, the CPCz was purged of hundreds of thousands of reformers, censorship was reimposed, the surveillance powers of the Czechoslovak secret police (the StB) increased, travel was restricted, and the planned economy reintroduced. These were not purges that led to imprisonment, but to expulsion from Party membership – Dubček himself was expelled in 1970.

Husák proved to be an effective manager who kept Czechoslovakia out of foreign debt while maintaining reasonable prosperity within his country. Czechoslovaks had more money to spend as they wished, and the State offset lower wages than in the West with social benefits (full employment, free healthcare, guaranteed pensions, and holidays subsidised by the State). But Husák was also inflexible, defensive, dogmatic, and resistant to change. Having experienced Soviet intervention in 1968, he stuck firmly to the idea of control through the Party. His leadership of Czechoslovakia stayed away from involvement with the West and Western investment, but did not introduce real economic reform either, coasting instead on the back of cheap energy from the USSR.

KEY PROFILE

Dr Gustáv Husák (1913–91) was born in what is now Slovakia and joined the Communist Party in his twenties. He was an organiser of the Slovak national rising against the Nazis in 1944. He was suspected of trying to establish a Slovak republic and was put in prison until 1960. Rehabilitated as part of Czechoslovak de-Stalinisation, he rose to be leader of the Slovak Communist Party and then, following Dubček's removal after the Prague Spring, to be First Secretary of the CPCz.

Policy changes and the extent of reform

Husák's commitment to 'normalising' Czechoslovakia was a significant policy change compared to the liberalisation promised by the Prague Spring, and actually marked a return to post-war Sovietisation. Rising living standards were coupled with less obvious everyday repression. Political reform was almost completely stifled and the activity of the StB against suspected political opponents was intensified. Husák grew increasingly reluctant to share power within the Party outside of his small leadership team. Like Brezhnev's regime in the USSR, Czechoslovakia under Husák stagnated (like Brezhnev's gerontocracy, his leadership team changed little over the years).

Apart from the active political agenda for squashing the dissident 'parallel culture' that began to emerge in the years after the Prague Spring, one other area did see further political development amidst Husák's otherwise deeply conservative rule – increased political power for Slovakia

Fig. 2 *Gustáv Husák visiting a poultry farm in 1972*

as part of a **federal** Czechoslovakia. Discontent over Prague's dominance in the country and the disproportionate amount of investment going to the Czechs led to Czechoslovakia being declared two 'equal fraternal nations': the Slovak Socialist Republic and the Czech Socialist Republic in October 1968. This reform had been one of the demands of the Prague Spring.

Hungary and the leadership of Kádár

János Kádár left Nagy's leadership on 3 November 1956 to set up a pro-USSR government in opposition to Nagy's liberal reforms. The Revolution was followed by a period of harsh repression during which 20,000 Hungarians were arrested and 2000 executed. It was dangerous to have any links to the Revolution – in fact, people were sacked from their jobs for even calling it a revolution: it was officially a counter-revolution.

Kádár then sought to bring the country and Party back together, reversing Rákosi's old statement that 'he who is not with us is against us' to 'he who is not against us is with us' (1962). Soviet troops were confined to their barracks; political prisoners began to be released. From being despised as the USSR's puppet leader in 1956, Kádár's 'New Economic Mechanism' reforms of 1968 meant most Hungarians saw him as 'better than most' leaders. He took a centrist position between hard-liners and a remnant of liberals in the Party: for example, economic reforms alongside the promotion of collectivisation. He was able to put Hungary on its own road to socialism, although it remained a country where open criticism of the USSR was strictly forbidden. These reforms went the furthest of the four satellite states under consideration in this book, and included more tolerance of opinions that competed with the Party line. The Party itself was seen as having a 'serving' rather than a 'leading' role. One important development happened in 1971, when electoral reform allowed more than one candidate to stand in most constituencies. Like Gierek, Kádár used foreign loans to subsidise living standards in Hungary, leaving Hungary with a national debt of $8 billion in the early 1980s that had grown to $15 billion by 1986.

ACTIVITY

Make a horizontal timeline to compare political developments in Czechoslovakia with those in Poland for the same period of 1968–80. Place events in one country above, and one below, the line.

KEY TERM

federal: relating to a system of government in which several states form a unity but remain independent in internal affairs; Czechoslovakia became a federation, comprising Slovakia and the Czech Republic, in October 1968

CROSS-REFERENCE

Read about the context of Kádár's rise to power in Chapter 13, page 110.

CROSS-REFERENCE

Contested elections in Hungary are discussed in Chapter 19, page 159.

ACTIVITY

Hungary and Poland both saw political change following popular uprisings. Draw a chart to identify and account for the similarities and differences in the way their respective leaderships reimposed control and then introduced reform.

Fig. 3 *General Secretary János Kádár addresses the Hungarian parliament in 1980. The men in the row behind him held senior positions in the Hungarian Socialist Workers' Party*

ACTIVITY

Select some memorable images of each leader mentioned in this chapter to create a display.

Policy changes and the extent of reform

Although the leader of the Soviet-backed 'counter-revolution', Kádár's initial return to repression and purges did not continue: his leadership did not mark a return to Stalinist policies, and he accepted that non-communists should not necessarily be excluded from involvement in politics. His economic reforms meant considerably-increased living standards, and some political liberalisation occurred alongside them, meaning that, by 1980, Hungary was significantly more liberal than the other satellite states. Without a formal secret police, human rights were under less pressure, there was greater tolerance of *samizdat* publication, and travel was less restricted than in other satellite states. Hungary remained, however, effectively a single-Party state, as the other parties and election candidates under the National Assembly followed the lead of the Hungarian Socialist Workers' Party and approved all its decisions.

KEY PROFILE

Erich Honecker (1912–94) had been an active communist in his youth and was imprisoned in a concentration camp between 1935 and 1945. After liberation, he became chairman of the Free German Youth in the Soviet zone. He rose in office and joined the GDR Politburo in 1956. He initiated the overthrow of Ulbricht and replaced him as leader from 1971, becoming head of state in 1976. In 1989, he lost office and fled to the USSR in 1990. He was returned for trial in Germany, but was spared due to ill health.

The GDR and the leadership of Honecker

Erich Honecker succeeded Walter Ulbricht in 1971. Honecker's arrival marked a revival in East Germany 's political and economic fortunes. Consumer goods became more widely available, services improved, and life became a little easier. 'Real existing socialism' seemed for a short while to be beginning to work, although the State remained structurally unsound – living on Western loans, yet dependent on the USSR.

Fig. 4 *Erich Honecker greets Leonid Brezhnev with a fraternal kiss in 1979, at a celebration for the thirtieth anniversary of the GDR*

Border protection after 1961, coupled with the FRG's new policy of **Ostpolitik**, which gave the GDR both much-needed cash and international recognition, encouraged Honecker to press ahead with a generous package of welfare reforms and an increase in consumer goods such as cars, fridges, and televisions. In March 1978, Honecker came to an agreement with the Lutheran Church allowing discussion meetings on church premises. These meetings became important for dissidents within the GDR.

Policy changes and the extent of reform

The introduction of 'consumer socialism' and the increasing normalisation of international relations through Ostpolitik were successful reforms, with East Germany playing a role in the Helsinki Conference on Security and Co-operation in Europe in 1975 that led to the Helsinki Final Accords. However, for the people of the GDR, improved living standards were, politically speaking, a cosmetic reform only. Nothing had changed with regards to the power relationships in the state. The developments in the 1960s and 1970s contradicted any idea of a move towards more political freedom. The Berlin Wall, the policy of opening fire on East Germans trying to escape, the border guards, Soviet troops, the people's police (Vopo), the workers' militia groups, and, above all, the Stasi (which grew greatly in size during the 1970s and 1980s), all made it clear that the State relied heavily on repression.

The SED continued to dominate and whether through fear, political apathy, or support, the mass of the populace consented in that rule. This outward conformity bred self-confidence among Honecker's leadership so that when Mikhail Gorbachev took over leadership of the USSR in 1985 and began spreading ideas of *perestroika* and *glasnost*, the GDR establishment showed no signs of following suit.

A LEVEL PRACTICE QUESTION

'1968 was a turning point for the leadership of the satellite states of Eastern Europe.' Assess the validity of this view.

SOURCE 1

From János Kádár's report of the Central Committee to the Tenth Congress of the Hungarian Socialist Workers' Party, November 1970:

The State has an important role in building socialism. We do not accept views which question the role of the socialist state, underestimate its significance and, by weakening state power, in fact jeopardise the achievements of the people. Both our domestic tasks and international conditions demand that the socialist state be strengthened, that its role as an economic organiser and cultural educator be increased and that the work of state administration be improved and its standards raised. At the same time efforts must be made to draw in ever larger numbers of the population to take part in public life, in the work of state bodies and councils and in the work of other state organisations. The further development of state life, of socialist democracy, is a task which, if successfully solved, will give added impetus to our continued progress.

SOURCE 2

From a memoir by Milan Šimečka, a Czech academic, published in 1984. Milan Šimečka was a member of the Communist Party who had written articles in support of the Prague Spring and was expelled from the Party after being summoned before the Party District Commission in 1969:

I presented myself at a room where some fifteen gloomy and unfriendly men were already seated. I knew none of them, and none of them knew me,

A CLOSER LOOK

Ostpolitik

Ostpolitik was a West German policy that sought German reunification through the gradual improvement of relations between West and East Germany. This included trade deals between the two states, and also the formal recognition of the GDR's borders and existence as a sovereign state in the 1972 Basic Treaty.

ACTIVITY

Compare the different ways in which each of the four satellite states financed the move towards 'consumer socialism'. Which do you think was the most sustainable, and which the least?

STUDY TIP

Although this chapter begins by suggesting that 1968 was an important year, you will need to consider whether it justifies being called a 'turning point'. In your answer try to explore the extent to which the statement is true for the four different satellite states that you have studied. The summary chart on page 144 would be useful as a starting point.

apparently. They handed me several pages of pointedly-chosen quotations from my articles and papers. In glancing through the pages I immediately realised that nothing had been forged, everything was just as I had written it. And that was precisely the question they asked. I replied that the sentences, which had already been taken out of context and sounded so incredible to their ears, were indeed my own work. I realised that it was pointless to say any more, they liked me as little as I did them. What was there left to talk about? On my way out, I gave in my Party card to the secretary in the outer office.

SOURCE 3

From a book of interviews with people born in the GDR in or after 1961 (the year the Berlin Wall went up).

School was the most difficult time in Katharina's life. 'The teachers who supported the Party tended to be the worst,' Katharina recalls. 'They hated religion and projected that hatred onto me.' When Katharina failed to give the correct answer to a question, those teachers would humiliate her, asking in a mocking tone, 'Where is your God then?' Katharina believes she was also given worse marks and school reports as a result of her Christianity. And on one notable occasion, when the young Katharina refused to take off her crucifix in class, the school called in uniformed Stasi officers to reprimand her. 'I was treated like I was a serious criminal', she recalls.

STUDY TIP

In an A Level exam you will be asked to assess the value of three sources, but this question asks you to assess two. Key questions to consider about the sources:

- Who said/wrote the source?
- When was the source written/presented/said, and when was it written down or recorded?
- To whom was the source presented? Who was the intended audience?
- What tone and emphasis is adopted in the source?
- What is the content and argument of the source?
- How does the source fit with your own knowledge of this time?

A LEVEL PRACTICE QUESTION

Evaluating primary sources

With reference to Sources 1 and 2 and your understanding of the historical context, assess the value of these three sources to an historian studying changes in policy in the satellite states after 1968.

ACTIVITY

Summary: policy changes and the extent of reform

Use the information in this chapter and in Chapter 16, together with additional research, to compile a review of the changes in policy after 1968 and the extent of reform in Poland, Hungary, the GDR, and Czechoslovakia. A table like the following could help with this.

State and leader	What key problems did the new leader face?	To what extent did policy change to tackle the problems?	How far had the political system been reformed before 1968?	To what extent was there political reform after 1968?
Poland and Gierek				
Hungary and Kádár				
GDR and Honecker				
Czechoslovakia and Husák				

18 Economic and social developments in the Soviet satellite states

Economic reforms

Economic reforms in Poland

Gomułka's reforms had contained many of the 'free market' elements of decentralisation, small-scale private business, and consumer focus seen in the later economic reforms of the GDR and Hungary. But the social stability that these reforms and Gomułka's leadership had brought then broke down again in December 1970, after economic problems forced a 36 per cent food price rise.

Gierek's economic policy used loans from the West to pump more investment into industry and agriculture. The increase in investment was substantial (50 per cent more than before 1970) and much of it went on raising wages in the hope that higher wages would encourage harder work and therefore higher productivity. Higher consumption resulted (people spent more) and what they bought was largely products imported from the West. By 1974, half of Poland's trade was with the West.

The initial result was an economic boom, but the growth was not sustainable.

- Instead of investment being used to upgrade and expand Polish infrastructure, industry, and agriculture, much of it was funnelled into high-prestige, large-scale projects, such as the huge Katowice Steelworks, which took four years to come into production.
- Gierek's technical specialists came from the powerful and corrupt industrial lobbies that, like the 'steel eaters' of the USSR, blocked plans to invest in other parts of the economy and then swallowed up vast amounts of money with very little to show for it.
- Increasing wages caused inflation and the surge in purchases of Western imports caused problems with the **balance of trade** – imports exceeded exports throughout the 1970s.
- Most serious of all was the build-up of foreign debt. By 1979, over 90 per cent of what Poland earned from its exports was being used to pay the interest on its foreign loans.

Gierek did recognise the problems that were building up. Keeping food prices artificially low was a huge drain on the government's finances. In 1976, an enormous price rise (60 per cent) took place. Despite higher wages, the price increase was, again, met by strikes and unrest. Gierek turned first to police repression, but then quickly cancelled the price rises and granted an amnesty to all those arrested in the unrest.

By the end of the 1970s, Western banks had finally realised how insecure their Polish investments were. Interest rates rose and the conditions under which new loans could be made, and for paying interest on existing loans, tightened. By the early 1980s, Poland could no longer pay its debts.

The social and political implications of Gierek's incompetent economic management were very serious. There were large-scale cutbacks in healthcare and house building – a housing crisis resulted. At the same time, Poles saw that the *nomenklatura* were still living privileged lives, despite the country's humiliating debt problems. The legitimacy of Gierek's leadership and the PUWP was undermined and people looked to other leaders for help.

Economic reforms in Czechoslovakia

The Prague Spring followed directly from Dubček's economic reforms. Therefore, dismantling these reforms and reimposing centralised control was a key aim of normalisation under Husák. Obligatory targets of central planning were reintroduced in 1969, price reform was squashed, and any future price increases vetoed.

LEARNING OBJECTIVES

In this chapter you will learn about:

- economic reforms
- economic strengths and weaknesses
- the influence of the West, economically and socially.

KEY CHRONOLOGY

1968 New Economic Mechanism begins in Hungary

1973 OPEC embargo on oil production raises the global price of oil

1979 A second oil crisis, following the Iranian Revolution of February 1979

KEY TERM

balance of trade: the difference in value between a country's exports and its imports

ACTIVITY

Make a chart to show the strengths and weaknesses of Poland's economic reforms.

Fig. 1 *Skoda car workers in 1976. At this time, the factory was suffering as its technology lagged further and further behind the West*

Once the purges were completed, Husák then focused on improving the efficiency of central planning, driving up quality to improve exports, and effective investment (for example, in engineering and the chemical industry), in order to ensure Czechoslovak workers were relatively well paid and did not experience shortages. This strategy worked well in the first half of the 1970s, with good economic growth (5.7 per cent between 1971 and 1975), higher wages, and a wider range of consumer goods in the shops. Agriculture improved too, so that by 1975, the country was almost self-sufficient for key food products.

The period 1976 to 1980 was more difficult. Poor weather conditions meant that agricultural production faltered and big grain imports were needed. Problems in the global economy after the oil crisis of 1973 hit Czechoslovak exports very badly, and the USSR, which supplied Czechoslovakia with fuel and raw materials for its industries, raised its prices. The government responded by putting a larger share of its production into export, but that meant fewer products for the domestic market, causing shortages in shops. Imports from Western countries were also reduced, which starved industries of raw materials and shops of Western products. Prices rose higher than wages, causing people to buy less.

The next Five Year Plan period, from 1981, saw the low-key reintroduction of elements of Dubček's reforms – some decentralisation to enterprise management, but without any reduction in the level of central planned control. The reforms coincided with a modest improvement in the Czechoslovak economy in the early 1980s, but did not address some basic problems of outdated technology, low worker productivity, and inefficient production techniques in both industry and agriculture.

ACTIVITY

Make a chart to show the strengths and weaknesses of Czechoslovakia's economic reforms.

KEY TERM

goulash: a traditional Hungarian stew that mixes meat and vegetables; 'goulash communism' describes a uniquely Hungarian mix of socialist and capitalist 'ingredients'

Economic reforms in Hungary

Hungary's economic reforms earned the nickname '**goulash** communism', though their official name was the New Economic Mechanism. They were launched on 1 January 1968. Brezhnev approved the reforms, against opposition from some in his Politburo, in return for Hungary's loyalty to the Warsaw Pact – Hungarian troops took part in the repression of the Prague Spring.

Key elements of the reforms included:

- decentralisation to enterprises
- prices adjusted to match equivalent world market prices
- promotion of consumer industries rather than heavy industry
- encouragement of private farms
- small businesses (e.g. newspaper kiosks) allowed to set prices and keep profits
- substantial increase in imports of Western consumer goods
- Hungary becoming more open to the West in general: for example, a Hilton hotel opened in Budapest in 1976.

Economic growth rose to an impressive 6 per cent in 1969 and trade with other countries increased by 14 per cent. Unfortunately, the global oil crisis in 1973 hit the Hungarian economy very hard, due to its reliance on imports. The USSR took the opportunity of higher Middle Eastern oil prices to raise its oil prices too, even for its satellite state clients. Kádár's government responded in two ways: by restoring direct governmental control on the country's biggest industries and by subsidising prices to ensure they stayed low for consumers – financing the latter with loans from the West.

ACTIVITY

How was the role of enterprise different under the New Economic Mechanism from under the old centrally planned system?

SOURCE 1

From a speech by János Kádár to the Seventh Congress of the Patriotic People's Front in March 1981:

I do not like to use the expression that we should work more. I would rather say that we have to work more efficiently and more rationally. Here the reserves are still very large. In the initial period of laying the foundations of socialism and of building socialism we were preoccupied with ensuring we had what we needed and nobody counted how much it cost. That period is behind us. It continues to be important to have what is necessary at our disposal, but now how much it costs also counts, how much labour, material and energy is needed for it and of what quality it is. If for no other reason, quality is of great significance because we have to trade with practically the whole world. It is obvious that nobody is going to accept goods of bad quality from us to do us a favour. The capitalist firms sometimes hardly accept even goods of good quality.

Fig. 2 *Customers in a hairdresser's in Debrecen, Hungary, in 1971. Private firms were encouraged under Kádár's reforms, but state-run enterprises continued, too*

SOURCE 2

From a Radio Free Europe research report of 18 March 1975. The report featured highlights from Kádár's opening speech to the Eleventh Congress of the Hungarian Socialist Workers' Party:

Kádár frankly stated that the Hungarian economy would have to work very hard to cope with worldwide inflation, and, at the same time, to achieve its plan goals. He stated that the targets of the current, fourth Five Year Plan would be met, but would require the mobilisation of all forces. It is interesting to note that he did not speak about any overfulfilment of the original plan targets. He promised to continue the party's cooperative and agrarian policies. He emphasised that, because of the deterioration of the terms of trade with Western countries, the national economy must do its utmost to remain competitive. "We cannot make international economic life responsible for the shortcomings of our own economic activity." The State, he said, should not hesitate to exercise its right of control or to give instructions whenever necessary.

ACTIVITY

Make a chart to show the strengths and weaknesses of Hungary's economic reforms.

SOURCE 3

From a report called 'Economic Performance Under Kádár: Miracle or Myth' by Cam Hudson. The report was written for Radio Free Europe's background report series, 25 May 1982:

It is evident that the widespread "image" of Hungary as a prosperous and rapidly growing economy during the "reform era" of the 1970s is difficult to confirm. Official statistics indicate that throughout the 1970s Hungary had one of the slowest growing economies of the region [and]in 1976–1980 Hungary's growth rates dropped more rapidly than elsewhere, giving it the second lowest growth rate in the region after Poland. National Net Material Product (the closest equivalent to GNP) increased over the 1976–1978 period, but this was followed by three successive years of decline. At the end of 1981 Hungary's net debt to Western banks and governments is estimated to have amounted to 7,800 million dollars, giving Hungary the highest per capita debt of all CMEA (Comecon) member countries.

CROSS-REFERENCE

Comecon is discussed in Chapter 13, pages 104–05.

A LEVEL PRACTICE QUESTION

Evaluating primary sources

With reference to Sources 1, 2, and 3 and your understanding of the historical context, assess the value of these three sources to an historian studying economic reform in Hungary under Kádár.

STUDY TIP

An interesting aspect of all three sources is their reference to external factors – the global downturn following the oil crises during this period. Try to demonstrate an awareness of context when answering this question.

Economic reforms in the GDR

Honecker's main economic reform was called 'The Unity of Social and Economic Policy'. Its aim was to increase production enough to finance an ambitious home-building programme and social reform. The initiative combined central planning, to ensure the overall direction of the economy, with a more flexible decision-making process at a local level.

Honecker nationalised all remaining independent firms in 1972, leaving only a very few craft activities in private hands, and introduced a higher degree of specialisation in both agriculture and industry. In industry, the VEBs of the post-war era were replaced by combines which linked technological research, production, and market research to make for more efficient production. In farming, collectives concentrated on either crops or animals, and 'cooperation councils' were established to coordinate the work of individual farms with their district administrators.

By the 1970s, nearly a third of the GDR's trade was with the developed economies of Western Europe. Thanks to the West German **Ostpolitik policy**, trade barriers between the two Germanys had been dismantled. This meant that the GDR effectively became an 'extra member' of the EEC. The GDR was able to obtain West German credit to cover trade deficits, and if there was a hold-up in supplies from Eastern Europe, it could turn to the FRG instead. With loans from the FRG provided on easy terms, the GDR was far better able to cope with the economic problems of the 1970s and 1980s than its Eastern European neighbours.

Overall, the GDR economy was relatively successful – at least in comparison with those of other Eastern bloc countries. East Germany achieved a high degree of agricultural self-sufficiency, needing only to import grain and animal feed, and the Honecker years saw big advances in consumer production and, in the 1980s, in microelectronics, electrical engineering, and

A CLOSER LOOK

VEBs (*Volkseigene Betriebe*)

After the war, the SED nationalised Nazi-owned industries and named them 'People's Enterprises' (VEBs). Over 75 per cent of industries were VEBs, although some of the biggest and most important were turned over entirely to production for reparations: everything they made went straight to the USSR as compensation for the damage done by Germany in the war. These were called SAGs.

CROSS-REFERENCE

Read about the West Germany Ostpolitik policy in Chapter 17, page 143.

computer production. The chemical industry and vehicle manufacture also grew, and there were attempts to develop nuclear energy. The East Germans enjoyed the highest standard of living in the Eastern bloc, and ownership of fridges, TVs, and cars continued to grow.

A CLOSER LOOK

The European Economic Community (EEC)

The EEC was created in 1957 by West Germany, Italy, France, the Netherlands, Luxemburg, and Belgium. By strengthening economic links between European countries it was hoped that another European war would be less likely. By 1968, trade tariffs between member countries had been removed, there was a common policy on agriculture that protected EEC members from cheap foreign competition, and there was a common external trade policy. Trade between member countries boomed.

However, it was not all rosy. The GDR's reliance on foreign trade made it particularly sensitive to the oil price rise in 1973 and, during 1972 to 1975, while import prices rose by 34 per cent, export values rose by only 17 per cent. The GDR was forced to import oil, coal, and gas from the USSR at unfavourable rates. The costs of welfare provision also proved a drag on the economy. They amounted to twice the rise in the national income between 1971 and 1979. By the early 1980s, the GDR's economy was almost totally dependent on loans from the FRG, although Honecker refused to face up to this reality.

Economic strengths and weaknesses

Lying behind these economic reforms was the fundamental weakness of the central planning system. Economic growth through the central planning system relied on pulling in more inputs each year and turning them into more 'stuff'. A key input was labour: pulling people off the land and putting them to work in industry. Once the supplies of inputs started to dwindle, so too did economic growth. Reformers could attempt to improve the effectiveness of central planning, but the deterrents to productivity within the system itself were too great for this to have any real effect.

There were also external challenges. The developments driving growth in Western economies in the 1970s were no longer the mass labour production lines of heavy industry, but consumer and service industries that innovated rapidly in response to competition for customers. The central planning system had no way of copying this. For example, in the 1970s, there were only 16 kinds of shoe made in Hungary. In Poland, during the 1970s, no hairpins were made, having been left out of the plan by mistake.

The reasons why the satellite states were able to carry on *despite* central planning included:

- loans from the West – Western banks needed new markets to invest in; by the early 1980s, Eastern Europe owed the West nearly $70 billion
- imports of Western technology – this enabled satellite states to improve their manufacturing and agricultural productivity without needing to innovate themselves
- economic reforms that, bit by bit, introduced elements of the market economy: decentralisation – so enterprises had more of a say in what they produced, were able to keep some of the profits from what they produced, and so on.

ACTIVITY

Make a chart to show the strengths and weaknesses of East Germany's economic reforms.

The influence of the West, economically and socially

- Loans from Western banks to governments of the satellite states allowed governments like Poland's to 'bribe' their populations with higher wages.
- Imports of Western technology allowed satellite state governments to modernise manufacturing.
- Western imports provided people in satellite states with a wider range of consumer goods and gave governments access to grain and industrial raw materials.
- Trade with the West meant that satellite states could earn foreign currency with their exports.

When economic conditions worsened in the late 1970s, the influence of the West became critically important, as debts were called in and credit conditions tightened.

Socially, the influence of the West was also very strong. Socialism was defined in opposition to Western capitalism, so that people in the satellite states were taught that the West was a miserable place to live, with extreme poverty alongside fabulous wealth, its society stricken by class conflict, crime, racism, drugs, prostitution. Any contact with the West, whether personal or through TV or radio broadcasts, inevitably challenged this picture, which in turn had the potential to make people cynical about Party propaganda.

The West had social influence in other ways. Access to Western culture through cultural exchange visits, media broadcasts, and imports (both legal and black market) allowed people, especially young people, to express a degree of non-conformity. These cultural exchanges happened across the satellite states; the following examples were not restricted to individual states therefore.

ACTIVITY

Research

Research Western fashions in the early 1980s. To what extent were the teen fashions shown in Figures 3 and 4 influenced by the West?

Fig. 3 *A Czechoslovak dance class in 1981*

Rock music in Poland

Rock music was very popular in Poland in the late 1970s and 1980s, and thousands of young people travelled across Poland to attend rock festivals. The groups were usually Polish, but were heavily influenced by Western rock, punk, and reggae, heard on Radio Free Europe or on records smuggled into the country. Lyrics often reflected young people's frustration and disenchantment, and allowed them to express their defiance of the system which, some historians feel, contributed greatly to the creation of a rebellious attitude towards authority in Poland. The PUWP was concerned about Western influence on young people, which went against official youth policies, but tended to see rock concerts as a way for Polish youth to let off steam: a distraction from getting involved in actual protest.

Czechoslovakia and Western influence: environmental movement

The environmental movement became popular in Czechoslovakia from the 1970s, especially among students and particularly, in its earliest days, in Slovakia, as criticism of heavy industry and central planning was not as directly confrontational with the Party as demands over human rights or political participation. Although concerns for protection of the natural environment had a long history, they became more mainstream in the twentieth century with the publication in the USA of Rachel Carson's *Silent Spring* (1962), which identified the link between pollution and environmental damage.

Hungary and Western fashion

In Hungary, as was the case across the satellite states, socialist ideology considered fashion, especially women's fashion, to be a bourgeois affectation that was wasteful of resources. Wearing Western clothes or making clothes based on Western fashions was a statement of individualism. A centrally planned economy ensured that only a very small range of clothes was available, making it easier to plan and promote a collective society. When occupations had regulation dress codes, women would often modify them to make them fit better, or wore more fashionable clothes underneath official coats or uniforms. Young men also often dressed fashionably, making them a target for police attention. There was a concerted effort by the authorities to develop socialist fashion, as part of socialist consumerism, to counter Western influences. This had only limited success.

Fig. 4 *East German punks in 1982*

The GDR and Western television

From the 1960s, around 80 per cent of GDR households were able to receive a TV signal from West Germany. Research suggests that many households watched more West German TV than the West Germans did. Although the leadership tried hard, through propaganda, to dissuade GDR citizens from watching Western TV, this failed completely and, by 1973, Honecker publically announced that people could watch and listen to whatever they chose. Propaganda then shifted towards both scheduling programmes on GDR TV that directly criticised Western TV shows or sought to expose the truth about life in the West, and to importing programming ideas so that by the 1980s, GDR TV looked more like Western TV. The difficulty for Honecker's leadership was that access to Western TV brought not only Western entertainment shows and films, but also news and information that was at odds with the claims made by state propaganda.

A LEVEL PRACTICE QUESTION

To what extent did Western influence impact upon social values in the satellite states in the 1970s?

STUDY TIP

Consider the ways in which Western influence acted to support the leaderships in the satellite states, as well as to undermine them. For example, to what extent did Western investment and loans, exports of Western technology and consumer goods play a role in sustaining Communist Party power through the 1970s?

Summary

'Real existing socialism' after 1968 was a recognition that the painful sacrifices of 'building socialism' were no longer sustainable against growing popular discontent. The Communist Parties of the satellite states could not allow their people the political liberalisation that had begun to blossom in the Prague Spring. Economic liberalisation was only possible to a very limited degree within the confines of the planned economy. The market laws of supply and demand required flexible prices; however, fixed prices for staple food products were at the heart of what 'real existing socialism' amounted to: subsidised standards of living (cheap food, cheap accommodation), job security, free healthcare and education, established career prospects, and the new emphasis on consumer products of 'socialist consumerism.' In all this, the influence of the West was critical – as a market for exports, for imported consumer goods and technological innovation, for the loans and investments of Western banks and governments. Although socialist alternatives were developed, the individualism of Western culture (and not just in fashion or music or film) was hugely influential. Western support for human rights in the satellite states was very important in the growth of opposition to Party control.

19 Challenges to Soviet control in the Soviet satellite states

Western influence and the media

The authorities in the satellite states had concerns about the impact of Western media on cultural life because of its potential to counteract the Communist idea of society.

Fig. 1 *An East German children's TV show from 1976. This format (and the fashions) were very similar to children's TV in the West*

The major concern for authorities in the satellite states was the influence of Western media on news and information. Since socialist media promoted a single, Party-directed view on news events, the legitimacy of the Party was severely undermined by contradictory information being broadcast to citizens of the satellite states by Western media. There were three main ways in which authorities attempted to reduce this influence:

- When possible, Western broadcast signals were jammed, but this was not possible all the time or in all areas. The **Helsinki Accords** specifically targeted this attempt to hinder communication between West and East.
- Popular shows were scheduled to coincide with influential Western programmes (at this time, the ability to record programmes was limited or non-existent).
- The legitimacy of the Western media was attacked as propaganda that attempted to deceive citizens of the satellite states.

These attempts had no significant impact, and there are numerous accounts of people turning to Western media sources for more accurate information about current events in their countries. A key source of information was Radio Free Europe (RFE).

LEARNING OBJECTIVES

In this chapter you will learn about:

- Western influence and the media
- the impact of the Helsinki Accords
- political activism, including Charter 77 and KOR (Czechoslovakia and Poland); church organisations (Poland and the GDR); contested elections (Hungary).

KEY CHRONOLOGY

1975	Helsinki Final Act signed
1976	KOR formed in response to repression of Polish strikes and unrest
1977 Oct	members of the Czechoslovak dissident group, Charter 77, imprisoned
1978	Karol Wojtyła, Archibishop of Kraków, elected Pope
1979 June	Pope John Paul II returns to Poland

CROSS-REFERENCE

Government concerns about the impact of Western media in the satellite states are discussed in Chapter 18.

The Helsinki Accords are discussed on pages 54 and 62.

RFE's influence on political opposition in the satellite states

Historians agree that RFE played a significant role in encouraging political opposition in the satellite states, as it was intended to do:

- Audience numbers for RFE in the GDR increased dramatically after the 1953 riots.
- Hungarians heard about the Polish uprising in Poznań in 1956 via RFE, which influenced the Hungarian Revolution.
- During the Hungarian Revolution in 1956, RFE broadcasts implied that Western support for the Revolution was coming. Although this proved to be wrong, it is thought to have encouraged many Hungarians to fight.
- As a result of the irresponsible broadcasting by RFE's Hungarian service in 1956, major changes were implemented to ensure that information was more accurate and impartial.
- RFE broadcast news of the Warsaw Pact Five's **invasion of Czechoslovakia** on 21 August 1968. When the invading soldiers reached central Prague, one of their first acts was to shut down Czechoslovak state radio. Journalists from within Czechoslovakia sent their reports to RFE to broadcast.
- The Helsinki Accords of 1975 were initially seen in the West as a victory for the USSR, but it was RFE and Radio Liberty broadcasts that told citizens of the USSR and satellite states that their leaders had signed up to agreements guaranteeing a number of human rights, prompting the formation of Helsinki Watch organisations which, in turn, sent their reports to RFE.
- The rise of the **Solidarity movement** in Poland in the 1980s was extensively covered by RFE broadcasts both in Poland and throughout the satellite states.
- RFE broadcasts about the **Chernobyl nuclear disaster** were the main source of information for people in the satellite states for the two days after the accident in April 1986 when Soviet media employed a news blackout. The broadcasts gave information on how people could protect themselves and about decontamination.
- **Gorbachev's reforms** in the late 1980s were not featured in the news media of some satellite states (e.g. the GDR and Czechoslovakia); RFE provided extensive coverage.

A CLOSER LOOK

Radio Free Europe (RFE) was established in 1949 in America as an anti-communist propaganda tool. Funded by the CIA until 1972, it had its headquarters in Munich, in West Germany (since 1995 it has been based in Prague). RFE and Radio Liberty (broadcasting to the USSR) were modelled on Radio in the American Sector (RIAS). (Originally targeted at Germans living in the US sector of Berlin, RIAS was widely listened to across East Germany.) RFE was infiltrated by Eastern bloc security services and was the target of a bomb attack in 1981, which sources show was funded by Nicolae Ceauşescu, Romania's leader.

CROSS-REFERENCE

The Soviet invasion of Czechoslovakia is covered in Chapter 16.

Read more about the Solidarity movement in Chapter 20.

The Chernobyl nuclear disaster is discussed in Chapter 10.

Gorbachev's reforms feature in Chapter 9.

SOURCE 1

From a report to the Hungarian Socialist Workers' Party Central Committee on 22 May 1973. The report was about the need to strengthen the Party's fight against Western propaganda:

The decrease in the listening rate of the programmes of Radio Free Europe, and in general, Western radio broadcasts, is due – in addition to the stable political situation in Hungary – to the fact that the work of [our own] mass media is much more efficient and up-to-date, and the level of providing information for the people has improved significantly. However, the viewing and listening rate to hostile radio stations and television programmes that can be received easily in the Western and southern parts of the country may temporarily increase in relation to some domestic or international events that are ignored by the national mass media for some reason, or to which their reaction is subdued and tardy.

SOURCE 2

From Ministry of the Interior report for the PUWP on the Polish-language broadcasts of Western radio stations Radio Free Europe, BBC World Service, Deutsche Wells, Deutschlandfunk, and Radio Vatican in January 1976:

In general, analysis of the propaganda of all the broadcasting stations indicates the following:

a. A clear increase in propaganda aimed at casting doubt on the existence of basic citizens' rights, and the functioning of democratic mechanisms in Poland and the Soviet Union.
b. An increase in the tendency to exploit alleged discontent with the policies of the authorities regarding the freedom of citizens in Poland and the Soviet Union and attempts to grant them the rank of a political opposition.
c. Exaggerating the temporary economic difficulties in Poland and the Soviet Union and using them to criticise the socialist system and the socio-economic policies of the Party and government in those countries.
d. Criticising Soviet policies in relation to other socialist countries, West European Communist and workers' parties, and capitalist countries.

SOURCE 3

From a report made by Colonel Kovach, Interior Minister of Czechoslovakia, on 23 April 1980, to a meeting of counter-intelligence operatives from the satellite states and the USSR about hostile actions by Western countries, including Western radio broadcasting:

The enemy's special bureaus and its centres for ideological sabotage use different kinds of committees and groups to organise many anti-Czechoslovak and anti-Soviet provocations in the capitalist countries, such as protest rallies in front of the buildings of our country's official representation agencies, different demonstrations, and so on, or else provisions are made for publishing anti-socialist lampoons, using for this such subversive publications as "Index" and "Dialogue" in the German Federal Republic, "Confrontation" in Switzerland, and other similar ones, acting closely with the radio stations Free Europe, Liberty, BBC, the Voice of America.

We will give special attention to churches, church organisations, and religious fanatics and their contact with the Vatican to avoid national politics being disturbed with respect to the church, and so that a tie is not formed between the reactionary clergy and the anti-socialist groups in the republic.

ACTIVITY

Read Sources 1, 2, and 3.

1. Identify at least three different ways in which Western media influenced people in the Soviet satellite states.
2. Outline the difficulties that access to Western media posed for governments in the satellite states.

A LEVEL PRACTICE QUESTION

Evaluating primary sources

With reference to Sources 1, 2, and 3 and your understanding of the historical context, assess the value of these sources to an historian studying Western media influences on the satellite states.

STUDY TIP

When evaluating three sources, try to comment in equal depth on all three rather than focusing on just one or two. This relates to your evaluation of provenance and content and context: try to give approximately equal attention to each for all the sources, but this evaluation also needs to be convincing, not vague or generalised.

The impact of the Helsinki Accords

The Helsinki Accords were initially seen in the West as a diplomatic triumph for the Soviet Union, which obtained the long-sought international recognition of the borders of its European satellites. However, since 1989, historians have recognised the signing of the Helsinki Final Act on 1 August 1975 as a turning point in the history of Eastern Europe because of the impetus it gave to dissident movements.

The Helsinki Final Act, the result of the Conference on Security and Co-operation in Europe, had four main outcomes:

CROSS-REFERENCE

See Chapters 7 and 8, pages 54 and 62 for more on the Helsinki Final Act.

ACTIVITY

Read points 3 and 4 in the text about the Helsinki Final Act; they quote what the Act said about human rights and the freedom of the individual.

1. Put both these quotes into your own words (in the 1970s, it was common for writers to use 'he' and 'his' to refer to both men and women).
2. Explain how these agreements could be related to the right for dissidents to express opposition to the Party leaderships of the satellite states.

CROSS-REFERENCE

For a discussion of **Helsinki Watch groups** in the USSR, see Chapter 7, page 62.

1. The participating states accepted the frontiers of all European states and undertook never to assault those frontiers. This was a major success for the GDR as it meant its existence as a state was now internationally recognised, and gave the USSR the recognition it craved for the borders of its European satellites.
2. The participating states undertook to refrain from any intervention (explicitly armed intervention) in the internal or external affairs of another participating state, regardless of any pacts or agreements between them. This was designed to prevent another intervention like that of Czechoslovakia in 1968.
3. The participating states undertook to 'respect human rights and fundamental freedoms, including the freedom of thought, conscience, religion or belief, for all without distinction as to race, sex, language, or religion.'
4. As part of this, the participating states agreed to recognise and respect the freedom of the individual 'to profess and practise, alone or in community with others, religion or belief acting in accordance with the dictates of his own conscience.'

Signing up to a commitment on human rights did not mean that the satellite states actually now allowed people to act 'in accordance with the dictates of [their] own conscience'. The 'moral' agreements of the Final Act were not legally binding, and there were no existing sanctions to be imposed on those who failed to uphold the terms of these agreements. Suspected dissidents continued to be harassed and spied on by the secret police. However, it made it harder for people to be mistreated, because **'Helsinki Watch' groups** monitored the satellite governments for any infringement of the Helsinki Final Act. As in the USSR, these Watch groups aimed to publically 'name and shame' their governments in the Western media, and broadcast to the satellite states and the West. This boosted support among Western Helsinki Watch organisations, communities of émigrés from the satellite states, and influential Western political groups (who could also increase pressure on satellite state leaderships). Within the satellite states there was significant sensitivity to how their countries were perceived in the West as this had, among other things, an impact on Western investment and trade. At times, international concerns about human rights in the satellite states could transfer into trade restrictions or sanctions.

A CLOSER LOOK

Helsinki Watch groups in the satellite states

Following the formation of the first Helsinki Watch group in Moscow in 1976, Charter 77 was set up in Prague in 1977, and a Watch group was established in Poland in 1979 after the director of Helsinki Watch, Jeri Laber, visited a member of KOR (see page 157). Thus, the link between Helsinki and the emerging political opposition in these satellite states was very strong. When martial law was declared in Poland, Warsaw's Helsinki Watch group members were arrested, but activists continued to compile reports and to smuggle them abroad. Helsinki Watch reports also came in from across the satellite states.

Political activism

Charter 77, Czechoslovakia

The process of normalisation following the Prague Spring had created a problem for the leadership in the form of a large number of well-educated people who had been expelled from the Party after 1968. Surveillance of these people by the StB (secret police), whether real or just suspected, only increased their anti-authoritarian feelings. When the Party leadership signed the Helsinki Final Act, a small group from this disaffected section of society realised that the leadership could now be held to account for its mistreatment of dissidents. In January 1977, they set up Charter 77: a human rights pressure group comprised of artists, writers and musicians. Charter 77 described itself in its founding Proclamation as follows:

'Charter 77 is an association of people united by the will to strive for the respecting of human rights in our country and throughout the world – rights accorded to all by the Helsinki Charter.'

- On 1 January 1977, Charter 77 produced a Proclamation describing examples of the many ways in which human rights in Czechoslovakia were infringed and suppressed; detailing the ways in which the StB harassed and spied on people.
- The security forces intercepted the Proclamation, arrested the leaders of Charter 77, imprisoned key spokesperson, Václav Havel, intimidated the group's members, and began a **smear campaign** to discredit the group.
- Radio Free Europe publicised Charter 77's Proclamation in Czechoslovakia, and news of the group's suppression.
- Interest in the group surged in the West after one of the founders of Charter 77 died after an interrogation session with the StB.
- Charter 77 members went underground and published many ***samizdat*** articles. An especially famous one by Havel, entitled 'The Power of the Powerless', described the way Czechoslovak people were 'living within a lie'.

Fig. 2 *Members of Charter 77, photographed in Prague in 1979; Václav Havel is seen top left*

KEY TERM

smear campaign: a campaign to discredit a person or a group by false information or accusations

CROSS-REFERENCE

See page 60 for a definition of ***samizdat***.

ACTIVITY

Extension

Havel's essay 'The Power of the Powerless' described how the CPCz's net of lies, created opponents among ordinary, powerless people. He uses the example of a greengrocer displaying the communist slogan 'Workers of the world, unite!' in his shop.

1. Read Havel's essay (or a summary of it) online and explain why he felt the greengrocer represented much that was wrong about life under Party control.
2. A Solidarity representative said that Havel's essay gave him and his co-workers motivation to resist repression from factory management and the police. Why do you think an essay by a Czech academic had this impact on shipworkers in Poland?

KOR, Poland

KOR stood for the Workers' Defence Committee, set up in the aftermath of the 1976 strikes and unrest in Poland that had followed the announcement of price rises on 24 June. The factory workers at the Ursus tractor factory went on strike in protest. A military crackdown followed, with hundreds of arrests and beatings and thousands being sacked. This violent response prompted Polish intellectuals to join the workers' cause. Set up by one such intellectual, Jacek Kuroń, KOR managed to connect with the workers in a way that had not happened before.

KOR was the first open opposition to the Soviet system in the whole Eastern bloc and aimed to support those persecuted for participation in strikes, and to protect workers' rights generally. In a socialist state, this is what the Party was supposed to do. KOR was thus a direct challenge to the Party's ideological basis and its position of power. KOR paved the way for independent trade unions in Poland, which in turn enabled Solidarity to directly challenge the Party's leading role in running the country. Serious

KEY PROFILE

Lech Wałęsa (b. 1943) worked at the Gdańsk shipyard until he was sacked following the 1976 unrest and his involvement in illegal unions and strike organisation. He continued to fight for workers' rights (working with KOR), was constantly under police supervision, and was arrested several times. When the 1980 strikes began at the Gdańsk shipyard, Wałęsa was quickly chosen as the head of the Strike Coordinating Committee. Following the government's agreement to legal trade unions, Wałęsa was chosen as chairman of Solidarity. When General Jaruzelski imposed martial law, Wałęsa was imprisoned for 11 months. In 1983, he was awarded the Nobel Peace Prize.

economic problems in 1980 prompted a strike at the Gdańsk shipyard. The strike organiser, a KOR activist, chose a worker called **Lech Wałęsa** to lead the strike committee.

Church organisations in Poland and the GDR

Church organisations in Poland

Like KOR, the Church in Poland also put its support behind the workers in 1976. The Catholic Church's influence in Poland, always strong, intensified still further with the election to the papacy of Karol Wojtyła of Kraków, who became John Paul II, the first Polish pope, in 1978. His visit to his homeland in 1979 had an enormous effect on the way many Polish people thought about their country and its place in the world. Although the Pope was careful not to directly criticise the PUWP, his message was clear: it was impossible, he said, to be fully human without religion and any attempt to exclude Christ from people's lives was therefore to fundamentally alienate people from what was really important in life.

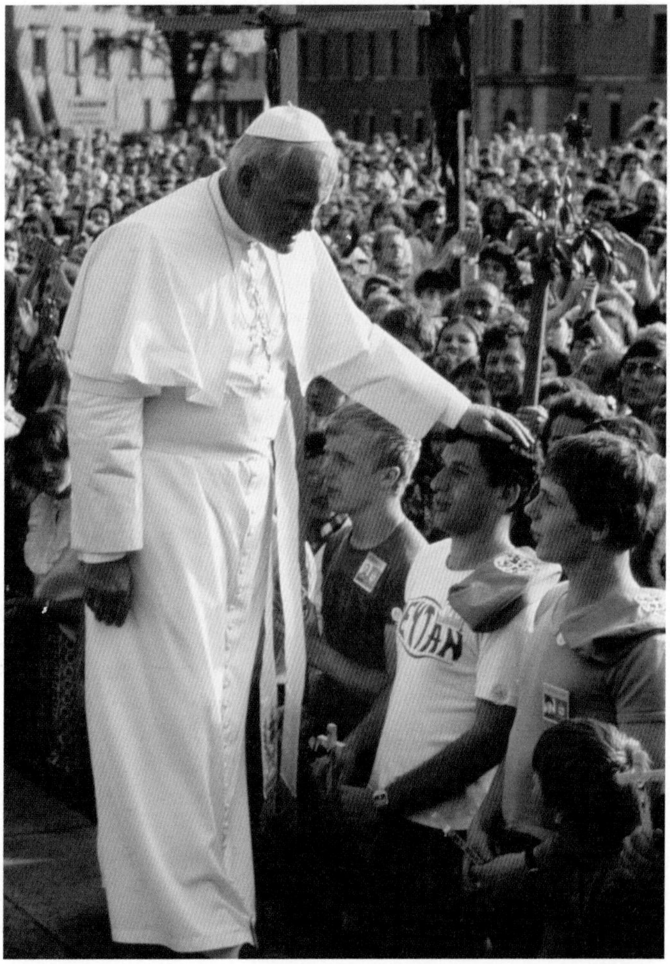

Fig. 3 *News reports stated that thousands of the 13 million Poles who turned out to see John Paul II in 1979 chanted 'We want God! We want God!'*

ACTIVITY

Research

Find John Paul II's speech from his 1979 visit to Poland online. How might this speech have given support to opponents of the PUWP and Marxist–Leninist ideology?

CROSS-REFERENCE

Riots in Poznań in 1956 prompted liberalising reforms under Poland's new leader, Gomułka. These are discussed in Chapter 16, pages 131–32.

The reforms won from the USSR after 1956 included a new level of freedom for the Catholic Church. Although Marxist–Leninism was atheist and restrictions on religious education in schools tried to remove the influence of the Church, the fact remained that even in the PUWP, 50 per cent of members were regular churchgoers (even as Church organisations became increasingly open in their opposition to communism). As in the GDR, the Church provided a space where dissident intellectual groups could meet and, in turn, the Church was influenced by arguments about human rights. However, the Church was a moderating influence on dissident groups, too. When, in 1980, the recurrent cycle of price rises, uprisings, repressions, and concessions meant the government needed allies who could help with talks with the workers' organisations, the Church tried to make sure the tensions did not lead to bloodshed.

Church organisations in the GDR

The **March 1978 agreement** with the Lutheran Church that allowed meetings on church premises gave dissidents a space for debate. While Honecker's intention had been to limit their influence under a compliant Church leadership, this agreement was to provide the seed from which the reform movement of the late 1980s would grow.

Initially, the agreement seemed to work in the government's favour as the Church adopted a conciliatory role. **Manfred Stolpe**, who from 1962 to 1989 was the lay head of the Protestant Churches of the GDR, was also a Stasi agent. There were occasional demonstrations, but the Stasi ensured that such activities were either suppressed before they could begin or were tightly controlled by the State.

A tiny minority of political activists sought reform in the late 1970s and 1980s and began forming organised groups and networks, usually under the aegis of the Church. However, it was only in the dramatically changed circumstances of 1989 that larger numbers found cause to speak out against the regime.

CROSS-REFERENCE

See page 143 for more on the **March 1978 agreement** with the Lutheran Church.

KEY PROFILE

Manfred Stolpe (b. 1936) was a lawyer who became active in the Protestant Evangelical Church in the GDR. He was head of the Secretariat of the Evangelical Churches between 1962 and 1981, and sat on the governing body of the Churches as President of the Eastern Region between 1982 and 1990. In 1990, he joined the SPD and became the Premier of the State of Brandenburg until 2002.

Contested elections in Hungary

In Hungary, the **umbrella group**, the People's Patriotic Front (PPF), organised representation from different social groups, including religious groups, in support of the Party programme. Since 1966, more than one candidate had been permitted for each constituency, although the PPF, under the leadership of the Party, controlled the selection process to ensure that the 'right' candidates stood for election. After 1971, that exclusive selection process was removed, but that did not lead to significant change. Candidates were still only those who would always vote in support of the Hungarian Socialist Workers' Party programme, and elections were only a contest between personalities, never about policies. Nor were there many cases of multiple candidacies: in the general elections, there were only 9 multiple candidacies in 1967, 49 in 1971, 34 in 1975, and 15 in 1980 – out of a total of 352 candidacies. Kádár explained this lack of opposing candidates as being because no one wanted to risk the shame of defeat. In 1983, a new electoral law required a minimum of two candidates for each national and local constituency in general elections. As Source 5 indicates, however, the new system still guaranteed that Party policy would always be voted through.

KEY TERM

umbrella group: a group of organisations that all have common interests

ACTIVITY

Summary

Keeping developments in each satellite state clear in your head is difficult when some states show similar developments. Using information in this chapter, compile separate timelines and revision diagrams for each state to help build up your knowledge and understanding. You can add to these as you continue through this book.

ACTIVITY

Pair discussion

Were Hungarian contested elections democratic?

SOURCE 5

From a report by the international news organisation, the Christian Science Monitor, on the 1985 Hungarian elections. The Christian Science Monitor is owned by a Christian organisation, but states that its aims are journalistic rather than evangelistic:

[A]ll candidates had to pledge to accept that program before they were finally approved for the ballot. This was true whether they belonged to the vast majority approved by the Communist Party's watchdog organization, the People's Patriotic Front (PPF), or to the 'independent' handful. The lawmakers balked at any concession to party plurality. There is no need in Hungary for this 'bourgeois' concept, party spokesmen say. The new law requiring at least two candidates for each seat, they say, opens the door to participation by diverse interests – party and nonparty members, labor unions, churches, and the arts. Nonetheless, the ruling Hungarian Socialist Workers Party – the Communist Party, that is – is assured of a working majority. It was apportioned 60 percent of the 352 seats in the parliamentary chamber in advance. The rest are ostensibly open to 'nonparty' individuals and organizations.

STUDY TIP

You will need to evaluate different examples of activism. Using this book to help you, you could prepare for answering this question by making a spider-diagram of the activist groups in the satellite states, with notes on the key features and achievements of each.

A LEVEL PRACTICE QUESTION

'Political activism in the satellite states was due to Western influence.' Assess the validity of this view.

20 Strikes and demonstrations in Poland

Fig. 1 *Strikers in Warsaw, 1980*

LEARNING OBJECTIVES

In this chapter you will learn about:

- the emergence of Solidarity in 1980
- the reaction of the Polish government and of the USSR.

KEY CHRONOLOGY

Events of 1980

July	Increase in meat prices leads to strikes
14 Aug	Gdańsk shipyard workers demand independent trade union; Lech Wałęsa elected leader of strike committee
31 Aug	The Gdańsk Agreements signed by Polish government, permitting independent trade unions and other concessions
Sept	Solidarity formed as a national confederation of free trade unions
Oct	Catholic Church backs Solidarity

The strike as a means of putting pressure on the government to meet worker demands was highly significant as part of a long campaign in Poland to improve both working conditions and pay and, increasingly, access to political power for the workers in whose name the PUWP supposedly ran the country. The first strikes and demonstrations in communist Poland were those of 1956, and it was the violent repression of these protests against working conditions that brought Polish intellectuals, many with Party memberships, into political opposition. Gierek's leadership had resulted from the large-scale protests against Gomułka's price rises and the cancellation of Christmas bonuses in December 1970, and though his reforms saw a reduction in strikes and demonstrations through the early 1970s, when worsening economic conditions forced the leadership to announce a new set of price rises in 1976, worker protests broke out in Warsaw that were, again, brutally suppressed with police beatings. The planned price rises were then cancelled. There was, therefore, an established pattern of price rises, strikes and demonstrations, and police repression, often followed by concessions to the workers. In 1980, however, the pattern changed.

The emergence of Solidarity in 1980

The emergence of Solidarity was a response to the economic crisis of 1980. The leadership struggled to assert any legitimacy based on its dire handling of the economy or assert its authority via crackdowns and harassment. All that Polish workers could see was a Party elite that looked after itself, while everyone else suffered.

The trigger for the formation of Solidarity came when a crane operator and activist at the Gdańsk shipyward, **Anna Walentynowicz**, was fired in August 1980, only five months before she was due to retire, for her membership of an illegal workers' organisation called Free Trade Unions of the Coast (WZZ). The shipyard workers went on strike, demanding she be given her job back. Under the leadership of Lech Wałęsa, the strike also demanded workers' rights and the legalisation of independent trade unions.

CROSS-REFERENCE

The Poznań uprising of 1956 began with worker demonstrations for better working conditions, and is discussed in Chapter 16, pages 131–32.

The causes of the economic crisis facing Poland by 1980 are discussed in Chapter 18, page 145.

KEY PROFILE

Anna Walentynowicz (1929–2010) never joined the PUWP, though she was a committed socialist who fought against the oppression and corruption she saw in the management of her workplace by PUWP Party apparatchiks. She was a devout Catholic who developed a close connection to Pope John Paul II.

Fig. 2 *Anna Walentynowicz and Lech Wałęsa at the 1980 strike at Gdańsk shipyard*

ACTIVITY

1. Which of the eight demands from the 'Twenty-One Demands' would you class as 'traditional' economic strike demands?
2. Which of them are political?
3. The PUWP and CPSU diligently described Solidarity as 'counter-revolutionary'. To what extent was Solidarity opposed to a socialist Poland?
4. Given what you know of the context of Poland's economic position in 1980, how realistic were these demands?

The Gdańsk strike committee made 'Twenty-One Demands' in August 1980, which included:

- acceptance of free trade unions independent of both the Party and employers (a step on from the freedom to form unions which had been ratified by the Polish government)
- a guarantee of the right to strike and that strikers and their supporters would not be attacked for striking
- the release of all political prisoners
- real measures to get the country out of its present crisis, starting with the public release of reliable information on the economy and then giving every section of society the opportunity to participate in open discussions about economic reform
- a wage increase for every worker of 2000 zlotys per month (the average monthly wage was around 8000 zlotys) to compensate for price rises to date, and automatic pay rises to match inflation
- managers to be appointed on the basis of qualifications rather than Party membership; special shops for Party members only to be abolished
- reducing the waiting time for apartments
- Saturdays to be days off from work.

Supported by other strike committees, Polish priests, **KOR**, and significant media attention both in Poland and internationally, the strike brought Poland's economy to a standstill. The government was forced to agree to many of the strikers' demands, including the legal right to strike and the legality of a workers' union that was independent of the Party.

CROSS-REFERENCE

KOR, the Workers' Defence Committee, is featured in Chapter 19 on pages 157–58.

Solidarity's tactics

Solidarity – Poland's first legal, independent trade union – was formed on 17 September 1980. Its tactics included:

- Non-violence – influenced by Church organisations and the recognition that violence was what the security forces (and the USSR) wanted in order to justify repression.
- Politicised – not only an organisation for workers' rights, Solidarity's programme was broad enough to appeal to the intellectuals, Church organisations, and nationalists.

- General strikes – the economy was very fragile and any loss of economic output threatened the government's ability to meet its international loan obligations. This made general strikes very effective.
- Concessions – Solidarity's leadership aimed for a partnership with the government and the Church and accepted compromises on its demands. (More radical elements in Solidarity found these concessions deeply frustrating.)
- Using the PUWP against itself – Solidarity members sought to gain control of local Party organisations and to use these as a base for putting pressure on the Party leadership.

The reaction of the Polish government and of the USSR

The government's initial response in September 1980 was to cut off Gdańsk from all means of communication, including road, rail, and telephone, and then offer to negotiate. It was these negotiations that resulted in the 'Twenty-one Demands'. At this point, on 6 September 1980, Gierek resigned (officially for health reasons, but his repeated failure to control the striking workers had made his position untenable). His replacement was **Stanisław Kania**. As Gierek had done after Gomułka's failure to control the protests of 1970, so Kania met with Wałęsa and the striking workers and admitted to faults in the Party's handling of the crisis. The accepted pattern then was for concessions to be accepted and the protests to be halted. That did not happen this time.

KEY PROFILE

Stanisław Kania (b. 1927) had risen through the ranks of the PUWP since joining in 1945, becoming a Politburo member in 1975. He replaced Gierek as First Secretary of the PUWP in September 1980, following the surge in strike activity in respond to Gierek's price rises at the start of the year.

Instead, Solidarity's influence spread throughout Polish society. Because Solidarity was an umbrella organisation, rather than a union or pressure group linked to one specific part of the economy, it was open to a wide range of protesting groups, including Rural Solidarity (representing private peasant farmers), student unions, professional organisations (including the police), and unions of craftsmen. Membership of Solidarity quickly grew to an astonishing 10 million by the start of 1981 – around 80 per cent of the Polish workforce and a quarter of the entire population of the country.

This mass movement within Polish society, with a self-declared aim of making Poland into a self-governing republic, was deeply alarming to the Soviet leadership. By August 1980, the Soviets had recognised that the strike had reached a national scale and had begun to move tanks and troops up to the border with Poland in case military assistance was requested by the PUWP – or, potentially, even if it were not requested but still deemed necessary. Brezhnev's leadership were increasingly frustrated, however, by Kania's unwillingness to take decisive action against Solidarity. By December 1980, Soviet warships were anchored off Poland's coast and its troops were carrying out manoeuvres on the border. Alongside this, as Table 1 indicates, the USSR was doing a great deal to prop up Poland economically, at very significant expense.

KEY CHRONOLOGY

1980	Sept	Stanisław Kania replaces Gierek as leader in Poland
1981	Feb	General Wojciech Jaruzelski appointed Prime Minister of Poland
	Mar	Solidarity calls for four-hour general strike
	Mar	Soviet Army carries out manoeuvres on Poland's border
	May	Assassination attempt on Pope John Paul II
	Oct	Kania is replaced by General Jaruzelski
	Dec	**Martial law** declared in Poland

KEY TERM

martial law: government by the military: all state powers, including justice and law-making, are taken over by the military

Fig. 3 *Lech Wałęsa addressing a crowd in Bydgoszcz on 21 March 1980; a demonstration on 16 March in support of legal status for Rural Solidarity in Bydgoszcz was harshly repressed, prompting Solidarity to call for a general strike on 24 March*

However, despite Soviet pressure, Kania continued to stall, hoping that continued negotiations with Wałęsa would reduce tensions or that popular support for Solidarity would begin to wane (or both). Solidarity's leaders had always stressed the importance of non-violent protest, so as not to give the security forces an excuse for a crackdown and general repression of the movement. In March 1981, Solidarity members were beaten up by police in the town of Bydgoszcz. A general strike was called. While the Soviet Politburo demanded the imposition of martial law, the Polish government responded with negotiations between Wałęsa and the Deputy Premier. Further concessions followed:

- In July, the PUWP's ninth congress voted members of Solidarity onto its Central Committee.
- On 3 October, Solidarity's first national congress directly challenged the PUWP's leading role with a referendum on Party reform. A one-hour general strike was called. Kania offered a 12 per cent pay rise for workers.

The Soviet Politburo had had enough. On 18 October 1980, Kania was replaced by **General Wojciech Jaruzelski**. Kania had been caught, on a bugging device, criticising the Soviet economic model (central planning), and this was the final straw. The USSR hoped that Jaruzelski would bring about the resolution that the situation required.

There are conflicting accounts about Jaruzelski's declaration of martial law, which came in December 1981. Jaruzelski himself stated that he feared that the USSR would have invaded if martial law had not been imposed. This position was contradicted by the Soviet leadership, including the commander-in-chief of the Warsaw Pact forces, Marshal Kulikov, and by minutes from the CPSU's Politburo meetings which were released following the collapse of the USSR. These minutes made it clear that Soviets never intended to invade – the USSR had too much to lose (not least the possibility of conflict with NATO, as the USA had warned the USSR against invasion). Marshal Kulikov had made 22 separate visits to Poland since December 1980 and his role had always been to convince the PUWP to impose martial law. The Warsaw Pact manoeuvres were a smokescreen to enable the PUWP to retain legitimacy with the Polish

KEY PROFILE

Wojciech Jaruzelski (1923–2014) was the final First Secretary of the PUWP. It was Jaruzelski who implemented martial law in Poland in December 1981.

people. In 1984, in Moscow, Jaruzelski was awarded the Order of Lenin for 'strengthening socialism on Polish soil'.

When martial law was declared, 100 people were killed in disturbances and 10,000 arrested, as Solidarity was banned, its leaders detained, and its activities driven underground. All civil rights were suspended and the media was placed under military supervision. Communications were blocked, troops were used to surround the factories, mines, and shipyards at the centre of the strikes, and peaceful demonstrations were broken up by police in riot gear. The operation went relatively smoothly, suggesting it had been carefully planned well in advance.

A LEVEL PRACTICE QUESTION

'The Polish government underestimated the threat posed by the Solidarity movement in 1980–81.' Assess the validity of this view.

STUDY TIP

This question includes very specific parameters: be sure to relate your answer to the period 1980–81. Consider why the Polish government 'under-reacted'. Try not to conflate the Soviet reaction with that of the Polish government.

SOURCE 1

From the minutes of a session of the CPSU CC Politburo, 2 April 1981, recording a discussion between General Secretary Brezhnev and Yuri Andropov, head of the KGB:

ANDROPOV: We must seriously ask the Polish friends whether they will hold Solidarity accountable for what's going on in Poland. How do things stand now? Economic chaos, confusion, and all manner of shortcomings in the supply of consumer goods and other things can be attributed to the strikes sponsored by Solidarity, but it's the government that's being held accountable for this. An absurd situation has emerged. Yet none of the members of the Politburo, and no one from the PPR [Polish People's Republic] leadership, is speaking out and telling the workers that the leaders of Solidarity are chiefly responsible for the shortcomings and economic devastation.

BREZHNEV. We must tell them this means the introduction of martial law and explain it all very plainly.

ANDROPOV. That's right, we must tell them precisely that the introduction of martial law means the establishment of a curfew, limitations on movement along city streets, and stepped-up protection for state and Party institutions, enterprises, etc.

SOURCE 2

From the minutes of a session of the CPSU CC Politburo, 10 December 1981, in which KGB head, Andropov, discusses the report that Marshal Kulikov threatened the invasion of Poland:

ANDROPOV: If Comrade Kulikov actually did speak about the introduction of troops, then I believe he did this incorrectly. We can't risk such a step. We don't intend to introduce troops into Poland. That is the proper position, and we must adhere to it until the end. I don't know how things will turn out in Poland, but even if Poland falls under the control of "Solidarity," that's the way it will be. And if the capitalist countries pounce on the Soviet Union, and you know they have already reached agreement on a variety of economic and political sanctions, that will be very burdensome for us. We must be concerned above all with our own country and about the strengthening of the Soviet Union. That is our main line. As concerns the lines of communication between the Soviet Union and the GDR that run through Poland, then we of course must do something to provide for their safekeeping.

ACTIVITY

Extension

The Digital Archive of the Wilson Center (available online) has a collection of documents which would be worth consulting to learn more about the 1980–81 Polish crisis.

Fig. 4 *General Wojciech Jaruzelski in December 1981, preparing to make his announcement of the declaration of martial law to the Polish people*

SOURCE 3

From a radio address by Wojciech Jaruzelski announcing the imposition of martial law on Poland, 13 December 1981:

I declare that today the army Council of National Salvation has been constituted, and the Council of State obeying the Polish Constitution declared a state of emergency at midnight on the territory of Poland.

In the name of national interests, a group of people threatening the safety of the country has been interned. The extremists of Solidarity are included in this group as well as other members of illegal organisations. On the demand of the military council, several people responsible for pushing the country into the crisis in the 1970s and abusing their posts for personal profit have been interned. Among them are Edward Gierek.

Despite all the failures and mistakes we made, the party is still the leading and creative force in the process of changes to fulfil its mission. We shall clean up the everlasting sources of our ideals from deformations and deviations. We shall protect universal values of socialism, enriching it with our national elements and traditions.

ACTIVITY

Watch the first part of the television address made by General Jaruzelski in December 1981 to declare martial law (on YouTube, with subtitles).

A LEVEL PRACTICE QUESTION

Evaluating primary sources

With reference to Sources 1, 2, and 3 and your understanding of the historical context, assess the value of these sources to an historian studying the reaction of the Polish government to the 'Polish crisis' of 1980–81.

STUDY TIP

The opening up of archives in the former satellite states and former Soviet Union has enabled historians to be much more certain about the intentions of leaderships in the USSR and satellite states than was previously possible. While you could argue that the value of such sources is undeniable, try to give a balanced appraisal of all sources provided.

Summary

Strikes crippled Poland both economically and ideologically, undermining the PUWP's legitimation as the Party of the workers, for whose benefit it was supposed to run the country.

While strikes happened in other satellite states and in the USSR itself, the ability of Solidarity to act as an umbrella organisation for every kind of Polish worker was unprecedented.

Solidarity's main weapon, the general strike, was powerful enough under the dire economic conditions of 1980 to force the PUWP into allowing Solidarity to become Poland's first legal, independent trade union. This now meant that the PUWP could not continue to rule Poland without the use of force.

Once 'real existing socialism' in Poland collapsed, people's tolerance of the regime ended and it was only coercion, backed by the threat of Soviet invasion, that allowed the PUWP to retain its hold on power.

6 The collapse of the Soviet Empire, 1980–2000

21 Political developments and activism within the satellite states 1980–1989

KEY CHRONOLOGY

1981	**December**	Declaration of martial law in Poland
1982	**December**	Death of Leonid Brezhnev
1983	**July**	Martial law ends in Poland; amnesty for political crimes
1984	**October**	Father Jerzy Popiełuszko is kidnapped and murdered
1985	**March**	Mikhail Gorbachev elected leader of the USSR
		Elections in Hungary see 43 independents voted into parliament
1987	**December**	Miloš Jakeš replaces Gustáv Husák in Czechoslovakia
		Wildcat strikes in Poland throughout the year
1988	**January**	Communist parade turns into demonstration for greater freedoms in the GDR
	May	Károly Grósz replaces János Kádár as leader in Hungary
	August	Negotiations between Solidarity and the Polish government
1989	**April**	Solidarity legalised
	June	Solidarity wins all but one of the seats available in Poland's elections
	July	Gorbachev declares the USSR will not interfere in internal affairs of the satellite states

LEARNING OBJECTIVES

In this chapter you will learn about:

- Jaruzelski and attempts to restrain Solidarity in Poland
- pressure groups in Czechoslovakia and electoral contests in Hungary
- regional peace workshops
- the IFN and environmental groups in the GDR.

KEY TERM

wildcat strikes: strikes that happen without the authorisation of a union

Jaruzelski and attempts to restrain Solidarity in Poland

Jaruzelski's imposition of martial law in Poland in December 1981 made Solidarity an illegal organisation; his justification being the need to act firmly to prevent the USSR leading a Warsaw Pact invasion. In the years after 1981, Solidarity was driven underground.

Jaruzelski and the conservatives in the Polish United Workers' Party (PUWP) had blamed Solidarity for the strikes of 1980, and it seems unlikely that worker discontent would have resulted in such strikes without Solidarity's organisational role. With its leaders detained and its open communication networks severed, Solidarity's attempts to continue its opposition failed to make headway. The security services shut down demonstrations in August 1982 organised by Solidarity to mark the anniversary of its formation; four people were killed in clashes with security forces and thousands arrested. In October, all Polish trade unions, including Solidarity, were made illegal. Despite its millions of members, a general strike called by Solidarity in November 1982 to oppose the ban was a failure.

This was not the same process as normalisation in Czechoslovakia after 1968, however. As soon as Jaruzelski's martial law looked to have succeeded in demoralising open opposition, martial law was lifted (on 21 July 1983), and an amnesty granted to all political detainees. In 1984, Jaruzelski acted to

CROSS-REFERENCE

See Chapter 20 for coverage of the build-up to the imposition of martial law, and its immediate consequences, under General Wojciech Jaruzelski.

KEY PROFILE

Father Jerzy Popiełuszko (1947–84) was a Catholic priest who encouraged opposition to the Communist Party in his sermons (often broadcast on Radio Free Europe) and who was an active supporter of Solidarity. He was beaten to death by three secret policemen. His funeral was attended by 250,000 people.

ACTIVITY

Evaluating primary sources

What is the value of Source 1 in providing evidence of the extent of Solidarity's challenge to the PUWP and of Soviet influence in Poland?

ACTIVITY

Look back at Chapter 20 and compare Jaruzelski's response to the strikes and unrest of 1980–81 with the aftermath of 1956 in Hungary and 1968 in Czechoslovakia. What are the similarities and the differences?

CROSS-REFERENCE

Samizdat, the secret copying and distribution of unauthorised publications, is discussed in Chapter 8, page 60.

The Hungarian Revolution of 1956 is discussed on pages 132–33, and the Prague Spring in Czechoslovakia on pages 135–37.

'**Goulash communism**' was the nickname given to the mix of planned economics and market economics developed in Hungary under Kádár's leadership and is discussed in Chapter 18, page 146.

distance himself from the murder of **Father Jerzy Popiełuszko**: putting the security force personnel involved on trial and taking control himself of the security services.

Fig. 1 *Former Internal Ministry officers, accused of kidnapping and murdering Father Jerzy Popiełuszko, photographed at the opening of their trial on 27 December 1984*

SOURCE 1

From Lech Wałęsa's acceptance speech for the Nobel Peace Prize in 1983:

We shall not yield to violence. We shall not be deprived of union freedoms. We shall never agree with sending people to prison for their convictions. The gates of prisons must be thrown open and persons sentenced for defending union and civic rights must be set free.

As a nation we have the right to decide our own affairs, to mould our own future. This does not pose any danger to anybody. Our nation is fully aware of the responsibility for its own fate in the complicated situation of the contemporary world.

Despite everything that has been going on in my country during the past two years, I am still convinced that we have no alternative but to come to an agreement, and that the difficult problems which Poland is now facing can be resolved only through a real dialogue between state authorities and the people.

Although Solidarity had been restrained, Jaruzelski did not seek to destroy it. Solidarity, though operating underground, sponsored a huge amount of dissident ***samizdat***, but the military government did not move in to bring this to a halt. There were no purges of Party members with links to the unions or the Church, although troublemakers did get sacked. Unlike the authoritarian governments of the GDR and Czechoslovakia, Poland's leadership had, since 1956, looked for consensus rather than the hard line, including the Church in social policy.

Jaruzelski introduced economic reforms in 1982 that were an attempt to improve living conditions through a '**goulash communism**' route of decentralisation of decision-making to enterprises, although without any real change to the state controls that kept prices artificially low.

The results of the reforms were not good: managers used their freedom from central control to increase wages, while prices remained low. This was the opposite of what Poland's Western creditors wanted. They wanted austerity so that the government could meet its interest payments. Martial law had also provoked a hostile Western reaction, including international censure, trade sanctions, and intensified pressure on Poland for the repayment of its loans. When a second round of economic reforms was put to a public **referendum** in November 1987, the Polish people rejected them. The government was still forced into price rises at the start of 1988. Strikes resulted and the strike demands included re-legalisation for Solidarity.

From trying to restrain Solidarity, in 1989 Jaruzelski set up **'Round Table' talks** with Wałęsa and other moderates in Solidarity and Church organisations. The result was that Solidarity achieved one of its key aims: free elections. Although 38 per cent of seats in the Sejm were guaranteed to the PUWP, Solidarity won every seat that was open to them in an extraordinary electoral victory. Although technically the PUWP retained control, in reality their legitimacy and authority were entirely undermined. On 24 August 1989, the first non-communist Polish prime minister since 1945, **Tadeusz Mazowiecki**, took up his post. Under Brezhnev, this sort of direct threat to socialism would not have been tolerated, but under Gorbachev, the situation was entirely different.

KEY TERM

referendum: a vote by the general public on a specific question

A CLOSER LOOK

'Round Table' talks, first developed in Poland, were discussion forums used throughout Eastern Europe as opposition groups negotiated with Communist Parties on power-sharing agreements.

KEY PROFILE

Tadeusz Mazowiecki (1927–2013) was a leading dissident with strong links to the Catholic Church and one of the last political prisoners to be released in the amnesty of 1983. He was committed to negotiating a transfer of power from the PUWP, rather than any attempt to take it by force. It was under Mazowiecki's premiership that the 'shock therapy' approach to restoring capitalism in Poland was first introduced.

Gorbachev, by his own account, told the leaders of the Warsaw Pact countries that the USSR would not intervene in their internal affairs when he became General Secretary in March 1985. This policy was motivated by Gorbachev's belief that socialism needed to become more democratically accountable. The Brezhnev Doctrine, in Gorbachev's view, hampered the ability of the satellite states to make choices that reflected the wishes of their own peoples. Likewise, the responsibility of maintaining thousands of elite troops in Eastern Europe was a burden, both financial and psychological, for the Soviet Union. It, he thought, should no longer be the Soviet Union's ultimate responsibility to decide what model of socialism would work best in all situations. He rejected the idea that socialism was too fragile, within individual countries, to be left to fend off the preying capitalist West (as had been one of the excuses for the imposition of martial law).

Pressure groups in Czechoslovakia and electoral contests in Hungary

Pressure groups in Czechoslovakia

Czechoslovakia's main pressure group remained Charter 77 – only a small group of dissidents throughout the 1980s (under sustained pressure from the security services), but representing many of those ousted from the Party after 1968. In 1987 Husák resigned as General Secretary, to be replaced by **Miloš Jakeš**. Due to the purges after 1968, the Party was predominantly made up of conservatives and lacked the reformist groups that characterised the CPSU, the PUWP, and the Hungarian Socialist Workers' Party (MSzP). When the Soviet Empire collapsed, most of the new leaders of Czechoslovakia came from Charter 77. Through the 1980s, the only response the CPCz had to

CROSS-REFERENCE

Charter 77, the Czech dissident group set up in 1977, is discussed in Chapter 19, page 156.

events in Poland, Hungary, and the USSR itself was to increase StB activity against Charter 77 members.

While Charter 77 was boosted in difficult times by Solidarity's challenges to the PUWP, in Slovakia (the predominantly Catholic part of Czechoslovakia), the Church also put pressure on the government, inspired by the reformist role of the Catholic Church in Poland. A petition for more religious freedom gathered more than half a million signatures in 1987 and 1988. Signing this petition was a risk for anyone, not just known dissidents under StB surveillance, so the size of this response is significant. In March 1988, a demonstration for the same cause, in which a large crowd mostly made up of older women held a candlelit vigil in a Bratislava square, was violently broken up by the StB.

Slovaks had benefited from Husák's long leadership. He was a Slovak himself, and the region had seen a lot of investment to close the gap between it and the industrialised Czech region. However, fear about the consequences of the Chernobyl accident in April 1986 led to the formation of environmental groups with strong Church backing, which started to hold the government to account for the pollution and environmental damage done by inefficient, ageing heavy industry across Eastern Europe.

Public meetings and demonstrations linked to these concerns (religious, environmental, and human rights) increased in number through 1988 and into 1989, mostly in the capital, Prague. The security forces tolerated some and disrupted others, seemingly at random. These demonstrations culminated in the 'Velvet Revolution' of 1989 that is covered in Chapter 23.

Electoral contests in Hungary

The collapse of communism in Hungary had a long evolution. Under Kádár, initial repression after 1956 moved relatively swiftly into tolerance of differing opinions, and by the 1980s Hungary was the most liberal of all the satellite states, both economically (following the reforms that Gorbachev greatly admired) and politically (with multi-candidacies encouraged in national elections). State censorship was almost non-existent, although people were still advised to stay away from criticism of the USSR. Human rights organisations recognised that Hungary's record was significantly better than in other satellite states, although individual freedoms were still limited by the power of the State.

Hungary was also economically successful relative to most of the other satellite states, but by 1980 problems were impacting on living standards there, too. Its export-led economy was hit hard by the recessions of the 1970s. Debts to the West rose from $1 billion in 1970 to over $9 billion in 1979. Kádár's government extended austerity measures, including raising prices. Unlike Geirek's sudden lurches in policy in Poland, though, Kádár prepared the population well in advance for a number of phased price rises. They were still unpopular with the people, of course, but there was no rioting and strike action as in Poland.

Economic liberalisation also played a part in the development of a political opposition to the MSZMP (Hungarian Socialist Workers' Party). The numbers of independent small businesses increased substantially and a scheme allowed skilled workers to contract out their labour, often to their same employer, after their day job was complete. These schemes were very successful in encouraging a large number of Hungarians to act as independent-minded **entrepreneurs**. However, for those not working in two jobs a day (and even for some that were), living standards began to decline. The ageing Kádár (he was 73 in 1985) failed to convince Hungarians that he knew how best to respond to the growing economic difficulties.

There were three other main areas over which opposition to the government grew:

KEY PROFILE

Miloš Jakeš (b. 1922) was General Secretary of the CPCz from 1987 to 1989. Educated in Moscow, he was involved in the 'normalisation' of Czechoslovakia after 1968. Gorbachev's reforms put increasing pressure on the ageing Husák because of a split in the Party between moderates who wanted to follow Gorbachev's example, and hardliners who wanted nothing to do with them. Jakeš was selected as a younger man better able to manage the pressure for change but, in fact, although he talked about *glasnost* and *perestroika*, he resisted any real reform and refused to meet with Charter 77 leaders.

CROSS-REFERENCE

For more on the Chernobyl accident, see Chapter 10, page 77.

KEY TERM

entrepreneur: someone who sets up a business for themselves, taking financial risks in the hope of making profits

ACTIVITY

1. Design a poster for a group linked to one of the issues causing growing opposition in Hungary.
2. Why do you think political opposition groups often found it easier to gain popular support over environmental issues than for challenging the State on human rights issues?

- Environmental issues, especially over the building of an enormous dam, the Nagymaros Dam, on the Danube river, which would have flooded large areas and completely changed the ecology of the river.
- Treatment of Hungarians living in Romania (in Transylvania) by Ceauşescu's regime.
- Conflict over official representations of Hungary's past, especially of the Revolution (officially counter-revolution) of 1956. Imre Nagy had been executed on 16 June, and the government struggled to contain popular celebrations on the anniversary of that day, in his honour, and on 30 October, popularly seen as the starting date of the 1956 Revolution. In 1988, the Committee for Historical Justice was formed, calling for complete rehabilitation of all victims of repression in 1956.

Within the Party, the main impetus for contested elections came from **Imre Pozsgay**'s chairmanship of the Party-backed Patriotic People's Front (PPF). The election of 1985 saw 43 independents elected to the Hungarian parliament – even if that independence was pretty limited (all candidates had to conform to the PPF political programme if they were to be approved). These elections were contested, but only in a very limited way. Campaigns were focused on removing bureaucracy and corruption rather than anything like opposition to the leading role of the Party.

CROSS-REFERENCE

The Patriotic People's Front (PPF) organised local and national elections in Hungary. See Chapter 19, page 159 for more information.

KEY PROFILE

Imre Pozsgay (b. 1933) worked his way up through the Hungarian Socialist Workers' Party, becoming a deputy minister in 1975 and a member of the Politburo. He was an influential figure in the reform of the Party, being the first Party member (let alone a Politburo member) to publically describe the Hungarian Revolution of 1956 as a 'popular uprising' rather than the officially sanctioned 'counter-revolution'. He was largely responsible for opening the border between Hungary and Austria, which was a turning point in the lead-up to the Revolutions of 1989.

Fig. 3 *Imre Pozsgay in Budapest in 1989. Pozsgay was described at the time as 'Hungary's Gorbachev' in the Western media.*

In 1987, Pozsgay commissioned a report entitled 'Turning Point and Reform' from the PPF into the problems of Hungary's economy, which argued that the problem was, in fact, the central planning system. The report's authors proposed a market economy, backed by a legal system that was above any Party or parties: 'a constitutional guarantee eliminating the right of political and administrative organisations to interfere with and inhibit the operation of a self-regulating marketplace' – that is, an end to central planning, although the Party would still provide a leadership role. This report also linked radical economic reform to democratisation.

In 1987, an opposition group of non-Party intellectual dissidents published an article calling for true **pluralism** in politics: a legislature made up of freely elected representatives of the people that had the power to hold the government (still Party-run) to account, rather than being merely a rubber

KEY TERM

pluralism: the dispersal of power between different institutes, groups, and people; the development of several or many different political parties, reflecting different political views

stamp for government decisions. This took ideas from another report from Pozsgay's PPF, 'Change and Reform' (1986), which also foresaw a 'duopoly' of power sharing between the Party and parliament.

Kádár was not receptive to such radical proposals from within his own Party, and moved to have the reformists expelled. However, in 1988 he was removed from the leadership, partly because he was getting senile and partly because investigations into the execution of Imre Nagy and deaths of other Hungarians in 1956 had reminded people of their initial disgust at Kádár's complicity in the repressions following 1956. From being an early supporter of Gorbachev, Kádár also started to issue warnings that Gorbachev's reforms would cause the collapse of the USSR.

Kádár was replaced as General Secretary in May 1988 by **Károly Grósz** who brought reformers, Pozsgay included, into the Politburo – with Gorbachev's approval. Economic reforms that introduced more marketisation followed in 1988, together with political reforms. Like Gorbachev, Grósz saw democratisation as part of the process of achieving the reconstruction of the economy, and hoped that allowing the people to have more of a say in how the Party governed the country would reconnect them to the socialist project. In July 1988, following Gorbachev's proposals for the creation of the Congress of People's Deputies in the USSR, Grósz announced he was working on a law that would allow opposition parties. Opposition groups began to form in anticipation of elections in 1990, including:

- the Hungarian Democratic Forum (MDF) – a grouping of nationalists and populists; the largest of the groups, with around 12,000 members (still tiny compared to Solidarity's membership)
- the Alliance of Free Democrats (SZDSZ) – the political wing of the Democratic Opposition, an intellectual organisation formed in support of Charter 77; a Western-orientated, anti-communist liberal party
- Fidesz (the Federation of Young Democrats) – with membership restricted to those between 16 and 35, this was a democratic alternative to the Pioneers
- the Independent Smallholders Party (KKGP) – refounded in 1988 after being shut down in 1948.

In 1989, the reformers within the Party began open criticism of socialism itself, led by Pozsgay. This was the point at which Pozsgay called the Revolution of 1956 'a popular uprising against an oligarchic system of power which had humiliated [Hungary]'. In February, the Party relinquished its leading role and permitted the reburial, with full honours, of Imre Nagy on 16 June 1989, attended by 200,000 Hungarians.

CROSS-REFERENCE

The creation of the Congress of People's Deputies in the USSR (first elections occurred in May 1990) is described in Chapter 10, page 80.

KEY PROFILE

Károly Grósz (1930–96) was a Communist Party member from the age of 14. In the Hungarian Revolution, he had acted in defence of the Party and was rewarded afterwards by increasingly senior positions, joining the Politburo in 1985 and becoming Prime Minister in 1987. Kádár recommended him as his replacement. Grósz's key concern was to ensure reform was controlled as much as possible and happened under the control of the Party rather than by the Party being replaced.

Fig. 4 *A scene from Imre Nagy's official, national funeral (reburial) on 16 June 1989*

Regional peace workshops; the IFN and environmental groups in the GDR

From the mid-1980s, with the arrival of Gorbachev as First Secretary of the USSR, dissident movements within the GDR became increasingly irritated with the conservative Church leadership, which lost the limited control it had exerted over them. As movements grew bolder, the only way to control the developing pressure for reform was by the use of the Stasi. This in turn brought further political activism (which even spread to some of the lower-level members of the political elite). There also seemed to be some indications of greater tolerance on the part of the State.

Typical of the new types of reform initiatives were:

- the IFN (Freedom and Civil Rights Movement) founded in January 1986 as the first truly independent political group outside the Church
- the regional peace workshops of the mid-1980s, which went beyond 'peace' to a discussion of human rights
- the Women's Peace Movement, bringing together peace groups from all over the GDR (from 1984)
- environmental groups, such as the UB (Environmental Library) of 1986, formed in response to the Chernobyl disaster.

The cause of peace had been championed by socialist states since the war, but peace groups outside the Party were still a challenge, especially when peace campaigners criticised the militarisation of young people in the GDR (for example, PE exercises that practised grenade-throwing skills). Environmental issues were also a sensitive matter to the GDR, which stopped publishing air pollution information in the 1970s. There was also influence from the West, where environmental groups directly criticised the SED's atrocious environmental record. But these groups were relatively moderate, certainly compared to the demands of Solidarity or even to the criticisms of Charter 77 in Czechoslovakia.

However, in the winter of 1987–88, there was a further clampdown. The traditional Luxemburg-Liebknecht parade of January 1988 was used as an excuse for a demonstration in favour of greater freedom in the GDR. Large numbers were arrested. This only encouraged more to join the incipient 'civic movement', and organised, non-violent demonstrations of sympathy and solidarity took place all over the GDR. There were candlelit meetings, concerts, church vigils, and, in Leipzig, Monday prayer services that became an important regular event. In 1989, both church groups and peace groups called on people to boycott local single-candidate elections.

Honecker's mistake was to resist any dialogue. Pretending that all was well, the regime relied on repression. However, the activism could not be totally repressed and as changes began to take place in the other communist states of Eastern Europe, the political opposition movement in Germany entered a new phase. Gorbachev grew increasingly irritated with Honecker, whose refusal to consider reform in the GDR went against all he was trying to do. Gorbachev had made his message clear from the start of his leadership of the USSR in 1985, and by July 1989 was saying it in public: the GDR had to take responsibility for its own future and change was unavoidable.

A CLOSER LOOK

Luxemburg-Liebknecht parade

This parade was an important ceremony in the East German state, commemorating the murder, in 1919, of German communists Rosa Luxemburg and Karl Liebknecht by the right-wing Freikorps. Workers were required to attend.

SOURCE 2

From a debate in Poland between Lech Wałęsa of Solidarity and Alfred Miodowicz, the leader of the official Communist (PUWP) trade union, on 30 November 1988:

Wałęsa: I say, let us not discuss whether Solidarity is necessary, only how to get it moving again.

Miodowicz: Is trade union reform the only solution to all Polish problems? It is also necessary to see opportunities in the party, where significant transformations are happening and will be happening. You understand that, given the very impulsive nature of Poles, diversity must be found in unity. Otherwise, we will tear each other apart.

Wałęsa: We will not make people happy by force. Give them freedom, and we will stop stumbling in place. Just look at Hungary, at how far forward they have gone.

Miodowicz: Do you not see here essential structural changes moving in the direction of democracy?

Wałęsa: What I see is that we are going by foot, while others go by car.

SOURCE 3

From the minutes of a meeting of the PUWP Central Committee on 5 June 1989. Solidarity won a landslide victory in the elections on 4 June 1989:

Comrade S. Ciosek: I don't understand the reasons for the defeat. Guilt is on our side. We trusted the Church, and they have turned against us. We overestimated our possibilities and have turned out to be deprived of support expected from Party members, which did not materialise. We have to keep in mind that very soon various claims and pressures will be rising like an avalanche – e.g., against the mass media. Radical changes must take place in the party.

Comrade Z. Michalek: What does it mean – radical changes in the party?

Comrade M.F. Rakowski: The party in its present structure is not in a position to stand up to current challenges. Talks with the opposition are necessary. It has proven to be trustworthy. What has happened in Poland is going to have tremendous impact outside. This may lead to upheavals in the whole camp.

SOURCE 4

From a speech in February 1990 by British Prime Minister Margaret Thatcher welcoming Poland's Prime Minister Tadeusz Mazowiecki to the UK:

We are welcoming the first non-communist Prime Minister of a government in Eastern Europe since 1948. History is being made this evening. It is hard to imagine circumstances more difficult than those under which you took the leadership of Poland's government. But you have not flinched for a moment from hard decisions. You have not promised your people easy solutions or painless remedies. Rather, you have told them the plain, unvarnished truth and they have responded to that.

It was your example – Poland's example – which inspired the other peoples of Eastern Europe to claim their freedom in the great peaceful revolution which has transformed our continent. So we honour you, Prime Minister, and we honour Solidarity's leader, Lech Wałęsa, who for millions of people round the world symbolised Poland's refusal to be cowed and her yearning to be free.

STUDY TIP

Knowledge of specialist vocabulary will be helpful for unpicking the value of these type of sources; for example, 'pluralism' – which means the dispersal of power between different institutes, groups, and people.

A LEVEL PRACTICE QUESTION

Evaluating primary sources

With reference to Sources 2, 3, and 4 and your understanding of the historical context, assess the value of these three sources to an historian studying change in Poland in the years 1988–90.

A LEVEL PRACTICE QUESTION

'By the end of 1988, the survival of the Communist regimes in Poland, Czechoslovakia, and the GDR was entirely dependent on repression.' Assess the validity of this view.

STUDY TIP

This question makes specific mention of three satellite states. Try to make detailed and valid reference to each of them in your answer. This does not mean that each state has to support your argument in the same way, however. Try to compare the relative importance of repression in each.

ACTIVITY

Summary

Draw a flow chart to show the build-up of opposition in Czechoslovakia, the GDR, Hungary, and Poland between 1980 and 1989. Include for each country:

- examples of opposition
- the extent to which opposition was repressed or restrained
- whether opposition came from outside the Party or from within it (or both)
- the nature of the opposition.

22 The state of communism in the satellite states of Romania and Bulgaria by 1989

The leadership of Zhivkov in Bulgaria

Historian Gale Stokes starts her description of Zhivkov's leadership in Bulgaria by saying 'There is not a great deal to be said about the development of Bulgarian politics under **Todor Zhivkov**'. This was all credit to Zhivkov's leadership skills, honed through a General Secretaryship that stretched from 1954 to 10 November 1989.

Fig. 1 *Todor Zhivkov in 1986. His nickname in Bulgaria was 'Old Uncle Tosho'. He was often mocked (in secret) for his uneducated ways; the quotation 'We must make a radical turn, at 360 degrees' is often attributed to Zhivkov*

KEY PROFILE

Todor Zhivkov (1911–98) was the longest-serving leader of any of the Soviet satellite states. Bulgaria had a home-grown Communist Party, which Zhivkov joined in 1928. He fought in the resistance to the Nazis in the war, and rose to the leadership of Bulgaria. As well as being First Secretary from 1954 until 1989, he was also premier of Bulgaria (First Chairman of the State Council) from 1962 to 1989.

Socialism under Zhivkov was kept very close to the Soviet line: collectivisation was completed in 1958, industry was centrally planned, with experimentation with decentralisation during the mid-1960s that ended following the suppression of the Prague Spring in 1968. Zhivkov loyally followed the foreign policy dictated by the USSR, and ties between the two countries grew so close during the Brezhnev era that Zhivkov even asked whether Bulgaria could become a part of the Soviet Union. Like Poland and Hungary, Bulgaria also found itself mired in foreign debt at the end of the 1970s. In the mid-1980s, Gorbachev invited Bulgaria to implement *perestroika*-style reforms, which Zhivkov obediently complied with. In short, if there was a model satellite state in the period from Stalin's death to the end of the Soviet Empire, Bulgaria was it.

Surprisingly, Zhivkov did not suppress opposition through the coercion of the secret police and security forces. Although the secret police, the CSS, were active in Bulgaria, those who overstepped the mark (for example, making fun of Zhivkov in a cartoon) might be forced out of their job or made to live in rural exile, but this punishment was often not lengthy and people were then allowed

LEARNING OBJECTIVES

In this chapter you will learn about:

- the leadership of Zhivkov in Bulgaria and Ceauşescu in Romania
- political and economic problems in Bulgaria and Romania.

KEY CHRONOLOGY

1954	March	Todor Zhivkov becomes General Secretary of the Bulgarian Communist Party
1965	March	Nicolae **Ceauşescu** becomes General Secretary of the Romanian Communist Party
1988		Activists in Bulgaria start to campaign in the town of Ruse against environmental pollution

to return to their jobs. Travel restrictions were much lighter than elsewhere, meaning Bulgarians who were rich enough could travel abroad, and thousands of Western tourists came to Bulgaria's Black Sea coasts each year. There were serious exceptions to this more relaxed regime, most notably the assassination of Bulgarian émigré writer **Georgi Markov** in London in 1978. However, relative to other satellite states where significant opposition to Communist Party rule developed, fear of the CSS could not have been the only reason for the very low levels of public political opposition in Bulgaria before 1989.

There are several factors that are important in explaining the success of Zhivkov's leadership in minimising opposition:

- The USSR was not seen as an oppressor in Bulgaria – Russian troops had helped bring about Bulgarian independence in the Russo-Turkish War (1877–78).
- Bulgaria had been directly ruled by the Ottoman Empire for 500 years before its liberation in 1878, which had isolated it from developments in West and Central Europe. For much of Ottoman rule, Bulgarian people suffered significant injustices, misrule, and loss of their national identity: they were treated no better than slaves. Therefore, although nationalism developed in the nineteenth century, there was an absence of a strong national identity that could stand in opposition to a Soviet-imposed system.
- Starting from a low base, rapid industrialisation and collectivisation had brought rapid growth to the Bulgarian economy in the 1950s and 1960s, and living standards in Bulgaria were among the highest of the satellite states through the 1970s.
- Bulgaria's economy was closely tied to the USSR, with imports of oil and raw materials and exports of machinery (including computers). Although it used foreign loans to finance the imports of Western technology it needed to innovate, its relationship with the USSR cushioned it from the drop in demand for Eastern European exports in the West in the 1970s and competition from the developing world.
- While Bulgaria faced the same foreign debt issues as other satellite states at the end of the 1970s, it reduced its balance of trade problems by boosting agricultural exports (from its cost-effective, efficient, huge collective farms) and, chiefly, by cleverly importing oil cheaply from the USSR and then reselling it at a much higher price to international markets. By 1983, foreign debt had been cut to $1.8 billion.
- Intellectuals (often the force for dissidence in other satellite states) almost all owed the Party and the socialist education system for their rise in society. Party organisations carried enormous benefits (for writers, for example), but also the requirement that members followed the Party line.
- Zhivkov himself came from the self-same poor background as the bureaucrats and intellectuals around him, and knew what was needed to gain their support. This included promoting patriotism in relation to Bulgaria's troubled history, and allowing the Orthodox Church a role in society. Zhivkov's daughter, **Lyudmila Zhivkova**, also proved popular with her lavish support of Bulgarian culture.

KEY PROFILE

Georgi Markov (1929–78) was a Bulgarian writer who defected to the West in 1969. He wrote critically about Zhivkov's regime and was a frequent broadcaster for the BBC and Radio Free Europe. He died in London in 1978 when someone, suspected to be from the KGB or Bulgarian CSS, injected him with the poison, ricin, which was apparently fired into his leg from a modified umbrella.

KEY PROFILE

Lyudmila Zhivkova (1942–81) was a key patron of the arts in Bulgaria, using her position to ensure museums and art galleries were well funded. She developed a keen interest in 'new age', mystical, and occult spirituality, which were in strong contrast to the Marxist–Leninist ideological line of Bulgaria in the 1970s and early 1980s. She died of a brain tumour in 1981.

Political and economic problems in Bulgaria

Political problems

Political and economic problems were closely intertwined in Bulgaria, as in the other satellite states. Leaders had far fewer problems of unrest and opposition when the economy was delivering increasing living standards, housing was being constructed to prevent housing shortages, and food was in

ACTIVITY

Why did Poland experience more opposition to the government than Bulgaria? With a partner, make a list of factors.

relatively good supply. But there were some political problems facing Zhivkov in the early 1980s that were not directly influenced by the economy:

- The treatment of ethnic Turks: since the start of his rule, Zhivkov had sought to make this ethnic minority take on a 'Bulgarian' identity. He ordered their ethnicity to be disregarded in censuses and then, from 1985, he launched a campaign of 'reconstruction of names' in which ethnic Turks were compelled, sometimes with violence, to change their Turkic or Arabic-sounding names to more 'Bulgarian' sounding ones. It is thought 100 people died as the army was used to enforce the campaign. When a group of Bulgarian Turks set up an opposition movement called the Democratic League for the Defence of Human Rights in 1989, Zhivkov ordered Bulgarian Turks to leave the country for Turkey: 300,000 people! (The economic impact of this was significant as Bulgarian Turks were among the most productive of Bulgaria's citizens.)
- Environmental problems: both those caused by its own industries and those caused by neighbouring Romania. Of particular concern was a chemical plant next to the Danube river which released quantities of highly toxic chlorine gas towards the Bulgarian town of Ruse. Activists in Ruse launched a campaign in late 1988 to curb the pollution, which, together with protests over a hydroelectric project near a historic monastery, led to the creation of the pressure group Ecoglasnost. The Chernobyl disaster in 1986 also raised concerns about Bulgaria's reliance on ageing Soviet-design nuclear reactors.
- *Glasnost* and *perestroika* were at the heart of a third political problem: the realisation that Zhivkov's enthusiastic adoption of Gorbachev's reforms was superficial and that he was actually doing almost nothing to share power (except perhaps with his son). Educated Bulgarians were almost all Russian speakers, and access to newspapers, radio, and television channels from the USSR clearly showed that political reform in Bulgaria was lagging far behind what was happening in the USSR. Criticism of Zhivkov began to be heard in intellectual circles (especially following the expulsion of ethnic Turks) and, within the Party, moves began to replace the old leader with someone able to take Bulgaria forward.

Fig. 2 *Members of the Bulgarian environmental pressure group, Ecoglasnost*

ACTIVITY

Extension

Treatment of minority ethnic groups was an issue around which political opposition coalesced in several satellite states, too. Find out more about the feelings of minority groups in Eastern Europe under Communism.

CROSS-REFERENCE

The Chernobyl disaster is covered in more detail in Chapter 10, page 77.

ACTIVITY

Thinking point

Make a spider diagram to show the reasons for opposition to Zhivkov's leadership. Consider which were the most significant, and highlight these.

Economic problems

Bulgaria's economic problems are simply stated: as Soviet oil prices began to rise through the 1980s, Zhivkov was no longer able to rely on the astute policy of reselling Soviet oil at a significant profit. Foreign loans bridged the investment gap, with the result that debt had grown again to over $10 billion by 1989 and the country's economy was in crisis.

The leadership of Ceauşescu in Romania

Todor Zhivkov and **Nicolae Ceauşescu** had very similar starts in life – both from peasant families and both only receiving a basic education. As leaders, though, the only real similarity was that both were in power for long periods: in the case of Ceauşescu from 1965 to 1989. While Zhivkov's deft economic and political management achieved compliance from Bulgarians until the very last years of the Soviet Empire, Ceauşescu developed a personality cult of grandiose proportions that was enforced by one of Eastern Europe's most extensive and brutal secret police forces, the Securitate. By the 1980s, it is estimated that one in forty Romanians, children included, were informers for the Securitate.

KEY PROFILE

Nicolae Ceauşescu (1918–89) was Romania's second General Secretary, and also its last. He came from a poor peasant family, ran away from his alcoholic father, and joined the Communist Party in his teens. He was imprisoned for his Party activities until 1940, which is when he met his wife Elena. Imprisoned again, he shared a cell with the future first leader of Romania as a socialist republic, Gheorghe Gheorghiu-Dej.

CROSS-REFERENCE

Stalin's personality cult was a major focus of Khrushchev's Secret Speech – see Chapter 2, page 10.

For more on Comecon, read Chapter 13, pages 104–105.

ACTIVITY

Using the Key Profile features in this book, together with your own research, produce a table comparing the Party leaders of the satellite states from 1953 to 1989. Your table could compare:

- dates of leadership (as First Secretary/General Secretary)
- family backgrounds
- war experiences
- education and training (which of the leaders were Russian-educated, for example)
- Party career
- political orientation (e.g. reformist, conservative)
- relationship with the USSR
- reasons for election
- reasons for resignation/leaving office.

Romania's Sovietisation had been a violent, grinding process: Soviet troops remained in occupation of the country until 1958 and any possible opponents of the regime – political, intellectual, or religious – had been purged to concentration camps and prison. At first, Ceauşescu was a reformer, encouraging feedback from workers and allowing limited moves towards small-scale businesses being able to operate for profit rather than to fulfil the central plan. In the West, he was viewed positively: Romania had, since the war, refused to toe the Soviet line. Comecon wanted it to be a primarily agricultural country that would supply the USSR and other satellite states, while Romania's leader, Gheorgiu-Dej, wanted Stalinist-style rapid industrialisation. Secondly, Ceauşescu had refused to allow Romanian troops to join the other Warsaw Pact forces in invading Czechoslovakia in 1968, linking his rationale to nationalist rhetoric – if the USSR ordered invasion of Czechoslovakia today, he said, then maybe it would be Romania's turn tomorrow: 'Be sure, comrades, be sure, citizens of Romania, that we shall never betray our homeland' (speaking on 22 August 1968).

As well as Western praise for his stance in 1968, the Romanian people also saw this as the start of radical moves away from the USSR, and support for the Romanian Communist Party surged. These hopes were ill-founded though, as Ceauşescu, fresh from a trip to China and North Korea in June 1971, began replicating the cults of personality he had seen on his travels. The 1971–75

Five Year Plan recentralised the economy, and Ceauşescu's plans for a return to strict ideological conformity in literature and art were expressed in a speech of 6 July 1971 that came to be known as his 'July Theses'. By December, a poet had been sentenced to 12 years in prison for writing critical poems.

Through the 1970s, the personality cult of Ceauşescu and his wife, Elena, ballooned to ludicrous proportions. Huge rallies were organised for which the only purpose was praise of the President of the Republic Nicolae Ceauşescu (as he was titled) and his wife, Comrade Academician Doctor Engineer Elena Ceauşescu (a grand title based on no discoverable qualifications).

ACTIVITY

Research

Find examples online of the personality cult of the Ceauşescus (e.g. propaganda paintings, posters, film clips, poems, songs) and create a display or a PowerPoint presentation.

Fig. 3 *The Ceauşescu personality cult was celebrated in images like this, where an oversized Ceauşescu is mobbed by grateful children; his supposed achievements are symbolised by doves of peace and the construction of apartments*

A CLOSER LOOK

The Ottoman Empire

Both Bulgaria and Romania had been part of the Ottoman Empire which, at its height in the seventeenth century, covered over 5 million square kilometres in Central and Southern Europe, the Middle East, northern Africa, and modern-day Turkey. The nineteenth century saw the Empire come under increasing economic and military pressure. Although the Empire lasted until the end of the First World War, Turkey's defeat in the Russo-Turkish War of 1877–78 saw Romania gain full independence and Bulgaria become a self-governing principality.

It is possible that Romania's complex history which included, as in Bulgaria, a long period under **Ottoman rule**, made open dissent less likely. However, the unparalleled intrusiveness of the Securitate must be the main reason for the lack of public opposition to Ceauşescu's miserable regime through the 1970s and 1980s. During the 1980s, the Securitate launched a huge campaign to root out dissidents (a title they attached to almost any educated Romanian). Censorship was very tight, telephone calls were listened to, and post was read. Propaganda pumped out the message that dissidents were everywhere, seeking to destroy Romania, and thousands of people were subjected to intimidation, blackmail, and public humiliation. There were assassination attempts against suspected dissidents.

Political and economic problems in Romania

The isolationism of Ceauşescu's Romania was a political problem in itself. As it grew increasingly out of step with reforms in the USSR and other satellite states, Western support dwindled for what had once been seen as a maverick East European state that dared defy the Soviet Empire. The extensive coercion of the Romanian people, resulting in violent change in 1989, was in contrast to the course of events in the other satellite states.

CROSS-REFERENCE

For more on violent change in Romania, see Chapter 23, pages 195–96.

In addition to the complete political and cultural domination of the Romanian people after 1971, Ceauşescu also introduced a much-resented policy in regard to abortion. As in other East European countries, abortion was the main form of birth control in Romania after its legalisation in 1957. The abortion rate in Romania soon rose to the highest of any country that reported such figures, and the Ceauşescus came to the decision that only a ban on abortion would solve the problem of declining birth rates. Without access to any other forms of contraception – which were not illegal but were impossible to obtain – the birth rate shot up initially, resulting in both a rapid increase in the use of dangerous, illegal abortion services and the abandonment of thousands of children in orphanages. Compulsory gynaecological examinations, overseen by the Securitate, were used to discover evidence of illegal abortions. While payment of a sizeable bribe could persuade Securitate officers not to press charges, those unable to pay could be sent to prison.

Economic problems were also closely linked to the Ceauşescus' simplistic views – which no one in the Party dared to question (since all senior positions were held either by sycophantic 'yes men' or the Ceauşescus' own relations, leading to the joke that, even better than 'socialism in one country', Romania had achieved socialism in one family.) Elena Ceauşescu's pretensions included industrial expertise, and she pushed for the development of huge, Stalinist, heavy industry projects that were out of step with global demand and which required costly imports of raw materials. Romania had Eastern Europe's most extensive oil supplies outside the USSR, but by the 1970s these were depleted. Rejecting any risk of dependence on the Soviet Union, Ceauşescu forged links with Middle Eastern oil suppliers. However, as oil prices rose in the 1970s, so did foreign debts: reaching $10 billion by 1981 and forcing Romania, like Poland, to **reschedule** its debts.

Ceauşescu's response was that Romania needed to pay back its debts and regain its independence. In order to do this, he cut imports and increased exports, but to the extent that the Romanian people were forced into serious poverty. Food rationing was introduced, which the Ceauşescus claimed had been scientifically calculated to ensure optimum nutrition. Meanwhile, the Ceauşescus continued their lavish lifestyle, the most public symbol of which was their enormous palace (built on land cleared of the homes of 40,000 people and of numerous churches, by 20,000 workers toiling for three shifts a day).

Fig. 4 *The Romanian parliament building, constructed as a private palace for the Ceauşescus*

A CLOSER LOOK

Romanian orphanages

The ban on abortion created a large number of children whose parents could not or did not want to look after them. Orphanages were quickly overwhelmed and conditions in them, which were basic to begin with, became inhumane. Basic sanitation was usually lacking and the children were often treated very badly in order to keep them compliant.

KEY TERM

reschedule [of debts]: obtain a longer time period before debt repayments have to be made or sometimes agreeing a reduction in the debt that allows some payment to be made

ACTIVITY

Research

To understand the scale and opulence of the Ceauşescus' palace, search for 'Romanian parliament building' on Google Maps. Street View and panoramic photos allow you to explore the exterior and interior of this building that was once the Ceauşescus' home.

SOURCE 1

From an essay entitled 'Romania: Three Lines with Commentary' written in 1989–90 by Norman Manea, a Romanian author who had published articles in the 1960s but then faced ruthless harassment by the Securitate:

Fear, exhaustion, disgust – at standing in lines, reading the same stupid newspaper all over again, watching the two hours of daily nausea on TV [news programmes in Romania in the 1980s consisted almost entirely of reports on the Ceauşescus]. The registration of your typewriter with the police [so the Securitate could trace *samizdat*], the underequipped and overused clinics, the feeling that you could die at any moment, and that every hour of survival merely retarded, prolonged, dismembered this slow dying, day after day, week after week. You would gradually stop seeing your friends because the buses ran very infrequently and were overcrowded, and it had become impossible to get from one end of the city to the other, and because you had nothing – food, drink or even cigarettes – to offer them when they came to visit. Because you were sick of repeating the same lament for the billionth time, and because you didn't want to face the other's defeat – marked each time by new wrinkles – and recognise it as your own.

SOURCE 2

From an interview in 1995 with Marius Mates, 27, who grew up in a city in Transylvania, Romania. The interview was part of an oral history project on the fall of communism in Eastern Europe:

During the early 80s, the situation deteriorated. Half a pound of butter had to last one month. It was the same thing with meat. There were huge lines to buy meat. I remember waiting in line for two or three days to be able to get ten pounds of meat that we would then try to store. I can't forget waiting in line day and night. I mean 24 hours a day. Our family would take shifts. By 1985 the situation was really bad and people started to feel a lot of pressure. We were afraid to speak, or say anything in public. The conversation at home was about how to get something – how to get coffee, how to get meat, how to get milk. My dad would say to my mom, 'Who do you know that we can give this piece of meat so we can get Marius some fruit?'

SOURCE 3

From an article entitled 'Birth and Death in Romania' by Pavel Câmpeanu, a former prison cellmate of Nicolae Ceauşescu during the Second World War, who managed to smuggle out this article to be published anonymously in *The New York Review of Books* in October 1986:

[People's problems increased] with the polar temperatures of the winter of 1984–1985, when heat was virtually cut off in every city. At twenty below zero people were freezing at home and in theaters, and, most of all, in hospitals. Schools were closed; women who had to go to work in the morning learned to do their cooking after midnight, when the power would occasionally be turned back on for one or two hours, on forbidden electric plates: the fine for doing so is five thousand lei, equivalent to the average salary for two months.

The right to keep warm becomes the obsession of most Romanians – the point where all the other rights invoked during the rest of the year tend to become forgotten. Thousands of people deprived of the right of free expression seem utterly indifferent to the fact. Very few remain indifferent about losing their right to keep warm.

STUDY TIP

You may find it helpful to start your assessment of the three sources by summarising what each says and noting key similarities and differences. For example, which of the sources include economic problems and which, social problems? What are the similarities and differences in terms of provenance?

A LEVEL PRACTICE QUESTION

Evaluating primary sources

With reference to Sources 1, 2, and 3 and your understanding of the historical context, assess the value of these three sources to an historian studying economic and political problems in Romania from 1984.

STUDY TIP

If a question asks about more than one state, then try to refer to each state mentioned in equal depth in your answer. If a question refers to a specific date range, try to stay within that range. This can be challenging, so consider planning your essay carefully beforehand.

AS LEVEL PRACTICE QUESTION

'The main problem faced by Bulgaria and Romania in the years 1980–89 was economic.' Assess the validity of this view.

ACTIVITY

Summary

Zhivkov's leadership and Ceaușescu's leadership show contrasting features. In pairs, role-play a hypothetical meeting between the two in which they discuss their different approaches and their attitudes towards the USSR. You could extent this role-play by inviting other leaders of satellite states to join the discussion.

Summary

Bulgaria was in many ways a model Soviet satellite state, from the USSR's point of view. Romania, also in many ways, was the West's poster child for a satellite state that resisted Soviet involvement as much as possible. The respective histories of both these countries, from the death of Stalin in 1953 to the revolutions of 1989, show the importance of the individual: Zhivkov in Bulgaria and Ceausescu in Romania. Zhivkov's pragmatic approach contributed significantly to a popular compliance/lack of open dissidence that meant the security services could stay low-key. Ceausescu's developing megalomania demanded the satellite states' most brutish secret police force to keep the Romanian people in line.

23 The collapse of communism within the satellite states in 1989

Reasons for and results of demonstrations and peaceful revolution in East Germany

Fig. 1 *In the summer of 1989, thousands of East Germans packed everything into cars and travelled to Hungary to escape over the border into Austria, and from there to West Germany*

KEY CHRONOLOGY

Events of 1989

2 May	Hungary starts to dismantle its 150-mile-long border fence with Austria
16 Aug	Poland's communist government collapses
10 Sept	Hungary allows thousands of East Germans to cross its border into Austria
Sept Oct	Leipzig peace marches grow in number each week: up to 300,000 marchers by the end of October
1 Oct	10,000 East Germans leave the GDR through West German embassies in Warsaw and Prague
6 Oct	Gorbachev visits Berlin for fortieth anniversary of the GDR
8 Nov	GDR's Politburo resigns
9 Nov	All border crossings, including the Berlin Wall, are opened
10 Nov	Todor Zhivkov resigns as General Secretary of Bulgarian Communist Party
17 Nov	Violent suppression of a demonstration in Prague leads to resignation of CPCz Politburo
24 Nov	Miloš Jakeš resigns as First Secretary of the CPCz
17 Dec	Ceauşescu orders troops to open fire on demonstrators
22 Dec	The Ceauşescu flee as the army joins opposition to their rule, but are given up
25 Dec	The Ceauşescus are shot after an improvised military trial

LEARNING OBJECTIVES

In this chapter you will learn about:

- reasons for and results of demonstrations and peaceful revolution in East Germany, Poland, Hungary, Czechoslovakia, and Bulgaria
- violent change in Romania.

A CLOSER LOOK

The 'freedom trains' and escape to the West

An agreement was reached between representatives of Czechoslovakia, East Germany, West Germany, and the USSR that the refugees in the Prague embassy would be allowed to travel to the West. Within hours of the announcement on 30 September, East German 'freedom trains' set off from Prague, taking the asylum seekers through East Germany to West Germany.

A CLOSER LOOK

Neues Forum

Neues Forum (New Forum) was founded in 1989 and was the first non-National Front party to be officially recognised in the GDR, after initial attempts had failed. It was pressure from large demonstrations that forced the SED to finally accept it as an official political party.

KEY TERM

civic movement: a movement devoted to defending the rights that protect individual freedoms from oppression, and of developing groups and organisations that represent the needs and interests of citizens

When in May 1989, the Hungarian government ordered frontier guards to dismantle the border fence with Austria, the first breach in the Iron Curtain was accomplished. Hungary had always been a popular holiday destination for East Germans, whose travel was restricted to the communist bloc countries. Some of those holidaying at Lake Balaton in the early summer of 1989 seized the opportunity to drive into Austria and then on to the FRG, where they could receive a West German passport and a small cash sum. Although the GDR government tried to halt this by prohibiting travel to Hungary, many simply defied the order.

By the end of August, the situation was growing out of control and to relieve the pressure, on 11 September, the Hungarians opened their border fully to East Germans. For weeks, trains made their way westwards laden with fleeing East Germans.

When the GDR government stopped travel to Hungary in September, more than 5000 would-be escapees set up camp in the grounds of the West German embassy in Prague. Altogether, approximately 15,000 refugees passed through the embassy in Prague before the border was closed on 9 November. Demonstrations against the border closure saw police cars set on fire.

German protest groups and the silent marches

In the summer and autumn of 1989, a number of new movements for reform and democratisation emerged in the GDR. These largely comprised educated urban professionals and became known as the **'civic movement'**. Some organisations were specifically political, others acted as debating forums, but they brought discussion out into the open and away from the confines of the Church.

Initially, the civic movement was limited in scope and lacked clear leadership. It was fragmented into so many different groups that each was vulnerable to Stasi infiltration. Nevertheless, there was some cooperation, such as when the Social Democrats, Democratic Awakening, Democracy Now, Neues Forum, and other pacifist groups met in Berlin on 4 October to address an audience of 2000. They issued a joint declaration –'We are united in our will to transform the State and society democratically' – and called on all GDR citizens to work for democratic renewal, human rights, pacificism, ecological improvements, intellectual freedom, and social solidarity.

Fig. 2 *A Neues Forum demonstration in Leipzig, 18 November 1989*

The centre of the freedom protests was Leipzig. The regular Monday prayer service in Leipzig's Nikolaikirche had already become a focus for peaceful change and greater personal liberty, and young peace protestors took to the streets after the service, waving banners that declared 'an open country with free people'. The Stasi took action to break this up, prompting the protestors to adopt a different approach. On 18 September, they emerged from their service, candles in hand, and marched silently, moving in different directions, offering no threat and presenting no easy target to the Stasi, who were unsure how to react.

There followed regular 'silent marches': 5000 marchers on 25 September; 20,000 on 2 October. On 7 October, during the celebration of the GDR's fortieth anniversary, the peaceful protest in Leipzig had water cannons turned on it and 210 protestors were arrested. Rumours began to circulate that the following Monday, 9 October, would see a massive crackdown, like that witnessed in Tiananmen Square in Beijing during June. Three local SED officials, fearing bloodshed, persuaded the Party to withdraw the massed security forces (all dressed in riot gear). The procession was allowed to pass peacefully. This was a turning point in the development of the protest movement. The following week, over 100,000 marchers appeared in Leipzig; on 23 October, there were more than 250,000; on 30 October, 350,000. The pattern was repeated elsewhere all over East Germany. The Stasi were held in check and the government tried to combat dissent politically instead.

ACTIVITY

Draw a spider diagram of the different factors that affected the way the SED responded to opposition to its control of the GDR during 1989.

A CLOSER LOOK

Tiananmen Square, June 1989

Student protests in Beijing's Tiananmen Square, through the spring of 1989, were harshly repressed by the Chinese government on 3 and 4 June. Hundreds of thousands of protestors and soldiers were involved, and the numbers killed as soldiers opened fire are thought to be between 400 and 800, though possibly higher.

Erich Honecker and internal collapse

Honecker underwent a gall-bladder operation on 18 August 1989, and the government floundered for six weeks while he recuperated. Honecker returned in time to preside over the GDR's fortieth anniversary celebrations.

SOURCE 1

From a speech by Honecker, and a response by Gorbachev, at the official celebration of the fortieth anniversary of the founding of the GDR which took place in Berlin on 6–7 October 1989:

Honecker: Today the GDR is an outpost of peace and civilisation in Europe. We will never forget this fact. Forty years of the GDR mark a totally new chapter in the history of our people. The GDR has paved its way with achievements serving to strengthen our people. Socialism and peace are, and remain, key words for that which we have achieved up to now, as well as that which we will continue to accomplish.

Gorbachev: Like every other country, the GDR, of course, has its own problems of development which must be considered and for which solutions must be found. We do not doubt the capability of the Socialist Unity Party of Germany, with all its intellectual potential, its rich experience and its political authority, in cooperation with all social forces, to find answers to the questions.

ACTIVITY

How do the two speeches in Source 1, given on 6 October 1989, differ? Can you account for this?

ACTIVITY

In October 1989, the GDR celebrated its fortieth anniversary, with dignitaries from across the Soviet bloc attending. Continue one of the speeches in Source 1 as might have been given by Honecker or Gorbachev for the occasion.

In the eyes of many East Germans, the staged celebrations merely exemplified Honecker's inability to face up to reality. Gorbachev's clear lack of support for the ageing leader signalled his loss of Soviet endorsement, as well as the loss of internal support. Consequently, some SED politicians came to accept that Honecker had to go. Those involved knew the Party's authority was in danger and believed in a more 'flexible' socialism. When the agenda for the closed Politburo meeting of 17 October was handed to him, Honecker found an additional item had been added – that he resign as General Secretary of the SED and associated state offices on the grounds of ill health.

The opening of the Berlin Wall

With Honecker 's departure, **Egon Krenz** assumed control. In his first address, he stated: 'The first requirement is a realistic appreciation of the position we are in. In the past months it is clear that we haven't always paid sufficient heed to the nature of the social evolution of our country and we haven't always drawn the appropriate conclusions at the right time. From today we shall be taking a different course, we are going to win back the political and ideological initiative.'

Krenz opened discussions with Church leaders and with Neues Forum. On 27 October, a ban on visa-free travel to Czechoslovakia imposed by Honecker earlier in the month was lifted and an amnesty given to all those convicted of trying to escape to the West. Krenz appeared on television on 3 November outlining an SED action plan of political reform, human rights, economic restructuring, and changes in education. However, he did not reverse the statements he had made two days earlier when he had rejected opening the Berlin Wall, moving towards reunification, or giving up the SED's claim to leadership. On 4 November, between 500,000 and 1 million people crowded onto the streets of East Berlin, calling for free elections and freedom of speech. A further 500,000 marched in Leipzig on Monday 6 November. It has been estimated that around 9000 people a day, or 375 an hour, left the GDR across the Czech border in early November.

On 7 November, the entire East German government resigned. Berlin marchers cheered and shouted, 'All power to the people and not to the SED.' On 8 November, the remainder of the Politburo resigned and a new, smaller Politburo was created, which included some moderate reformers, as well as old hardliners.

On 9 November, an SED official, Günter Schabowski, was asked whether the lifting of the travel ban had been a mistake. Schabowski sidestepped the question but then added, 'We have decided today to implement a regulation that allows every citizen of the GDR through any of the border crossings,' adding that this would be 'immediately, without delay'. It later transpired that the regulation had only been a draft proposal, but once the word was out, it could not be retracted.

No one had expected the announcement and border guards were not prepared for the ever-increasing crowds. They were, however, ordered to avoid bloodshed at all costs and so, around midnight, they gave up trying to control the crowds and let them through the Berlin Wall.

Fig. 3 *East Germans walk into West Germany in November 1989*

KEY PROFILE

Egon Krenz (b. 1937) joined the SED in 1955 and became leader of the Ernst Thälmann Pioneers (1971–74) and the Free German Youth (1974–83). He entered the SED Central Committee, the *Volkskammer* (People's Chamber), and finally the Politburo. He served as Secretary of the Central Committee from 1983 and was Honecker's deputy. He led the GDR from October until December 1989, when he was forced to resign. In 1997, he was sentenced to six and a half years in prison for the deaths of Berlin Wall would-be escapees and electoral fraud, but he never renounced his political views.

ACTIVITY

Research

Using online news reports for 9 November and the days after, put together a collection of sources describing the fall of the Berlin Wall in the Western media. Use them to develop information on the context of the fall of the Berlin Wall, and consider how valuable these sources are for historians working on the reasons for the collapse of SED authority in 1989.

The final attempts to reform and preserve the East German regime, and their failure

Within a week, 9 million East Germans had set out to visit the West. Most returned, but on average (through December, January, and February) over 2000 per day did not. The loss of nearly another million East Germans during this period weakened the economy.

The SED leadership desperately tried to curb increased opposition demands by promising free elections, freedom for the media, and economic reform. Many Party members thought such changes too radical, but many in the population at large felt they were not enough. If the Berlin Wall could go, it seemed that nothing was impossible any more, including reunification.

On 13 November, the moderate **Hans Modrow** became prime minister. Modrow offered concrete reforms rather than vague promises, and although he rejected reunification, he insisted on the separation of Party and state power, which meant that power shifted from the SED back to the *Volkskammer* and the newly appointed cabinet of government ministers, comprising 16 SED ministers and 12 from other parties. Hundreds of SED district leaders and lesser officials were also replaced.

The newly liberated media exposed Party corruption, the brutality of the Stasi, and the opulent lifestyle the Party elite had enjoyed while everyone else queued for food. The SED was terminally damaged. On 1 December, the *Volkskammer* formally removed the SED's leading role from the constitution and on 3 December, Krenz stepped down as Chairman of the Council of Ministers. Over the following winter months, Round Table talks took place between the Modrow government and the leaders of the main opposition groups, the Churches, and other parties.

At the first meeting, they set up four working groups to consider reforms and agreed that the GDR's first free elections would be held on 6 May 1990 (later moved to 18 March 1991). However, most of those who participated in the Round Table talks were still committed to a 'third way' – a society that was halfway between communism and capitalism. This was increasingly out of touch with the public mood. While in November 1989, 86 per cent of the population favoured socialist reform, by February 1990, this was down to 56 per cent, with 31 per cent wanting a return to capitalism.

The hated Ministry of State Security was replaced by the Office for National Security, but there was an alarming continuity of personnel and organisation. Only after the Normanenstrasse Stasi headquarters were stormed and occupied by disgruntled Berliners in January 1990 did the Modrow government climb down and dissolve the force entirely.

In the GDR, the economy was on the brink of collapse, and the early months of 1990 were ones of readjustment. True details about the state of the economy began to emerge, including a vast budget deficit of 17 billion marks. The government had huge foreign debts of around £12.9 billion (the highest debt per capita of any satellite state except Poland). Workers established independent unions and went on strike for higher wages. Public order in the GDR seemed on the verge of total collapse, too. In February, an interim **coalition** government, the 'government of national responsibility', was created, bringing together 13 different parties and groups, including Round Table members and the old SED, renamed as the PDS (Party of Democratic Socialism).

Modrow's mounting difficulties were not helped by the attitude of the FRG Chancellor **Helmut Kohl** who, sensing the mood of the East Germans, refused Modrow's requests for aid in the face of bankruptcy and rejected Modrow's own proposals for unification and the creation of a neutral German state.

KEY PROFILE

Hans Modrow (b. 1928) joined the SED after the war and had a long Party career, including being boss of Dresden. His criticism of Honecker, however, blocked him rising much higher in the Party hierarchy. Gorbachev favoured him over Krenz, but it was Krenz who took over from Honecker in 1989.

ACTIVITY

Pair discussion

How influential were Gorbachev's reforms in the collapse of one-party rule in the GDR? Was the collapse of communism inevitable by the end of the twentieth century?

CROSS-REFERENCE

Round Table talks, began in Poland. Read more details in Chapter 21, page 171.

KEY TERM

coalition: an alliance of political parties to form a government

KEY PROFILE

Helmut Kohl (b. 1930) was Chancellor of West Germany from 1982 to 1990, and of reunified Germany from 1990 to 1998. His achievements included both overseeing German reunification and the Maastricht Treaty of February 1992, which created the European Union.

By mid-February, East Germany had approximately 160 'parties' competing to take part in the election campaign, although only 24 finally took part. The real power came from the West German political parties, which backed different East German parties. The result on 18 March 1991 was an overwhelming endorsement for Helmut Kohl's 'Alliance for Germany', which gained 48.1 per cent of the vote, in contrast to the PDS's 21.9 per cent: East Germans had voted for a social market economy and for German reunification. **Lothar de Maizière** was elected the new head of the East German government and set about the task of 'democratising the GDR in order to dissolve it'.

The final months of the GDR's history were dominated by reunification negotiations. A currency union on 1 July only speeded up the GDR's collapse. A treaty of accession in October merged the Eastern states into the Federal Republic. Although de Maizière conducted some hard bargaining over the draft treaty, the huge disparity in power between the weak, disintegrating Eastern state and the dominant Western one made the act of reunification more of a takeover than a merging of equals.

KEY PROFILE

Lothar de Maizière (b. 1940) was elected to the *Volkskammer* in 1990 and was premier from 12 April to 2 October 1990. He signed the 'Two Plus Four ' treaty which ended Allied control over Berlin and Germany, and brought forward the German reunification of 3 October 1990. He was subsequently appointed Minister for Special Affairs under Kohl, but resigned on 17 December 1990 following rumours that he had worked for the Stasi.

ACTIVITY

The collapse of the East German state is actually quite hard to pinpoint and can cause confusion. Make a timeline diagram that shows:

- when and why the SED collapsed
- when and why the East German dictatorship collapsed
- when and why the GDR collapsed.

A LEVEL PRACTICE QUESTION

'The collapse of SED rule in East Germany was entirely the result of the Party's own failings within the GDR.' Assess the validity of this view.

STUDY TIP

Since essay questions could ask about any one of the satellite states for this period of study, try to ensure you have sufficient detail to be able to answer in depth on each. Detailed knowledge helps you to support your argument with relevant, appropriate examples and information.

Peaceful revolution in Poland

Following **Solidarity's** electoral victory in 1989, undermining any remaining PUWP legitimacy, there was much debate within Solidarity as to what its next move should be. Although it had more than demonstrated the strength of its popular support as an opposition movement, some within Solidarity doubted that they had the skills to run a country and recommended remaining in opposition, now backed with the political power to ensure reform. The Solidarity leadership stepped in to give Jaruzelski enough votes to become president, having decided that keeping him in a leading role would provide much-needed stability for Poland and reassurance to the USSR. Wałęsa proposed forming a Solidarity government in which the PUWP retained control of the ministries of the interior and of defence, together with a commitment to Poland remaining in the Warsaw Pact. Again, both these were designed to reassure the USSR. Wałęsa also proposed **Tadeusz Mazowiecki** as prime minister – a Catholic intellectual with the Church's support. With the PUWP leadership having obtained the tacit agreement of Gorbachev that the USSR would not intervene, Solidarity formed a coalition government in September 1989 with the PUWP and two other parties that had formerly supported the PUWP. Jaruzelski became president. It was a huge achievement for Solidarity, but now an organisation formed to protect workers from the government had become the government itself.

CROSS-REFERENCE

The factors that enabled **Solidarity** to take a leading role in Poland's government are discussed in Chapter 21. **Tadeusz Mazowiecki** is also featured on page 171.

ACTIVITY

Using the information here and in Chapter 21, identify the factors that enabled Solidarity to take a leading role in Poland's government in September 1989.

Peaceful revolution in Hungary

Having opened its border with Austria at the start of 1989, allowing Hungarians to travel freely between the two countries, Hungary was in the forefront among the satellite states when it came to reform. Its government, headed by Károly Grósz was being pushed along by demonstrations organised by the democratic opposition. Attempts by Grósz to corral the main new parties into an umbrella group supporting socialist aims (controlled by the Hungarian Socialist Workers' Party) failed, and led instead to eight of the main opposition parties forming a united front against Grósz. According to historian Gale Stokes: 'The success of the negotiated revolution in Hungary can be laid to the unity these disparate groups maintained for the next few months, which was just long enough to prevent the regime from ramming through a phony multiparty constitution and to create a workable political agreement.'

Round Table talks began in June 1989 between the Party (including Imre Pozsgay and other reformers), the Party's loyal satellite parties, and the opposition parties, with the expressed aim of introducing a democratic, multi-party parliamentary system. The opposition parties all had one aim in common – free elections. However, the Party also believed that it could win in a free vote, including the expectation that Imre Pozsgay would be elected president. The Party split: the old guard of conservatives kept the Hungarian Socialist Workers' Party name and the reformers became the Hungarian Socialist Party (confident that they would appear more attractive to voters having got rid of the old guard). Such hopes were dashed in the parliamentary elections of March and April 1990, when the reformed Communists got just 8.5 per cent of the seats and the unreformed Communists were wiped out.

CROSS-REFERENCE

The leadership of Károly Grósz is discussed in Chapter 21, page 174.

Reasons for and results of demonstrations and peaceful revolution in Czechoslovakia

Throughout 1989, the security forces notably reduced their attempts to break up demonstrations organised by dissidents, Church organisations, and student protestors. This changed on 17 November when a demonstration to mark International Students' Day turned into a show of opposition to the government.

The police reaction was a turning point. Václav Havel formed the Civic Forum in response to the police repression, thus combining Czech opposition in one umbrella group. In Slovakia, the equivalent body was called People Against Violence. Civic Forum put forward its demands to the CPCz, which had been shaken by the events of 17 November and was no longer even sure of support from the security forces. A general strike showed the protests spreading from dissidents and students to workers. The CPCz renounced its leading role and announced free elections. This is known as the 'Velvet Revolution'.

A CLOSER LOOK

International Students' Day: 17 November 1939

Demonstrations in Prague in October 1939, to mark the anniversary of the founding of the Czech Republic, turned into a protest against the Nazi occupation. A student called Jan Opletal was beaten up at the demonstration and later died. His funeral triggered another mass demonstration, to which the Nazis retaliated on 17 November: all Czech universities were closed, 1200 Czech students were sent to concentration camps, and nine students were executed.

SOURCE 2

From a speech by Czechoslovak premier Ladislav Adamec to the CPCz CC on 24 November 1989, in which, having rejected the use of force to put down the demonstrations, he set out the alternative:

I would clearly prefer the second alternative: a political solution. We must count on making certain acceptable concessions. I believe that we have not nearly exhausted these possibilities. I also rely on the fact that most of our people, including young people, have no reason to be against socialism. They are unsatisfied with many things, even stirred up by all kinds of disinformation, but are able and willing to repay trust with trust. To drive the young generation into the arms of the enemies of socialism would be an unforgivable mistake. This must be prevented under any circumstances. I also advocate political methods because the recent intervention of the forces of order has led to the radicalisation of youth, allowed the unification of various groups behind its condemnation, and has not contributed to the authority of either the Party or the State. This warning should not be understood as a call for concessions at any price, without regard to the loss of socialist values.

Fig. 4 *Václav Havel (right) and Alexander Dubček (left), with dissident pop singer Marta Kubisova (centre), join hands on 24 November 1989 on their way to address 200,000 protesters gathered on Wenceslas Square, calling for the resignation of the communist government.*

A CLOSER LOOK

On 28 December, Dubček was elected speaker of the new parliament and Havel was elected president.

SOURCE 3

From a speech by Václav Havel in Wenceslas Square, Prague, on 23 November 1989, to a crowd of 300,000 people. Wenceslas Square became the focus of the Velvet Revolution – demonstrators went there to get information and to hear daily speeches from opposition groups:

The Civic Forum is prepared to secure a dialogue between the public and the present leadership immediately and has at its disposal qualified forces [from] all areas of society, capable of carrying out a free and objective dialogue about real paths toward a change in the political and economic conditions in our country.

The situation is open now, there are many opportunities before us, and we have only two certainties.

The first is the certainty that there is no return to the previous totalitarian system of government, which led our country to the brink of an absolute spiritual, moral, political, economic, and ecological crisis.

Our second certainty is that we want to live in a free, democratic, and prosperous Czechoslovakia, which must return to Europe, and that we will never abandon this ideal, no matter what transpires in these next few days.

A LEVEL PRACTICE QUESTION

Evaluating primary sources

With reference to Sources 2 and 3 and your understanding of the historical context, assess the value of these sources to an historian studying the Velvet Revolution in Czechoslovakia.

STUDY TIP

In an A Level exam you will be asked to assess the value of three sources. In this question you need to assess the value of two. Historical context helps with unlocking a source and ascertaining its value and significance. For example, consider what Havel means by the 'CPCz monopoly', and what Adamec is referring to when he mentions 'the authority of the Party'. Also try to establish the tone of each source in your answer to this type of question.

A LEVEL PRACTICE QUESTION

'It was the ability of the opposition leaders that explains why the end of communism in most satellite states in 1989 was so peaceful.' Assess the validity of this view.

STUDY TIP

You will need to reflect on the end of communism in the GDR, Poland, Hungary, Czechoslovakia and Bulgaria, in order to assess the claim made in the question. For example, was the opposition leadership equally able in all states and was it only opposition leadership that made for the peaceful transitions?

Peaceful revolution in Bulgaria

The political and economic difficulties besetting Zhivkov's leadership were significant and by March 1989 there were a number of opposition groups, including those expressing opposition to the expulsion of Turkish Bulgarians and those, like Ecoglasnost, who protested against environmental damage. Ecoglasnost, in particular, was able to mobilise large demonstrations in early November 1989. Increasingly throughout 1989, Zhivkov was seen as out of touch within the Party, and on 9 November he found that a majority of the Politburo were requesting his resignation and that, moreover, they had the backing of the army. He resigned the next day. From that time on, events moved rapidly. His replacement, Petur Mladenov, announced the end of the Party's leading role, expelled Zhivkov from the Party, and called for free elections in 1990. Opposition parties, united as the Union of Democratic Forces, joined Round Table talks.

CROSS-REFERENCE

The problems of Zhivkov's leadership by the end of the 1980s are discussed in Chapter 22, page 179.

Reasons for and results of violent change in Romania

As discussed in Chapter 22, the Ceauşescus' determination to pay off Romania's national debt meant austerity on a scarcely imaginable scale for a post-war European country: food rationing, energy rationing (people even froze to death in unheated apartments in winter), requisition of food from family plots, enforced overtime with 24-hour shifts, together with the highly intrusive policy to increase the birth rate. Extreme repression by the security forces prevented opposition groups forming, and the outbreaks of worker discontent (demonstrations or riots) that sometimes followed wage cuts or food price increases were severely punished, with 'ringleaders' simply never seen again.

In 1989, pressure began to build against the Ceauşescu regime both from within Romania and from outside. International disquiet about human rights abuses, especially regarding treatment of the Hungarian minority population in Transylvania, meant that Ceauşescu turned down advantageous US trade terms to avoid investigation of claims against the regime by the US Congress. This meant a loss in trade valued at $250 million: foreign currency Ceauşescu needed to pay off Romania's debts. Romanian dissidents began to publish critical articles against him, some of which were broadcast throughout Romania via Radio Free Europe. Those dissidents still in Romania were arrested and put under house arrest; some were sentenced to death.

CROSS-REFERENCE

See Chapter 22, page 182 for discussion of the Ceauşescu leadership.

When in December 1989, in Timişoara, crowds protested at the exile of a dissident Hungarian Reformed Church minister called László Tőkés, Ceauşescu railed at the army for not taking firmer action against the protestors, which resulted in a massacre on 17 December. Around a hundred people were shot dead by the army, who then, perhaps appalled by orders to shoot their own countrymen, withdrew and let an opposition body called the Democratic Front take over the city by 22 December. Ceauşescu went on TV to promise more harsh repression and called for a televised rally to be organised for 21 December. This was packed with reliable members of the security forces dressed as ordinary people and factory workers assumed to be loyal to the regime. Unexpectedly, Ceauşescu was heckled by this 'reliable' part of the crowd – an event broadcast nationwide by the TV cameras.

It appears that what happened next was a disguised coup by an organisation calling itself the National Salvation Front, working together with Securitate forces. Although the latter was supposed to have been fighting the former, the fight was staged to remove the Democratic Front from contention, while still allowing the National Salvation Front to appear as liberators. In these confused and panicky times, on 22 December, the Ceauşescus only just escaped by helicopter from an angry crowd. However, it seems the pilot landed again in order for the Ceauşescus to be arrested by the National Salvation Front, tried by **kangaroo court,** and shot.

KEY TERM

kangaroo court: an improvised military tribunal that tries a person or people without the use of recognised legal standards

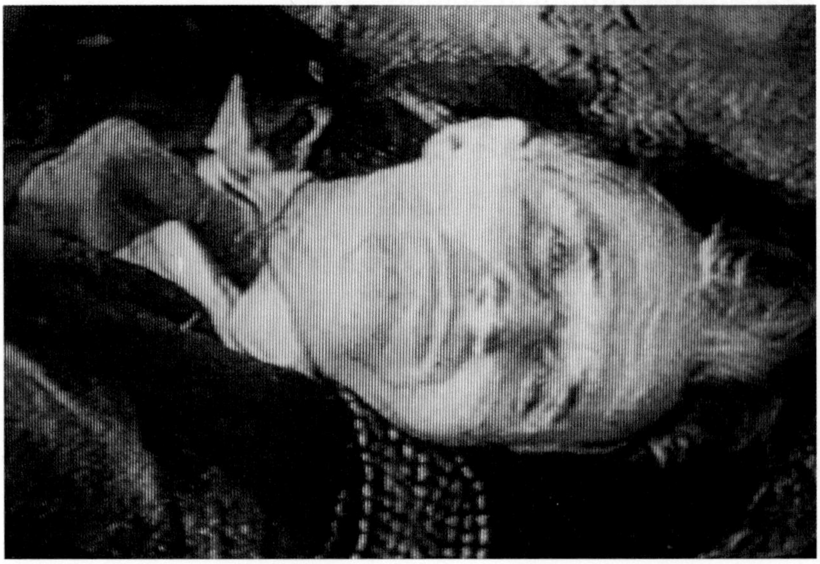

Fig.5 *The corpse of Nicolae Ceauşescu , after his execution during the Romanian revolution of December 1989*

There is no consensus on whether the violent change in Romania was the result of spontaneous revolution against the hated Ceauşescus or of a plot from inside the security forces, senior members of which did gain prominent positions in the new government. It is possible that it was the result of both.

STUDY TIP

To prepare for answering a question like this, make a list of external factors to consider, followed by a list of internal factors. Try to recall your knowledge of the historical context of the year 1989 in the satellite states and use that to inform your answer.

A LEVEL PRACTICE QUESTION

'The revolutions of 1989 in the Soviet satellite states in Central and Eastern Europe were caused more by external factors than internal pressures.' Assess the validity of this view.

ACTIVITY

Summary

Copy and complete a table like the one below, to record the key information about the revolutions of 1989.

Reasons for and results of the collapse of communism within the satellite states in 1989

Satellite state	Internal factors	Results and significance (out of 10)	External factors	Results and significance (out of 10)
East Germany				
Poland				
Hungary				
Czechoslovakia				
Bulgaria				
Romania				

24 The new national states of Eastern and Central Europe

Political issues: problems of creating united and stable governments

ACTIVITY

List the different types of political parties and try to find examples of each from within the new national states, i.e. former satellite states.

With the exception of Poland, which had already broadened its political base, 1990 was the year of free, multi-party parliamentary elections in Eastern Europe.

All the revolutions of 1989 demanded political freedom, producing an outpouring of multi-party democracy in the 1990 elections. There were dozens of political parties in the elections (82 in Romania), representing a huge variety of interests. These included parties that had been suppressed after the Second World War (or earlier), right-wing nationalists and conservative religious parties, left-wing socialists, including the old Communist Parties repackaged or reformed, parties advocating a **technocratic** path, those (like Solidarity and Civic Forum) who stood for a '**civic society**', centrists, environmentalists, and Westernisers – every colour of the political spectrum. They all had in common a commitment to democratic representation and most of them, even the socialists, believed the only solution to Eastern Europe's economic difficulties came from a move towards the opposite of the planned economy: the free market.

- One outcome was that it was hard for one party to achieve the majority required in parliament to pass laws, especially since legislatures were set up to make it difficult for any one party to dominate the leadership of the country. Coalition governments were common. In Hungary, for example, even a coalition of the two main opposition parties, the MDF and the SzDSz, did not have enough votes to pass laws on the most important national issues.
- Opposition groups had united against the monopoly of power of the Communist Parties, their corrupt cronyism, and their discredited economic systems, but after they had been defeated (outside of Romania and Bulgaria), parties had less in common than before. This was shown most graphically in Czechoslovakia, where Slovak people quickly began to resent the decisions being taken by the mostly Czech leaders of Civic Forum.
- Opposition groups came to power on a surge of optimism about political freedom, economic revival, a fairer and better way of living, and the repair of environmental damage. However, although political freedom was quickly achieved, the rest of these problems were very difficult to solve, and the new leaderships of the Eastern European countries were often no more, and sometimes less, successful than their Communist Party predecessors in making the changes their people wanted to see.
- Dealing with the legacy of the past was extremely problematic. How should those responsible for the crimes and human rights abuses committed under the old regime be punished, when so many people had collaborated in the system? Allegations of helping the secret police, or collaborating with the Soviets, proved an easy way for politicians to destroy each other's credibility.

LEARNING OBJECTIVES

In this chapter you will learn about:

- political issues: problems of creating united and stable governments, including the separation of Czech and Slovak republics
- the restoration of capitalism
- closer ties with the West
- political, economic, and social progress and continuing difficulties by 2000.

KEY CHRONOLOGY

1990	March	Hungarian parliamentary elections
	Oct	reunification of Germany
1991	Feb	Warsaw Pact dissolved
1992	Dec	Czechoslovakia breaks up
1993		Last Soviet troops leave Poland
1999	March	Czech Republic, Hungary, and Poland join NATO

KEY TERM

technocratic: when policies are put forward and implemented by those with relevant technological knowledge and understanding (for example, economists)

civic society: when community groups and organisations take on part or full responsibility for the provision of services and support for those who need it, rather than the State alone

- The Soviet system had attempted to eradicate ethnic and religious differences, but once Soviet control had gone, those differences often quickly reappeared and were a key cause of the unstable political environments of some Eastern European countries.

Table 1 *Selected data for the 1990 elections in Eastern Europe*

Date	Country	Last free election since . . .	Winner	% of vote of winning party	Where did the former Communist Party come?	Turnout
18 March	East Germany	1933	Alliance for Germany bloc	48%	Third (16%)	93%
28 March	Hungary	1945	MDF – the Hungarian Democratic Forum	42%	Fourth	65%
20 May	Romania	1937	National Salvation Front	85%	First? Since NSF leaders were mostly former communists	86%
8 and 9 June	Czechoslovakia	1946	Civic Forum	49.5%	Second (13%)	96%
10 June	Bulgaria	1931	Bulgarian Socialist Party	47%	First	90%
25 November	Polish presidential election	–	Lech Wałęsa of Solidarity	74%	–	60% first round, 53% second round

ACTIVITY

1. Which countries' elections were won by former Communist Parties (or ones that appeared to be very similar to them)? To what extent would you say these countries had factors in common that explained this?
2. Which countries had relatively low turnout rates compared to the rest? What factors might have been involved in this?
3. Lech Wałęsa had to go to a second round against Stanisław Tyminski, an independent candidate (Tadeusz Mazowiecki came third). Research Tyminski's result: why do you think he did so well?

Political fragmentation: Poland

Parliamentary elections in Poland in 1991 produced a deeply fragmented political situation, with 29 political parties gaining seats in the Sejm (from 111 parties that were seeking election) and no one party achieving more than 13 per cent of the vote. This fragmentation occurred after Solidarity was itself pulled apart by disagreement within its leadership as the country struggled to deal with the impact of economic 'shock therapy', with 'a war at the top' due to President Wałęsa's confrontational, authoritarian style, and with continuing accusations of historic collaboration with the USSR and other political scandals. Wałęsa himself was narrowly defeated as president, in elections in 1995, by Aleksander Kwaśniewski, the leader of the successor to the PUWP, the Social Democracy of the Republic of Poland.

CROSS-REFERENCE

'Shock therapy', the name given to the radical economic changes required by the IMF in return for large loans, is discussed in this chapter on page 203.

The legacy of the past: East Germany

Following the fall of the Berlin Wall, the Stasi, like secret police forces across the Eastern bloc, started to destroy their files. In many places, East German citizens occupied local Stasi offices to prevent this from happening. The new political leaders were unsure about this process. On the one hand, the files would be necessary for rehabilitating those unjustly convicted of crimes and for making recompense to those who had suffered under the old regime. But on the other, the same files would certainly implicate many people in collaboration with the Stasi,

KEY TERM

lustration: a process for filtering out/purging former communist officials from taking office in post-communist states including several of the new political leadership and those needed now to run local government, public services, and businesses. In 1990, a law was passed protecting the files, and making access to them a democratic right for every citizen. A **lustration** process was then set up, which meant that everyone applying for any kind of public office had to declare any involvement with the Stasi or face instant dismissal if undisclosed links were later discovered. Since links to the Stasi were likely to make election less likely, many would-be politicians did not own up to them, only to be mired in scandal once in office. Presumably, too, some East Germans with useful political and administrative experience under the old regime did not put themselves forward for public office because they did not want to go through the lustration process.

Nationalist tensions: the separation of the Czech and Slovak republics

A strong centralising, Soviet-backed state had constrained ethnic tensions within the former Yugoslavia and Czechoslovakia. However, the problems of creating stable and unified governments were most intense once that constraint was lifted.

The new name for what had been the Czechoslovak Socialist Republic, as put forward by Czech parliamentary delegates, was the Czechoslovak Federative Republic. Slovak delegates preferred the Czecho-Slovak Federative Republic. For the Czechs, this name was too reminiscent of the Munich Agreement (Czecho-Slovakia was the name used after the Nazis had annexed the Sudetenland), and the end decision was for 'The Czech and Slovak Federal Republic'. Although seemingly trivial, this dispute (the 'hyphen war') pointed to resentment from Slovaks and a determination not to let the Czechs assume control over their country, and prefigured the dissolution of Czechoslovakia in 1993.

Fig. 1 *Slovakians celebrate their independence at midnight on 31 December 1992*

SOURCE 1

From an article entitled 'Thousands cheer Slovak "freedom"', by journalist Adrian Bridge, writing for the UK newspaper *The Independent*, a British national newspaper that began in 1986 with the aim of reporting news without any bias towards a particular political party viewpoint. This article appeared in the newspaper on 1 January 1993:

VLADIMIR MECIAR, the Prime Minister of Slovakia, yesterday hailed his country's newly acquired independence, [calling it] an 'escape from assimilation and the loss of national identity'. Mr Meciar warned that there would be tough times ahead, but predicted that Slovaks would rise to the challenge.

In Prague, Vaclav Klaus, the Czech Prime Minister, said that Czechs had not wanted the split, but had effectively been left no choice following the victory of the nationalist Mr Meciar in elections last June. Mr Klaus[...] stressed that both countries would continue to have close ties.

With an economy which, by [Meciar's] own definition, is in a 'crisis' and an abrupt ending of federal budget subsidies, critics fear that, in order to divert attention from the scale of the problems, Mr Meciar's government will whip up tensions between Slovaks and the country's several ethnic minorities, particularly its 600,000-strong ethnic Hungarian community.

SOURCE 2

From an article by journalist Sandra Jordan in the British Sunday newspaper *The Observer*, published on 21 November 1999. Sandra Jordan witnessed, as a 19-year-old student, Czechoslovakia's Velvet Revolution in November 1989, and then revisited Prague a decade later. *The Observer* is a left of centre newspaper.

For those who live in Prague, life is still difficult. In theory, people are better off, it's just that they don't feel it. Life expectancy has risen, GDP has doubled since 1991 and inflation has fallen. [But] the days of subsidised accommodation are numbered. The centre of Prague has been emptied of many former residents to make way for valuable office and retail space. Rent has quadrupled since the revolution, as has the cost of property.

Post-revolution, the Communists who made life miserable for so long live to tell the tale, and quite a few have prospered. This is the hardest part to swallow for most Czechs. The rosy future hasn't materialised.

I meet Josef Fleisleber [who said:] 'The first years after the revolution were chaotic for the government. The freedom was so young, it was without borders, without edges. Everyone thought they could do what they wanted. But that's not possible, because democracy is chaos. And also, because of the unemployment problem, people are not happy.'

SOURCE 3

From a World Bank report called 'Slovakia: Restructuring for Recovery', published in 1994; the report was intended for use by governments, businesses, financial investment groups and academics with an interest in Slovakia's transition to a market economy:

The Slovak Republic started down the road to economic transformation with a legacy of policies and resources that are both favourable and unfavourable. Slovakia inherited low inflation, and modest debt. Its skilled and competitively priced labour force and strategic location in the centre of Europe hold out the promise of economic prosperity at the end of the transition to capitalism. But Slovakia also inherited an industrial structure not suited to its economic strength, weak banks and a large and inefficient system of social security. Thus the economy and its people inevitably face a great deal of adjustment, which has already been costly in social terms. Real incomes have plunged by 24 per cent since 1990. The major challenge for Slovakia will be to continue reforms while minimising the social costs and the number of people excluded from its benefits.

A LEVEL PRACTICE QUESTION

Evaluating primary sources

With reference to Sources 1, 2 and 3 and your understanding of the historical context, assess the value of these three sources to an historian studying Czechoslovakia after the collapse of communism.

STUDY TIP

With these types of sources there is good potential for considering their different provenance in your answer. The sources are from three different points chronologically, and it would be helpful to refer to this in your evaluation. Try to establish your own checklist for source evaluation to ensure you cover all relevant angles each time.

A LEVEL PRACTICE QUESTION

To what extent was the difficulty in creating united and stable governments in the former Soviet satellite states after the elections of 1990 due to their years of communist rule?

STUDY TIP

This might seem a question where a counter-argument does not immediately present itself, but remember that the question asks 'To what extent?' Consider why different states had different problems.

The restoration of capitalism

Expectations in Eastern Europe were that economic transformation could be achieved as quickly as the transformation to a multi-party democracy. There were two main options on offer for the restoration of capitalism: the rapid 'shock' transition and the 'gradualist' approach. Poland took the **shock therapy** approach and Hungary, the **gradualist approach**, and these two countries will be considered as case studies.

Poland and 'shock therapy'

Poland's plan for rapid transition to capitalism was put together in 1989 by a panel of economic experts in accordance with the requirements of the International Monetary Fund (IMF). Poland's foreign debt by 1989 had reached $42 billion and the IMF would only endorse access to its large stabilisation funds if Poland made radical economic changes that substantially reduced state spending. This is what Poland proceeded to do. In December 1989, the Sejm passed a package of ten acts that dismantled the planned economy. Measures included:

- freeing exchange rates, which made imports very expensive inside Poland and exports cheap outside Poland
- removing obstacles to foreign investment
- removing price controls and other subsidies
- privatising state industries and services
- heavy cuts to government spending.

The immediate social and economic impacts were severe:

- Many businesses collapsed once state support was removed. Oil prices increased once Soviet subsidies stopped, which also put industries out of business.
- Unemployment increased from an official level of zero before 1989 to a high of 16.4 per cent in 1993. Over a million people lost their jobs.
- Many of the newly unemployed required state benefits to survive, putting a strain on state finances and Poland's ability to make its debt repayments. Benefits were cut back.
- Poland's economy fell into a deep recession, with GDP dropping by nearly 12 per cent by 1993. Agricultural production declined steeply.

The social impact of the reforms undermined Solidarity's legitimacy, leading to its election defeat in September 1993. The new government reduced

KEY TERM

shock therapy: a sudden change in the way a state's economy is run, so that the influence of the State is rapidly reduced; for example, price controls are axed, protection from competition and free trade is removed, nationalised industries are privatised, and all this is done decisively and quickly

gradualist approach: making economic changes in small steps, over an extended period of time, allowing people to adapt to change, and for reform to respond flexibly to changing contexts

CROSS-REFERENCE

Read about the IMF's involvement in Russia's 'shock therapy' in Chapter 12, pages 94–95.

the pace of privitisation but, under pressure from the West, continued the reforms. However painful the shock therapy was in the short term, Western supporters of the approach were confident that in the longer term, Poland's economy would rebound and the pain would be worth it. And in fact, Poland's economy did recover. Inflation reached over 550 per cent in 1990, but had fallen back to 40 per cent by 1992; 600,000 new businesses were set up, employing hundreds of thousands of Poles and pushing economic growth up again so that by 1995 GDP, at 6.9 per cent, was higher than it had been under the old regime. Six thousand of the new businesses were foreign, with investors from Europe keen to take advantage of Poland's skilled but cheap workforce.

Fig. 2 *This giant advert for Coca-Cola was put up in August 2000 in Warsaw, despite protests from city authorities*

Hungary's 'gradualist' approach

In the first years after 1989, Hungary's government rejected the shock therapy approach recommended by Western experts, and sought a gradualist route that they hoped would protect citizens from some of the worst effects of rapid transition.

- While Poland tried to jump-start a market economy by selling shares in state industries to its citizens, Hungary sold off state industries and services to foreign investors in order to raise money to pay off some of its large debts.
- Like Poland, Hungary freed prices, leading to price rises of 30 per cent in the first few years of the transition. However, some prices remained subsidised, including energy and public transport. This helped industries to stay in business longer, and reduced the impact on living standards to a degree.
- The way the centrally planned economy 'hoarded' workers meant that the government found it was employing 30 per cent more workers than it could afford. Rather than just sack people, the government encouraged people to take early retirement and live on state pensions or accept disability benefits. This put enormous pressure on the benefits system.

As in Poland, the Hungarian economy went into recession in the first few years of the transition, though the impact was less severe.

- Hungary's GDP declined by 4 per cent in 1990, compared to nearly 12 per cent in Poland. The year after, both countries saw the same drop of 8 per cent.
- Unemployment also increased sharply: 8 per cent of the workforce were unemployed by the end of 1991 (compared to 11 per cent in Poland at the same time).
- Wages fell by 7 per cent in 1990 and again in 1991 (compared to 28 per cent in 1990 and 15 per cent in 1991 in Poland).

Although the gradualist approach did soften the impact of market reforms, it was not enough to prevent popular discontent; perhaps nothing could have done that, as expectations in all the post-communist states were very high – people assumed capitalism would almost immediately bring about Western-style living standards. The softened impact also had consequences for Hungary's longer-term economic development. While other factors were important too, Poland's economy grew faster in the mid- and late 1990s than Hungary's did. By 1994, economic growth in Hungary had stalled and there was widespread concern that the country would not be able to meet its foreign debt payment. The MDF government was voted out by the electorate and, as in Poland, replaced by reformed communists, although even this new government was forced to bring in severe austerity measures.

By the end of the twentieth century, many Hungarians, like people all over Eastern Europe, were expressing a preference for life under the

Communist Party compared to life under capitalism. Timothy Garton Ash, a leading historian of Eastern Europe, noted the painful irony that the Solidarity workers who started the process of revolution ended up working for private firms, often run by former colleagues, and in which no trade unions were allowed.

ACTIVITY

1. Create a graph comparing the results of Poland's and Hungary's transitions back to capitalism, using the data in this chapter on GDP and unemployment rates. What other indices could you research to add more detail?
2. Which do you consider to have been the more successful route to restoring capitalism in Eastern Europe – the 'shock therapy' approach of Poland or the 'gradualist' approach of Hungary?

The restoration of capitalism in other former satellite states

Bulgaria	Bulgaria took a similar route to Poland in the restoration of capitalism, but the fragile political situation exacerbated the problems of shock therapy. Waves of strikes and demonstrations made progress difficult to achieve and in 1997 the economy collapsed. Industries focused on local resources: agriculture, mining, chemicals, oil refining, steel production.
Czechoslovakia	Czechoslovakia took a two-stage approach to shock therapy that first privatised small-scale enterprises in 1990, before the 'big-scale' privatisation in 1991 of large companies that gave all citizens a share in the sell-off. However, corruption issues and scams meant valuable assets ended up going to key individuals and groups for knock-down prices. While the Czechs adjusted well to a market economy, with government policy cushioning the social impacts of the privatisations, in Slovakia the historic reliance on heavy industry meant shock therapy had much bigger impacts. By 1993, industrial output there had nearly halved, agricultural production had fallen by a third, and GDP by a quarter. Wages fell, too, while nearly a fifth of the population was unemployed by 1993.
East Germany	Reunification meant restoration of capitalism in East Germany took a different route from in the other former satellite states. An economic merger between East and West was one of the first steps in reunification, and East Germany's integration into Germany's developed capitalist economy was, over the decades that followed, funded with trillions of euros through a 'Solidarity surcharge'. Despite this subsidised development, East Germany struggled with the process of deindustrialisation due to its reliance on heavy industry. Although wages in East Germany had doubled by 1995, with living standards improving significantly, unemployment soared to twice the rate in the West. There was criticism that the speed of the transition (shock therapy) did not allow East German enterprises enough time to adapt to the new conditions.

ACTIVITY

Research

Research the ways the other former satellite states restored capitalism after 1989. You will find information to help you in the chart in this section. Consider:

- To what degree did each country follow a 'shock therapy' or a 'gradualist' approach to restoring capitalism?
- What factors, if any, can youd identify that worked in similar ways across the former satellite states as they sought to restore capitalism?
- What factors, if any, can you identify that were specific to individual states as they sought to restore capitalism?

Romania	The privatisation of state-owned industries was carried out from 1992 in a stepped programme: all adult Romanians received shares of ownership in 30% of state industries, with the remaining 70% held by the State; the aim being that the State would then sell off 10% of this state ownership fund each year. There were also buy-outs of enterprises by management and staff. Although designed to allow proper management of the transition, this gradualist approach failed to prevent the 1990s being characterised by high inflation, shortages of consumer goods, and high unemployment. As well as the massive problems of a largely defunct industrial base, the State managed the sale of assets poorly and management buy-outs tended to see the same inefficient methods being maintained.

Closer ties with the West

One of the many problems facing the post-communist states was the collapse in trade links with the former Soviet Union. Poland, Hungary, the Czech Republic, and Slovakia sought to shift their economies to greater integration with Europe and with the global market. European integration was most effectively to be gained by becoming part of the European Union (EU), which the Czech Republic, Slovakia, Hungary, and Poland achieved on 1 May 2004, and Bulgaria and Romania on 1 January 2007 (after a long build-up period through the 1990s). Like the EU, NATO was another key membership goal for the post-communist states, especially for those with particular concerns about their neighbour, Russia. Hungary, Poland, and the Czech Republic joined NATO on 12 March 1999, with Bulgaria, Slovakia, and Romania joining on 29 March 2004.

East Germany and reunification

It was with East Germany, of course, where ties with the West became closest, following reunification with West Germany. By the terms of reunification, the GDR became subject to all the economic, social, and labour laws of the FRG, and had a banking system controlled by the **Bundesbank**. The huge task of privatising all the state monopoly industries was carried through, but many industries simply collapsed without state support. It soon became clear that the economic integration of the two states would take far longer than originally expected, and since the Kohl government had promised not to raise taxes, in order to win support for unity, it was slow to institute the 'Eastern recovery programme' that the former GDR so needed.

This recovery programme was finally launched in March 1991, with government money going into housing, agriculture, and services, as well as the industrial infrastructure. However, when the economy of the old GDR was confronted with West German and EEC competition, the fall-out left large areas suffering structural long-term unemployment. In the short term, reunification certainly failed to perform the economic miracle that the Easterners had hoped for.

Socially, reunification had a massive impact. Compliance, passivity, and withdrawal into a private world had to give way to new qualities like initiative, drive, competitiveness, and a willingness to undertake responsibility. Those who were compromised by their former political sympathies lost their positions, and the legal and education systems were reformed along Western democratic lines.

There were also massive adjustments to be made in the world of work, where, within six months of unification, 21 per cent of the workforce had

A CLOSER LOOK

The Deutsche Bundesbank was the central bank of the FRG. It was set up in 1957. On 18 May 1990, East and West Germany formed a monetary union based on the deutschemark, and the Bundesbank was made responsible for monetary policy within the union.

moved to a new job, 8 per cent were unemployed, and 10 per cent had taken an early retirement. There was less need for unskilled manual labour, which particularly hit female employment.

For some, reunification brought immense rewards. The highly trained could do well and the independently minded could set up their own businesses. There were new opportunities for the young, and those who wanted to travel had their horizons suddenly opened up. However, living standards did not immediately rise to meet those in the West, and others lost out and were only saved by the Western safety net of unemployment insurance and retraining schemes. Rising crime rates and youth delinquency in the East accompanied growing disappointment and the sudden change in social control.

According to an opinion poll in the summer of 1991, a large majority on both sides believed that 'only since unification has it become evident how different Eastern and Western Germany are.' Resentment grew in the West over the tax rises needed to support Eastern economic development and, most particularly, the so-called 'solidarity tax' levied on all Germans from 1991 which, according to the journalist, Allan Hall, 'often seemed the equivalent of throwing money at an alcoholic to keep the bar open'.

One outcome of the two-state merger was the emergence of a new sense of GDR identity – a nostalgia for the old securities and the social cohesion of the communist state, once the restrictive and repressive aspects of the regime were no longer feared – *ostalgie*.

A CLOSER LOOK

Germany's relationship with Eastern Europe

Germany's relationship with the former Soviet states and Russia had also to be defined. Germany's main concern was the stability and prosperity of neighbouring Central and Eastern European states. Consequently, in the early 1990s, Germany offered aid, and became the single largest investor and the most important trading partner for the former Soviet bloc.

ACTIVITY

Prepare a balance sheet to quantify the successes and failures of German reunification by 1991. On one side, list the successes and the positive factors, and on the other, the failures and negatives.

Fig. 3 *A German museum caters for* ostalgie *with this reconstruction of a typical kitchen in a GDR apartment*

Political, economic, and social progress and continuing difficulties by 2000

The information in the charts below is taken from the country profiles of each of the satellite states, as compiled by the *CIA's World Factbook* in 2000, which is a valuable reference for studying the political, economic and social achievements and continuing difficulties of the satellite states by 2000.

The Czech Republic, 2000

Introduction	On 1 January 1993, the country underwent a "velvet divorce" into its two national components, the Czech Republic and Slovakia. In 1999 the Czech Republic became a member of NATO and moved toward integration in world markets, a development that posed both opportunities and risks.
Life expectancy at birth	74.51 years
Economy overview	Political and financial crises in 1997 shattered the Czech Republic's image as one of the most stable and prosperous of post-Communist states. Delays in enterprise restructuring and failure to develop a well-functioning capital market played major roles in Czech economic troubles, which culminated in a currency crisis in May. The government was forced to introduce two austerity packages which cut government spending by 2.5% of GDP. Growth dropped to 0.3% in 1997, –2.3% in 1998, and –0.5% in 1999. The difficulty with transition was blamed on too much government influence on the privatised economy. The government established a restructuring agency in 1999 and launched a revitalisation programme – to spur the sale of firms to foreign companies.
GDP growth rate	–0.5%
GDP per capita	$11,700
Unemployment rate	9%
External debt	$24.3 billion
Economic aid received	$351.6 million (1995)

Germany, 2000

Introduction	The decline of the USSR and the end of the Cold War allowed for German unification in 1990. Since then Germany has expended considerable funds to bring eastern productivity and wages up to western standards. In January 1999, Germany and 10 other EU countries formed a common European currency, the euro.
Life expectancy at birth	77.44 years
Economy overview	By 2000 Germany possessed the world's third most technologically powerful economy after the US and Japan, but its basic capitalistic economy had started to struggle under the burden of generous social benefits. The integration and upgrading of the eastern German economy remained a costly long-term problem, with annual transfers from the west amounting to roughly $100 billion. Growth slowed to 1.5% in 1999, largely due to lower export demand and still-low business confidence.
GDP growth rate	1.5%
GDP per capita	$22,700
Unemployment rate	10.5%
External debt	$0
Economic aid received	$0 – Germany is an aid donor: $5.6 billion

Hungary, 2000

Introduction	Following the collapse of the USSR in 1991, Hungary developed close political and economic ties to Western Europe. It joined NATO in 1999 and is a frontrunner in a future expansion of the EU.
Life expectancy at birth	71.37 years

Economy overview	By 2000 Hungary had shown strong economic growth and was working towards membership of the European Union. Over 85% of the economy had been privatised. Foreign ownership of and investment in Hungarian firms was widespread with cumulative foreign direct investment at $21 billion by 1999. GDP growth was 4% in 1999. Inflation, while diminished, was still high at 10%. Economic reform measures included regional development, encouragement of small- and medium-size enterprises, and support of housing.
GDP growth rate	4%
GDP per capita	$7,800
Unemployment rate	10%
External debt	$27 billion
Economic aid received	$122.7 million (1995)

Poland, 2000

Introduction	The "shock therapy" programme during the early 1990s enabled the country to transform its economy into one of the most robust in Central Europe, boosting hopes for early acceptance to the EU. Poland joined the NATO alliance in 1999.
Life expectancy at birth	73.19 years
Economy overview	Poland stands out as one of the most successful and open transition economies. The privatisation of small and medium state-owned companies and a liberal law on establishing new firms marked the rapid development of a private sector responsible for 70% of economic activity by 2000. In contrast to the vibrant expansion of private non-farm activity, the large agriculture component remains handicapped by structural problems, surplus labour, inefficient small farms, and lack of investment. The government's determination to enter the EU as soon as possible affected most aspects of its economic policies. Structural reforms advanced in pensions, healthcare, and public administration in 1999, but resulted in larger than anticipated fiscal pressures. Restructuring and privatisation of 'sensitive sectors' (e.g., coal and steel) had begun by 2000, but work remained to be done. Growth in 2000 was expected be moderately above 1999.
GDP growth rate	3.8%
GDP per capita	$7,200
Unemployment rate	11%
External debt	$44 billion (1998)
Economic aid received	$4.3 billion (1995)

Slovakia, 2000

Introduction	The Slovaks and the Czechs agreed to separate peacefully on 1 January 1993. Slovakia experienced more difficulty than the Czech Republic in developing a modern market economy.
Life expectancy at birth	73.74 years
Economy overview	By 2000 Slovakia was still experiencing a difficult transition from a centrally planned economy to a modern market economy. It started 1999 faced with a sharp slowdown in GDP growth, large budget and current account deficits, fast-growing external debt, and persisting corruption. Tough austerity measures implemented in May 1999 cut the overall fiscal deficit from 6% in 1998 to under 4% of GDP. However, Slovakia's fiscal position remained weak in 2000; inflation and unemployment remained high; and the government still had to address the structural problems inherited from the Mečiar period, such as large inefficient enterprises, and a banking sector that was unable to pay back the debts it owed. Furthermore, the government faced considerable public discontent over the austerity measures and, persistent high unemployment – which reached an all-time high of 20% in December 1999 – rising consumer prices, reduced social benefits, and declining living standards.
GDP growth rate	1.9%
GDP per capita	$8,500
Unemployment rate	20%
External debt	$10.6 billion
Economic aid received	$422 million (1995)

ACTIVITY

1. Using the data provided in the charts on pages 208–09, identify indications of political, economic, and social progress in the countries featured, and also of continuing difficulties in these same countries by 2000.
2. Compare the progress made between the countries. Use your contextual knowledge to explain the differences and similarities you see.

Fig. 4 *The industrial town of Martin in Slovakia, in 2000, where 70 per cent of inhabitants were living below Slovakia's average standard of living*

STUDY TIP

When preparing to answer this type of question it might be helpful to make a list of arguments in support of the view and arguments against it. for each of the areas mentioned – economic, political and social. Remember that some areas might have had fewer problems than others. Try not to simply list your points in your answer – aim for an answer that is effectively delivered, analytical and balanced, with a well-substantiated judgement.

A LEVEL PRACTICE QUESTION

'Rapid transition to capitalism brought grave economic, political, and social problems to the former Soviet satellite states in the years 1990 to 2000.' Assess the validity of this view.

Summary

The collapse of the Soviet Empire came very quickly, surprising everyone – including Western critics of the Soviet system who had watched every move made by the Soviet leadership in such obsessive detail. Once the Soviet Empire *had* collapsed, Western commentators scrambled to explain its inevitable demise and to claim victory for the superiority of Western capitalism and democracy.

The progress made by the former satellite states by 2000 was remarkable, especially when the most successful are compared with the worst performing former Soviet republics and the economic and social meltdown endured by Russians in the 1990s. Political freedom had been sustained, and the difficult transition (both economic and psychological) from a planned economy to a highly competitive, globalised, market economy was well advanced. Leading global economic expertise, together with substantial investment from Western banks, development funds, and the EU was readily available for this remarkable opportunity to put theory into practice.

The *ostalgie* felt by the former East Germans, though, was certainly mirrored in other states, too. The pain of austerity, the political fragmentation, the continued corruption scandals, the growth in inequality (between states as well as between people), and above all, the frustration with how long it was taking for the promise of a Western way of life for all to be realised, meant that people inevitably looked back at what they had lost as well as forward. Perhaps this was because the end of the communist experiment, when it had come, had been so sudden. Long resented, feared, and mocked for its glaring hypocrisy and everyday frustrations, its legitimacy was so hollowed out that by 1989 there was nothing solid enough to reform. As with a condemned building, everything needed to be torn down before rebuilding could begin.

Conclusion: the crisis of communism

Fig. 1 *A worker cleans a Soviet symbol on top of a Stalin-era skyscraper in Moscow in 2000.*

The leaders of the USSR and its satellite states dogmatically followed an ideology, Marxism–Leninism. Even Gorbachev's reforms were inspired by Lenin's last writings. One conclusion about the crisis of communism was that Marxism–Leninism fossilised the political, social, and economic status of the Soviet empire after the Second World War. As the capitalist West moved from traditional heavy industries and construction-line manufacturing to chemical industries and plastics, service industries, light industry, and computing, the Soviet system stagnated, unable to innovate.

Instead of looking for reasons why the Soviet system collapsed, it is perhaps easier to ask why it was able to last for so long. Explanations for this centre on the power of the socialist states to control their populations through fear. Under Stalin and his protégées in Eastern Europe, there was always the terrifying threat of arrest, imprisonment, hard labour, execution. After Stalin, the Gulag retreated, but still there were many ways in which people were forced to toe the line: the threat of losing a job was a very significant incentive, as was loss of privileges for Party members. Uprisings against Soviet control came when the grip of that control seemed to weaken: in 1953 in East Germany, following Stalin's death; in 1956 in Hungary, following Khrushchev's Secret Speech; in 1968 in Czechoslovakia as, for four months, the Prague Spring seemed free to blossom, and in the late 1980s as Gorbachev's reforms in the USSR sought to decentralise political power from the Party's grip.

There is much to say for this argument, too, although the willingness of people to go along with the system should also be considered: the *nomenklatura* who fought the reforms that stripped them of their power and privilege, and also the ordinary people who wanted the system to work better rather than to be replaced by something else. Many of the uprisings were essentially conservative ones: against higher work norms or higher prices (rather than against work norms themselves), as well as against control of prices by the State. Yet another question concerns the suddenness of the collapse of the Communist Parties in 1989. Why was 1989 so different from other years through the 1980s?

The role of Gorbachev and his reforms, building as they did on similar attempts to reform the Soviet system, were enormously significant. Gorbachev, like Khrushchev before him, was trying to return to the 'pure springs' of communism, before it had been polluted by Stalin's perversions. In the West, Stalinism *was* communism.

Gorbachev's reforms and the revolutions of 1989 in Eastern and Central Europe are clearly closely connected. Soviet reforms certainly seemed to have unintended consequences; for example, the unrest in the GDR in 1953 following the reforms of Malenkov and Beria, and in Poland and Hungary in 1956 following Khrushchev's reforms. In these cases, there would seem to be a relationship between the content and 'idea' of reforms and political discontent. Satellite states tried to avoid the 'contagion' of reform from other Warsaw Pact members, only then to have to work out their response to Gorbachev's growing reforms within the USSR.

By 2000, the USSR and the satellite states had been through a tumultuous experience. The initial euphoria of political freedom was followed, for many, by a desperate period of economic collapse in which the legacy of their obsolete economies combined with inexperienced and fragmented politicians seeking economic expertise from the West at a time when mainstream economic theory favoured shock therapy. The promise that things would get better but only after they had got much, much worse, was a strategy that politicians found difficult to sell to their electorate, especially as it soon became clear that a massive gap had opened up between the few who had done very well out of privatisation and the many who had been duped out of shares in the industries they had helped to build. Communist Parties began to win support again by 2000– something that would have been hard to imagine in 1989 and 1990 – as did parties linked to nationalist causes. Slowly, though, each country of the former Soviet system began to redefine its identity – some in relation to Russia, or against it; some in relation to the rest of Western Europe and the opportunities it offered. For Russia itself, the presidency of Vladimir Putin in 2000 offered something that looked familiar: a strong state, with a powerful military, keen to exploit its natural resources to increase its global significance; a democracy, but one where government controlled the oligarchs on one hand and the press on the other, to achieve stability under a commanding leader who promoted an image of a strong, patriotic Russian who could protect the country from the enemies all around it.

Glossary

A

absenteeism: regularly staying away from work

apparatchiks: ('agents of the apparatus') operators of the bureaucratic system; often these functionaries were moved from job to job rather than being specialists

B

balance of trade: the difference in value between a country's exports and its imports

black market: when products or services that are hard to obtain are traded illegally, usually for high prices

Bolshevik: the political party created by Lenin that managed to take control of Russia in the 1917 October Revolution

budget deficit: the amount a government has to borrow to fill the gap between what it spends and what it earns from taxes and other income

bureaucracy: complicated administrative procedures

C

cadres: groups of reliable, politically dependable activitists in responsible, influential positions within the Party and government

civic society: when community groups and organisations take on part or full responsibility for the provision of services and support for those who need it, rather than the State alone

client state: a state that is dependent on another state

Cold War: the state of political hostility that existed between the Soviet Empire and the Western powers from 1945 to 1990

collectivisation: a process by which individual peasant farms are made into one big collective farm; peasant resistance to this process in the 1930s meant collectivisation was enforced in USSR

command economy: another term for the Soviet planned economy – instead of market forces deciding what was produced and in what quantity, a command economy sees these decisions being made centrally by the State

communism: a classless society in which production is organised to provide for what people need, without any requirement for money; everything is owned by everyone, there is no private property

constituency: a particular area whose voters elect a representative to the legislature

consumerism: a culture or system that puts high value on being able to purchase and show off the new things you have bought to enhance your lifestyle

cooperatives: owned and run by their members; for example, by workers

coup: the overthrow of a government by force, often using a sudden, violent attack

cult of personality: the creation through propaganda of an attitude of extreme reverence towards a leader

D

defection: leaving one state to live in another one, in violation of emigration restrictions

defectors: people who independently give up allegiance to a state; a term used to describe those who escaped the Soviet Union

degenerates: immoral, corrupt people

de-Stalinisation: a term that was used in the West to describe attempts to remove the negative aspects of Stalinism from Soviet society, politics, and economy

détente: the diplomatic term used in the West to describe the easing of tensions between countries

devaluation: when the international value of a currency is set lower than previously

deviation: Soviet criticism for those who strayed from the proper ideological route

dissident: someone who opposes the official policy of an authoritarian state

dogmatist: person who fervently expresses ill-founded opinions

E

electorate: the people who can vote in an election

émigrés: people who have left one country to live in another

F

fascism: an authoritarian and nationalistic right-wing system of government that tends to include a belief in the supremacy of one national or ethnic group, a contempt for democracy, and an insistence on obedience to a powerful leader

Federal Republic of Germany (FRG) – West Germany: a state made up of the parts of Germany occupied by the USA, Britain, and France in 1945

federation: a union of states that accepts a federal government

G

GDP: (gross domestic product) the income of a country in one year; Soviet statisticians actually used a different measure which had to be adjusted for comparisons with GDP

German Democratic Republic (GDR) – East Germany: a state in Eastern Europe that governed the part of Germany occupied by the USSR in 1945

gerontocracy: when a country is led by a group of elderly people

goulash: a traditional Hungarian stew that mixes meat and vegetables; 'goulash communism' describes a uniquely Hungarian mix of socialist and capitalist 'ingredients'

gradualist approach: making economic changes in small steps, over an extended period of time, allowing people to adapt to change and for reform to respond flexibly to changing contexts

Gulag: the state organisation responsible for running the USSR's system of forced labour camps; Gulag was an acronym for Main Camp Administration

H

hard-line: unbending; so a hard-line Stalinist would not accept any deviation from Stalinist teachings, regardless of context; a hardliner would criticise those who suggested compromise or a different approach as deviationists or revisionists

head of state: a role that varies from country to country – in the USA, it is the very powerful role of the president; in other countries, it is more ceremonial; a person who represents the State and its legislature; in the USSR and its satellite states, real power lay in the Party, not in the legislature

I

ICBMs: intercontinental ballistic missiles; nuclear missiles capable of flying from one continent to another (for example, from launch sites in the USSR to targets in the USA)

inflation: happens when prices increase, reducing the value of the money people have to spend or in savings

J

joint enterprise: when two different companies combine together, often one from the home country and one from a foreign country

K

kangaroo court: an improvised military tribunal that tries a person or people without the use of recognised legal standards

KGB: the Committee for State Security; the successor to Stalin's feared NKVD

kolkhoz: a collective operated by a number of peasant families on state-owned land, where the peasants lived rent-free but had to fulfil state-procurement quotas; any surplus was divided between the families according to the amount of work put in, and each family also had a small private plot

kulaks: 'rich' peasants, blamed under Stalinism for resistance to collectivisation

L

legislature: an elected group of people who make, change, or repeal the laws of a state

legitimacy: public acceptance and recognition of a system of authority; communist regimes' claims to legitimacy were based on the predictions of Marxist–Leninist ideology, so when a gap opened up between the ideology and the reality of life under Communism, legitimacy became harder to achieve

lustration: a process for filtering out/purging former communist officials from taking office in post-communist states

M

market forces: economic factors that determine the price of, demand for, and availability of a product; for example, the price of something rises if demand for it rises

martial law: government by the military, in which the highest-ranking military leader takes over as the leader of the country, and all state powers, including justice and law-making, are taken over by the military

Marxism–Leninism: the social and economic principles of Marx as interpreted and put into effect by Vladimir Lenin in the Soviet Union; it was the guiding ideology, as suggested by Stalin, for the USSR and its satellite states

mujahideen: Muslims engaged in jihad, Islam's struggle against oppression

N

NATO – the North Atlantic Treaty Organization: an organisation based on a treaty of 1949 in which its members agreed to help defend each other from an armed attack by a state outside NATO

NKVD: Stalin's secret police, the People's Commissariat of Internal Affairs; replaced by the KGB – the Committee for State Security – in 1954

O

old Bolsheviks: people who had joined the Party in its early days and had taken part, with Lenin, in the October Revolution of 1917

oral history: recording and studying interviews with people recalling their experiences of the past

P

perestroika: restructuring (a Russian word made famous by Gorbachev's reforms)

peaceful coexistence: a policy of mutual toleration between states or groups that hold different beliefs, ideologies or outlooks; the foreign policy of the Soviet Union towards the countries of the capitalist West

pluralism: the dispersal of power between different institutes, groups, and people; the development of several or many different political parties, reflecting different political views

Politburo: short for Political Bureau, this was the executive committee carrying out the decisions of the Communist Party; under Khrushchev, the Politburo was called the Presidium of the Central Committee

Presidium: the committee which functioned as the legislative authority in the USSR between meetings of the Supreme Soviet

profit incentives: this implied allowing a small amount of free market economics into the planned economy; if enterprises were to keep some profits from production, they should produce what customers wanted, to maximise sales, and do so more efficiently, to minimise costs
proletarian: working people, the working class
protection money: a mafia speciality – business owners are told that they need to pay money to the mafia in order to prevent any 'accidents' happening to them or their businesses
protégée: someone who an older/ more experienced person supports and advances in their career
purge: literally a 'cleaning out of impurities'; under Stalin and the 'little Stalins' of the satellite states it came to mean the removal (often through imprisonment or execution) of anyone deemed a political enemy

R

rapid industrialisation: state-organised industrial growth, particularly heavy industry. Sometimes called 'crash industrialisation' to describe its sudden imposition into an economy
ratify: to make something official
red tape: describes overly complex bureaucratic requirements
reschedule [of debts]: obtaining a longer time period before debt repayments have to be made or sometimes agreeing a reduction in the debt that allows some payment to be made
revisionist: a criticism made of those who moved away from the official (orthodox) interpretation of Marxism
RSFSR: Russian Soviet Federalist Socialist Republic; commonly referred to as Soviet Russia
rubber-stamped: a phrase that describes the process where authorisation is given to something just as a matter of course, often because the decision to do that something has already been made somewhere else (where the real power is)

S

satellite states: states that are officially independent countries but which are in fact controlled or heavily influenced by another state
shock therapy: a sudden change in the way a state's economy is run, so that the influence of the State is rapidly reduced; for example, price controls are axed, protection from competition and free trade is removed, nationalised industries are privatised, and all this is done decisively and quickly
Sino–Soviet: relations between China and the Soviet Union
smear campaign: a campaign to discredit a person or a group by false information or accusations
socialism: when production is publically owned rather than owned by private individuals, and individuals are rewarded by the system according to their contribution
socialist legality: law in a socialist state was designed to protect the State's interests rather than private property, and often featured tribunals made up of ordinary people who decided on 'revolutionary justice' for certain types of crimes
socialist realism: a policy that required all art (e.g. literature, film, music) to educate the people about socialism and why it was good
sovereign state: a state that is run by its own government alone
Soviet: Russian word for council; workers' councils played an important part in the Bolshevik Revolution of 1917, which overthrew the temporary Russian government of the time
Soviet periphery: Cold War thinking was originally characterised by the idea of 'spheres of influence'; the Soviet periphery referred to developing countries that had followed the Soviet model of development
Stalinism: the term used to describe the methods and ideologies of Stalin's rule
subjectivism: Soviet criticism for letting personal feelings get in the way of objective decision-making

T

technocratic: when policies are put forward and implemented by those with relevant technological knowledge and understanding (for example, economists)
teetotaller: someone who never drinks alcohol
totalitarian: a state system in which everyone is compelled to follow a single ideology and any dissent or alternative political view is ruthlessly crushed by the police

U

umbrella group: a group of organisations that all have common interests

W

wildcat strikes: strikes that happen without the authorisation of a union
wreckers: a term used for 'enemies of the people' accused of sabotaging industrial production

Bibliography

Books for students

Brown, Archie, *The Rise & Fall of Communism*, Vintage Books, 2010

Cannon, Martin et al., *20th Century World History Couse Companion*, Oxford University Press, 2009

Figes, Orlando, *Revolutionary Russia, 1891–1991*, Penguin, 2014

Fulbrook, Mary, et al., *Democracy and Dictatorship in Germany 1919–1963*, Heinemann 2008

Klein, Naomi, *The Shock Doctrine*, Picador, 2007

Lovell, Stephen, *The Soviet Union: A Very Short Introduction*, Oxford University Press, 2009

Laver, John, *Triumph and Collapse: Russia and the USSR, 1941–1991*, Oxford University Press, 2009

Lewis, Ben, *Hammer and Tickle: A history of communism told through communist jokes*, Phoenix, 2008

Nutt, Stephen and Bottaro, Jean, *History for the IB Diploma: Nationalist and Independence Movements*, Cambridge University Press, 2011

Todd, Alan, *History for the IB Diploma: Communism in Crisis 1976–89*, Cambridge University Press, 2012

Waller, Sally, *From Defeat to Unity: Germany, 1945–1991*, Oxford University Press, 2010

Williamson, David, *Europe and the Cold War 1945–91*, Hodder Education 2006

Books for teachers and extension

Acton, Edward and Stableford, Tom, *The Soviet Union: A documentary history*, volume 2, University of Exeter Press, 2007

Ambrosius, Gerold, *A Social and Economic History of Twentieth-century Europe*, 1989, Harvard

Andrle, Vladimir, *A Social History of Twentieth-Century Russia*, Edward Arnold, 1994

Brezhnev, Leonid I., *Leonid Brezhnev: Pages from his Life*, Simon and Schuster, 1978

Cohen, Stephen F. and Vanden Heuvel, Katrina, *Voices of Glasnost: Interviews with Gorbachev's Reformers*, Norton & Company, 1989

Colton, Timothy J., *Yeltsin: A Life*, Basic Books, 2008

Curry, Jane Leftwich, *The Black Book of Polish Censorship*, Random House, 1984

Daniels, Robert V. (ed.), *A documentary history of communism in Russia*, University Press of New England, 1993

Fowkes, Ben, *The Rise and Fall of Communism in Eastern Europe* (2nd ed.), Macmillan Press Ltd, 1995

Frucht, Richard (ed.), *Encyclopedia of Eastern Europe*, Taylor and Francis, 2000

Fulbrook, Mary (ed.), *Europe since 1945*, Oxford University Press, 2001

Gorbachev, Mikhail, *Memoirs*, Transworld, 1995

Gorbachev, Mikhail, *Perestroika: New Thinking for Our Country and the World*, Collins, 1988

Hanhimaki, Jussi M. and Westad, Odd Arne, *The Cold War: A History in Documents and Eyewitness Accounts*, Oxford University Press, 2013

Hanson, Philip, *The Rise and Fall of the Soviet Economy*, Routledge, 2014

Heimann, Mary, *Czechoslovakia: The State That Failed*, Yale University Press, 2011

Hensel, Jana, *After the Wall: Confessions from an East German childhood and the life that came next*, Perseus Books Group, 2004

Kádár, János, *On the Road to Socialism: Selected Speeches and Interviews 1960–64*, Corvina Press, 1965

Khrushchev, Nikita, *Khrushchev Remembers*, translated by Strobe Talbott, Andre Deutsch, 1971

Leffler, Melvyn P. and Westad, Odd Arne (eds), *The Cambridge History of the Cold War*, vols I-III, Cambridge University Press, 2010

Lewis, Paul G., *Central Europe Since 1945*, Longman, 1994

Millar, James R. (ed.), *Politics, work and daily life in the USSR: A survey of former Soviet citizens*, Cambridge University Press, 1987

Nove, Alec, *Glasnost in Action: Cultural Renaissance in Russia*, Unwin Hyman, 1989

Prokhorova, Irina (ed.), *1990: Russians Remember a Turning Point*, Quercus, 2013

Raleigh, Donald J., *Soviet Baby Boomers: an oral history of Russia's Cold War generation*, Oxford University Press, 2012

Rothschild, Joseph and Wingfield, Nancy M., *Return to Diversity: A Political History of East Central Europe since World War II* (3rd edition), Oxford University Press, 2000

Sakwa, Richard, *Russian Politics and Society*, Routledge, 1993

Sebestyen, Victor, *Twelve Days: Revolution 1956*, Phoenix, 2007

Sebestyen, Victor, *Revolution 1989: The Fall of the Soviet Empire*, Orion, 2010

Shapiro, Susan G., *The Curtain Rises: Oral Histories of the Fall of Communism in Eastern Europe*, McFarland & Company, 2004

Stites, Richard, *Russian Popular Culture: Entertainment and Society since 1900*, Cambridge University Press 1995

Stokes, Gale, *The Walls Came Tumbling Down*, Oxford University Press 1993

Stone, Dan (ed.), *The Oxford Handbook of Postwar European History*, Oxford University Press, 2014

Suny, Ronald Grigor (ed.), *The Cambridge History of Russia, vol III The Twentieth Century*, Cambridge University Press 2006

Vaizey, Hester, *Born in the GDR: Living in the Shadow of the Wall*, Oxford University Press 2014

Webb, Adrian, *The Routledge Companion to Central and Eastern Europe since 1919*, 2008

White, Stephen, *After Gorbachev*, Cambridge University Press, 1993

Winkler, Allan M., *The Cold War: a history in documents*, Oxford University Press, 2003

Acknowledgements

The publisher would like to thank the following for permission to use their photographs:

pxv: (t) Mary Evans/Everett Collection, (b) Laski Diffusion/Getty Images; **p1**: Apic/Getty Images; **p4**: (t) Keystone-France/Gamma-Keystone via Getty Images, (tm) FPG/Archive Photos/Getty Images, (bm) Mary Evans/Everett Collection, (b) Mary Evans/Marx Memorial Library; **p9**: © RIA Novosti/Alamy; **p11**: Khrushchev's 'Secret Speech', 1956 (b/w photo), Russian Photographer (20th century)/Private Collection/RIA Novosti/Bridgeman Images; **p17**: © ITAR-TASS Photo Agency/Alamy; **p23**: © Heritage Image Partnership Ltd/Alamy; **p24**: Sovfoto/UIG via Getty Images; **p28**: Sovfoto/UIG via Getty Images; **p31**: © Everett Collection Historical/Alamy; **p33**: AFP/GettyImages; **p35**: Keystone-France/Gamma-Keystone via Getty Images); **p39**: © Constantine Manos/Magnum Photos; **p43**: Leonid Brezhnev And Alexei Kosygin In Budapest,./Tass/UIG/Bridgeman Images; **p46**: Sovfoto/UIG via Getty Images; **p47**: Mark Redkin/FotoSoyuz/Getty Images; **p48**: Viktor Budan/Photas/Tass/Press Association Images; **p54**: © Wally McNamee/CORBIS; **p55**: AP/Press Association Images; **p57**: © CORBIS; **p59**: © Mike Goldwater/Alamy; **p60**: DANIEL JANIN/AFP/Getty Images; **p65**: Express/Hulton Archive/Getty Images; **p69**: Michel SETBOUN/Gamma-Rapho via Getty Images; **p71**: (tl) Chris Niedenthal/The LIFE Images Collection/Getty Images, (tc, tr, bl, bc) © RIA Novosti/Alamy, (br) Kurita KAKU/Gamma-Rapho via Getty Images; **p73**: Vladimir Zavyalov/Photas/Tass/Press Association Images; **p77**: SHONE/GAMMA/Gamma-Rapho via Getty Images; **p79**: © David H. Wells/Corbis; **p80**: © Georges de Keerle/Sygma/Corbis; **p86**: Vladimir Musaelyan/Photas/Tass/Press Association Images; **p87**: ITAR-TASS/Photas/Tass/Press Association Images; **p88**: ITAR-TASS/Photas/Tass/Press Association Images; **p93**: YURI KADOBNOV/AFP/Getty Images; **p96**: Roman Denisov/Photas/Tass/Press Association Images; **p97**: ITAR-TASS/Photas/Tass/Press Association Images; **p99**: ITAR-TASS/Photas/Tass/Press Association Images; **p105**: © Bettmann/CORBIS; **p107**: © CTK/Alamy; **p110**: © Bettmann/CORBIS; **p112**: Wlocka/ullstein bild via Getty Images; **p118**: (l) Perlia/ullstein bild via Getty Images, (r) © CTK/Alamy; **p119**: Archive Photos/Getty Images; **p123**: © Iain Masterton/Alamy; **p125**: House of Terror Museum; **p127**: Erich Engel/ullstein bild via Getty Images; **p128**: Lisa Larsen/The LIFE Picture Collection/Getty Images; **p130**: Chronos Media GmbH/ullstein bild via Getty Images; **p132**: Hulton Archive/Getty Images; **p133**: Mario De Biasi/Mondadori Portfolio via Getty Images; **p136**: © Bettmann/CORBIS; **p140**: James P. Blair/National Geographic/Getty Images; **p141**: © Miroslav Zajíc/CORBIS; **p142**: (t) ATTILA MANEK/AFP/Getty Images, (b) © Regis Bossu/Sygma/Corbis; **p146**: © Miroslav Zajíc/CORBIS; **p147**: Albert Moldvay/National Geographic/Getty Images; **p150**: © Bettmann/CORBIS; **p151**: Danigel/ullstein bild via Getty Images; **p153**: Klaus Winkler/ullstein bild via Getty Images; **p157**: Ondrej Nemec/Lidove noviny/isifa/Getty Images; **p158**: © Henri Bureau/Sygma/Corbis; **p161**: PAI-Foto.pl/ullstein bild via Getty Images; **p162**: © Jean-Louis Atlan/Sygma/Corbis; **p164**: Lech Walesa, former president of Poland, creator and head of Solidarity, speaking in Bydgoszcz, after the Bydgoszcz crisis 21.03.1980./Forum/Bridgeman Images; **p166**; © PAP/epa/Corbis; **p170**: AFP/Getty Images; **p173**: Chris Niedenthal/The LIFE Images Collection/Getty Images; **p174**: © Thierry Orban/Sygma/Corbis; **p179**: Chris Niedenthal/The LIFE Images Collection/Getty Images; **p181**: Chris Niedenthal/The LIFE Images Collection/Getty Images; **p183**: DANIEL MIHAILESCU/AFP/Getty Images; **p184**: GERARD FOUET/AFP/Getty Images; **p187**: © Peter Turnley/Corbis; **p188**: Eric BOUVET/Gamma-Rapho via Getty Images; **p190**: © David Turnley/Corbis; **p194**: LUBOMIR KOTEK/AFP/Getty Images; **p196**: Christopher Pillitz/Getty Images; **p201**: Sovfoto/UIG via Getty Images; **p204**: Laski Diffusion/Newsmakers; **p207**: Ritter/ullstein bild via Getty Images; **p210**: Sean Gallup/Newsmakers; **p213**: ALEXANDER NEMENOV/AFP/Getty Images

Artwork by OKS and OUP.
We are grateful to the authors and publishers for use of extracts from their titles and in particular for the following:

Anonymous: *Birth and Death in Romania*, New York Review of Books, 33:16, (New York Review of Books, 1986). Reproduced with permission from The New York Review of Books., **T. S. Blanton:** *The Revolutions of 1989: New Documents from Soviet / East Europe Archives Reveal Why There Was No Crackdown*, 5th November 1999, translated by Jan Chowaniec (Document #2) and by Todd Hammond (Document #7) http://nsarchive.gwu.edu/news/19991105/#docs (National Security Archive, 1989) Reproduced with permission from the National Security Archive., **L. Brezhnev:** *Session of the CPSU CC Politburo, 02 April 1981 (excerpt)*, 2nd April 1981, http://digitalarchive.wilsoncenter.org/document/112758 (History and Public Policy Program Digital Archive, 2015). Reproduced with permission from Wilson Center, Cold War International History Project., **L. Brezhnev:** *Brezhnev Doctrine*, Speech by First Secretary of the Communist Party of the Soviet Union Leonid Brezhnev, http://www.isn.ethz.ch/Digital-Library/Publications/Detail/?id=125400 (ISN, ETH, 2015). Reproduced with permission from ISN ETH, Zurich., A Bridge: 'Thousands cheer Slovak Freedom', 1 January 1993, The Independent (1993). Reproduced with Permission from The Independent. www.independent.co.uk **S. Broadberry and A. Klein:** *Aggregate and per capita GDP in Europe, 1870–2000: continental, regional and national data with changing boundaries*, Scandinavian Economic History Review, 60:1, (Taylor & Francis, 2012). Reprinted by permission of Taylor & Francis Ltd.,
A. Chernyaev: *The Diary of an Assistant to the President of the USSR*, October 28, 1988, http://digitalarchive.wilsoncenter.org/document/112476 (History and Public Policy Program Digital Archive, 1991). Reproduced with permission from Wilson Center, Cold War International History Project., **T. J. Colton:** *Yeltsin: A Life*, (Basic Books, 2008). Reproduced with permission from Perseus Books., **Communist Party of the Soviet Union:** *Session of the CPSU CC Politburo*, 10th December 1981, translated by Mark Kramer, http://digitalarchive.wilsoncenter.org/document/110482 (History and Public Policy Program Digital Archive, 2015). Reproduced with permission from Wilson Center, Cold War International History Project., **R. V. Daniels:** *A Documentary History of Communism in Russia*, (IB Tauris, 1986) Reproduced with permission from I B Tauris & Co. Ltd., **V. Gransow and K. H. Jarausc:** *Uniting Germany: Documents and Debates 1944-1993*, (Berghahn Books, 1994). Reproduced with permission from Berghahn Books.,
J. M. Hanhimaki and O. A. Westad: *The Cold War: A History in Documents and Eyewitness Accounts*, (Oxford University Press, 2013). Reproduced with permission from Oxford University Press.,
N. Khrushchev: *Khrushchev Remembers*, translated by S. Talbott, (Andre Deutsch, 1971). Reproduced with permission from Carlton Books., **N. Khrushchev:** *The Cuban Missile Crisis, 1962: The 40th Anniversary*. Letter from Nikita Khrushchev to Fidel Castro, October 30, 1962. https://www2.gwu.edu/~nsarchiv/nsa/cuba_mis_cri/621030%20Letter%20to%20Castro.pdf (The National Security Archive, The George Washington University, 2015). Reproduced with permission from The National Security Archive., **Anton Luzny:** *Communism and the Church in Czechoslovakia*, The Tablet, 9th June 1962 (the Tablet, 2011). Reproduced with permission from The

Tablet., **J. R. Millar:** *Politics, Work and Daily Life in the USSR: A Survey of Former Soviet Citizens*, (Cambridge University Press, 1987). Reproduced with permission from Cambridge University Press., **OSCE:** *Russian Federation Presidential Election 26 March 2000, Final Report*, (Office for Democratic Institutions and Human Rights, 2000). Reproduced with permission from OSCE. *The information contained regarding the 2000 presidential election is based on the report from the OSCE Office for Democratic Institutions and Human Rights (OSCE/ODIHR), and not a direct quote.*, **Hungarian Socialist Workers' Party Central Committee:** *Hungarian Secretariat Report on Fight against 'Imperialist Propaganda*, 4th December 1978, document obtained by Csaba Bekes. and translated by András Bocz. http://digitalarchive.wilsoncenter.org/document/121501 (History and Public Policy Program Digital Archive, 2015). Reproduced with permission from Wilson Center, Cold War International History Project., **Institute for the Study of Contemporary Problems of Capitalism (Poland):** *Report, 'Trends of Western Radio Propaganda Broadcast in Polish'*, January, 1976, translated by Irena Czernichowska. http://digitalarchive.wilsoncenter.org/document/121506 (History and Public Policy Program Digital Archive, 2015). Reproduced with permission from Wilson Center, Cold War International History Project., **Radio Free Europe**: *Poland's Absenteeism Problem*, Munich 26th August 1957, http://hdl.handle.net/10891/osa:e3b64959-bb68-4ed3-9ce0-d3850aa056d1 (Radio Free Europe, 2015). Copyright holder not established at time of going to print., **Radio Free Europe**: *"Borba" on Catholic Clergy in Poland*, Munich 8th July 1958, http://hdl.handle.net/10891/osa:8480d146-719c-43d5-ba75-d02c72263df0 (Radio Free Europe, 2015). Copyright holder not established at time of going to print., **Radio Free Europe/Radio Liberty Research Institute**: *The Persecuted Church Appeals to the Pope*, 9th April 1955, http://www.osaarchivum.org/greenfield/repository/osa:a9be764e-6e7f-4b1e-bd76-97c3c120b0c9 (Radio Free Europe/Radio Liberty Research Institute, 2015). Copyright holder not established at time of going to print., **Radio Free Europe/Radio Liberty Research Institute**: *Situation Report: Hungary, 18 March 1975"*, 18th March 1975, http://www.osaarchivum.org/greenfield/repository/osa:4e9fc0bd-f8ec-430c-b5b0-a423f51f57da (Radio Free Europe/Radio Liberty Research Institute, 2015). Copyright holder not established at time of going to print., **Radio Free Europe/Radio Liberty Research Institute**: *Economic Performance under Kadar: Miracle or Myth?*, 25th May 1982, http://www.osaarchivum.org/greenfield/repository/osa:2123f19c-ee80-4893-9591-44637cb2f169 (Radio Free Europe/Radio Liberty Research Institute, 2015). Copyright holder not established at time of going to print., **D. J. Raleigh:** *Soviet Baby Boomers: an Oral History of Russia's Cold War Generation*, (Oxford University Press, 2012). Reproduced with permission from Oxford University Press., **Russian Public Opinion Research Centre:** *Nationwide VCIOM Survey*, 8-10th January 2000, (Russian Public Opinion Research Centre, 2000). Reproduced with permission from Russian Public Opinion Research Centre., **P. Schweizer:** *Victory: the Reagan Administration's Secret Strategy That Hastened the Collapse of the Soviet Union*, (Grove Press, 1996). Reproduced with permissions from Grove/Atlantic Inc. and Swagger., **S. G. Shapiro:** *The Curtain Rises: Oral Histories of the Fall of Communism in Eastern Europe*, (McFarland & Co., 2004). Reproduced with permission from McFarland & Co., Inc., **P. Shelest:** *Reports on Miloš Krno's Evaluation of the Czechoslovak Crisis*, June 06, 1968, TsDAHOU, F. 1, Op. 25, Spr. 30, Ll. 1-6. http://digitalarchive.wilsoncenter.org/document/113095 (History and Public Policy Program Digital Archive, 2015). Reproduced with permission from Wilson Center, Cold War International History Project., **Soviet Union. Ministry of Internal Affairs:** *Report by the Chairman of the Delegation of the Ministry of Internal Affairs of the Czechoslovak Socialist Republic, Comrade Colonel Jan Kovach, during Bloc Meeting on Western Radio*, 24th April 1980, document obtained by Jordan Baev and translated by Sveta Milusheva, http://digitalarchive.wilsoncenter.org/document/121524 (History and Public Policy Program Digital Archive, 2015). Reproduced with permission from Wilson Center, Cold War International History Project., **Ukrainian CP CC:** *Report on the Trip by a Delegation of Soviet Workers to the CSSR*, June 04, 1968, TsDAHOU, F. 1, Op. 25, Spr. 28, Ll. 180-189. http://digitalarchive.wilsoncenter.org/document/113088 (History and Public Policy Program Digital Archive, 2015). Reproduced with permission from Wilson Center, Cold War International History Project., **USSR Council of Ministers Order:** *On Measures to Improve the Health of the Political Situation in the GDR*, June 02, 1953, AP RF, f. 3, op. 64, d. 802, ll. 153-161. Document provided by Leonid Reshin (Moscow) and translated by Benjamin Aldrich-Moodie, http://digitalarchive.wilsoncenter.org/document/110023 (History and Public Policy Program Digital Archive, 2015). Reproduced with permission from Wilson Center, Cold War International History Project., **H. Vaizey:** *Born in the GDR: Living in the Shadow of the Wall*, (Oxford University Press, 2014). Reproduced with permission from Oxford University Press., **L. Wałęsa:** Speech in Accepting the Nobel Peace Prize, Nobelprize.org (The Nobel Foundation, 1983). Copyright ©The Nobel Foundation (1983), reproduced with permission from The Nobel Foundation., **S. White:** *After Gorbachev*, (Cambridge University Press, 1993). Reproduced with permission from Cambridge University Press.

We have made every effort to trace and contact all copyright holders before publication, but if notified of any errors or omissions, the publisher will be happy to rectify these at the earliest opportunity.

N. Bethell: *Gomulka: His Poland and His Communism*, (Penguin, 1969). Copyright holder not established at time of going to print., **E. Bourne:** *Hungarians get a small chance to challenge the Establishment*, Special to The Christian Science Monitor, 7th June 1985, www.csmonitor.com/1985/0607/oview.html (Christian Science Monitor, 1985). Copyright holder not established at time of going to print., **W. M. Brinton and A. Rinzler:** *Without Force or Lies: Voices from the Revolution of Central Europe in 1989-90*, (Mercury House, 1990). Copyright holder not established at time of going to print., **K. Chernenko:** *Selected Speeches and Writings*, (Pergamon 1982). Copyright holder not established at time of going to print., **M. Gorbachev:** *Socialism, Peace and Democracy*, (Zwan Publications, 1987). Copyright holder not established at time of going to print., **C. Kiado:** *Janos Kadar: Socialism and Democracy in Hungary*, (Kner Printing House, 1984). Copyright holder not established at time of going to print., **Y. Ligachev:** *Inside Gorbachev's Kremlin*, (Pantheon Books, 1993). Copyright holder not established at time of going to print., **M. Simecka:** *The Restoration of Order: The Normalization of Czechoslovakia 1969-1976*, from *Czechoslovakia: The State That Failed*, edited by Mary Heimann (Yale University Press, 2011). Copyright holder not established at time of going to print., **L. Wałęsa:** *Droga do wolności*, (Editions Spotkania, 1991). Copyright holder not established at time of going to print., **Y. Yevtushenko:** *Stalin's Heirs*, Translator unknown. Copyright holder not established at time of going to print.

The author would like to thank Sally Waller, Roy Whittle, Jane Wood, Becky Ayre, Janice Chan, Sarah Flynn, Rachel, Maisie and Shadow.

The publisher would like to thank the following people for offering their contribution in the development of this book: Sally Waller and Roy Whittle.

Index